#SHOSPLE COLUPIS

WHEN THE SOCIAL NOTWORKS

TO IPAN

This series of illustrations intend to be a testimony of the social network time we are living through.

Show this thread

Sign up

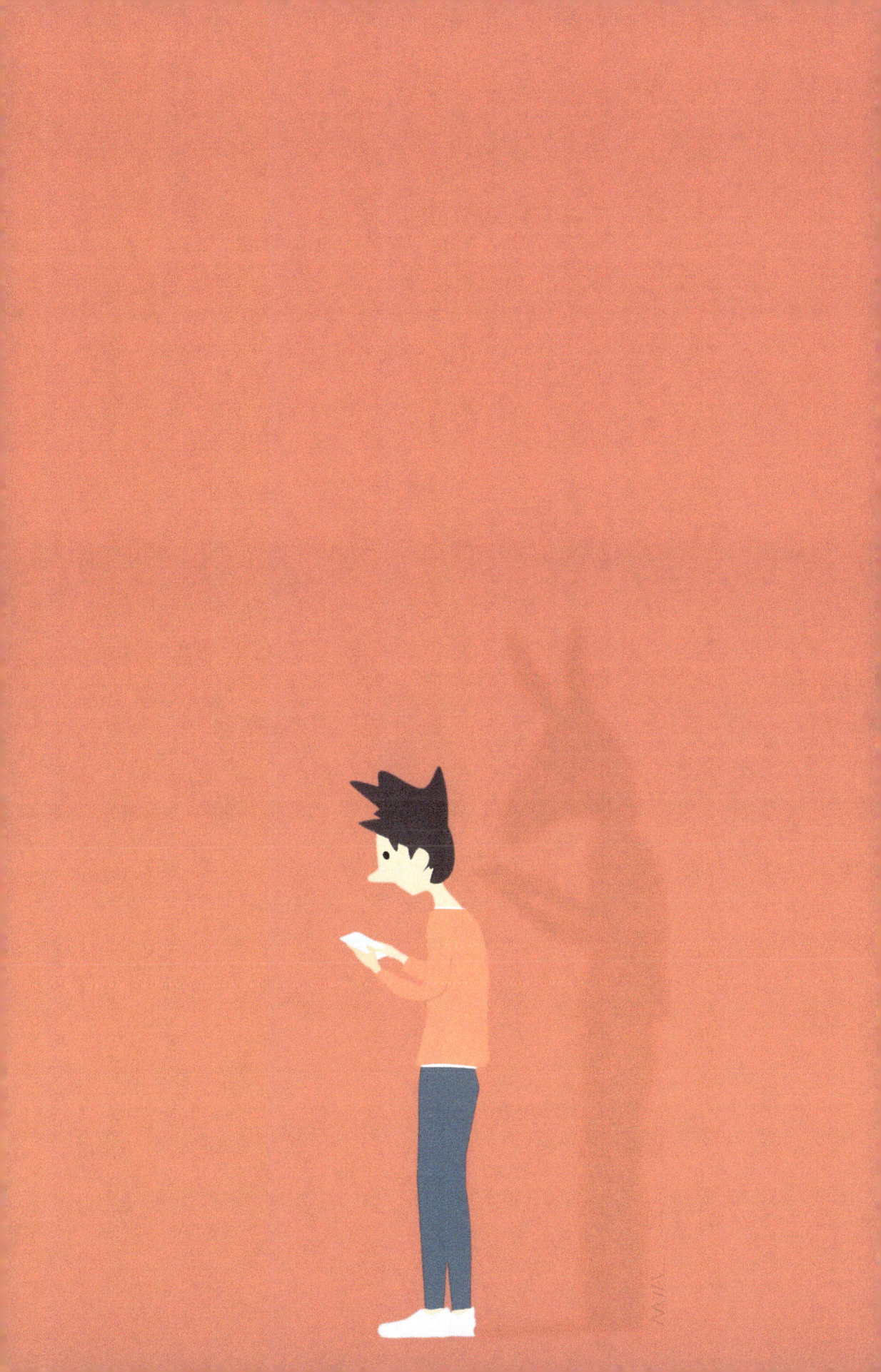

Simon says

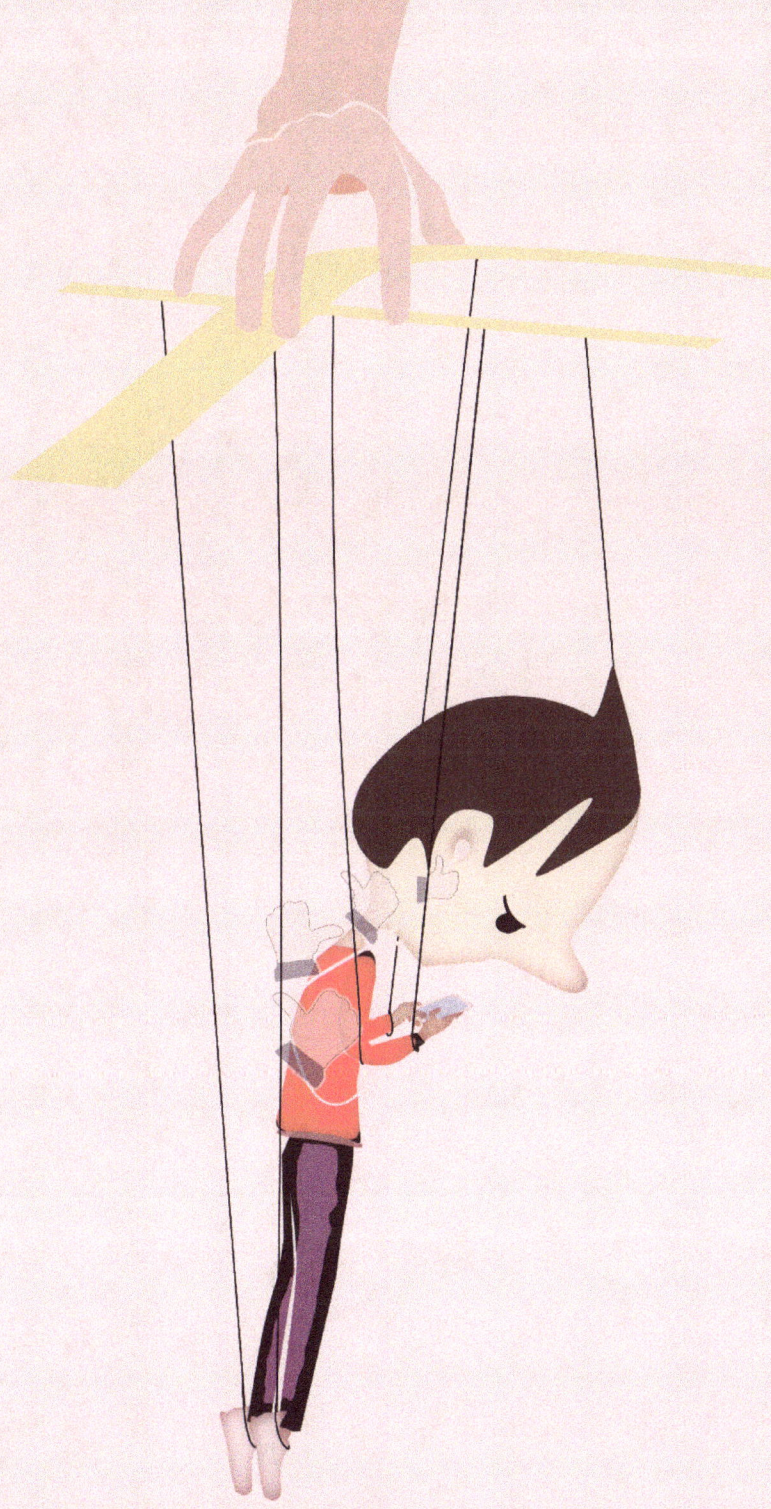

Find Friends

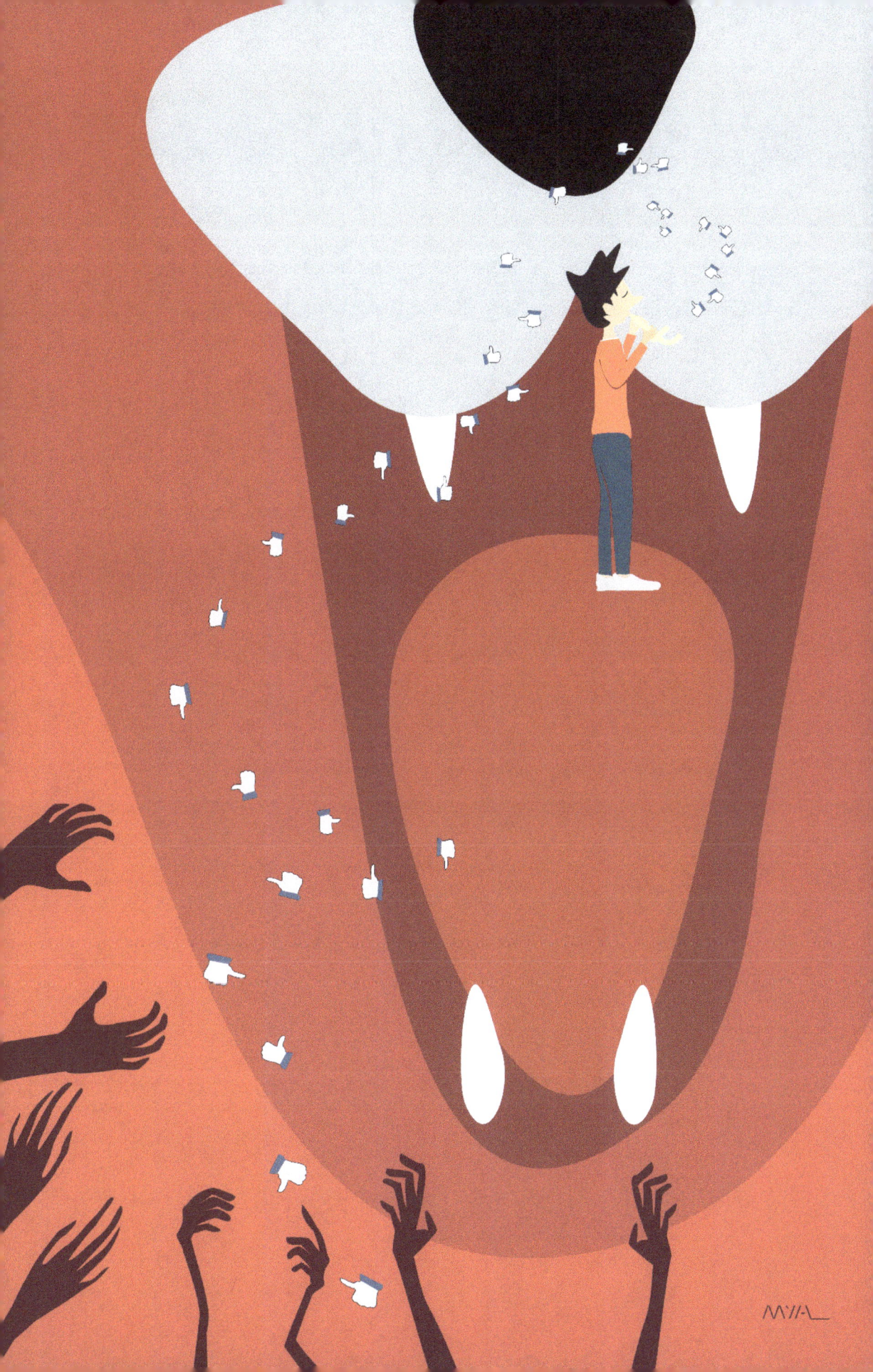

Log in

freakshow

User/loser/abusername or E-mail

Password

Log In

Forgot Password? 😆

MYA

Settings

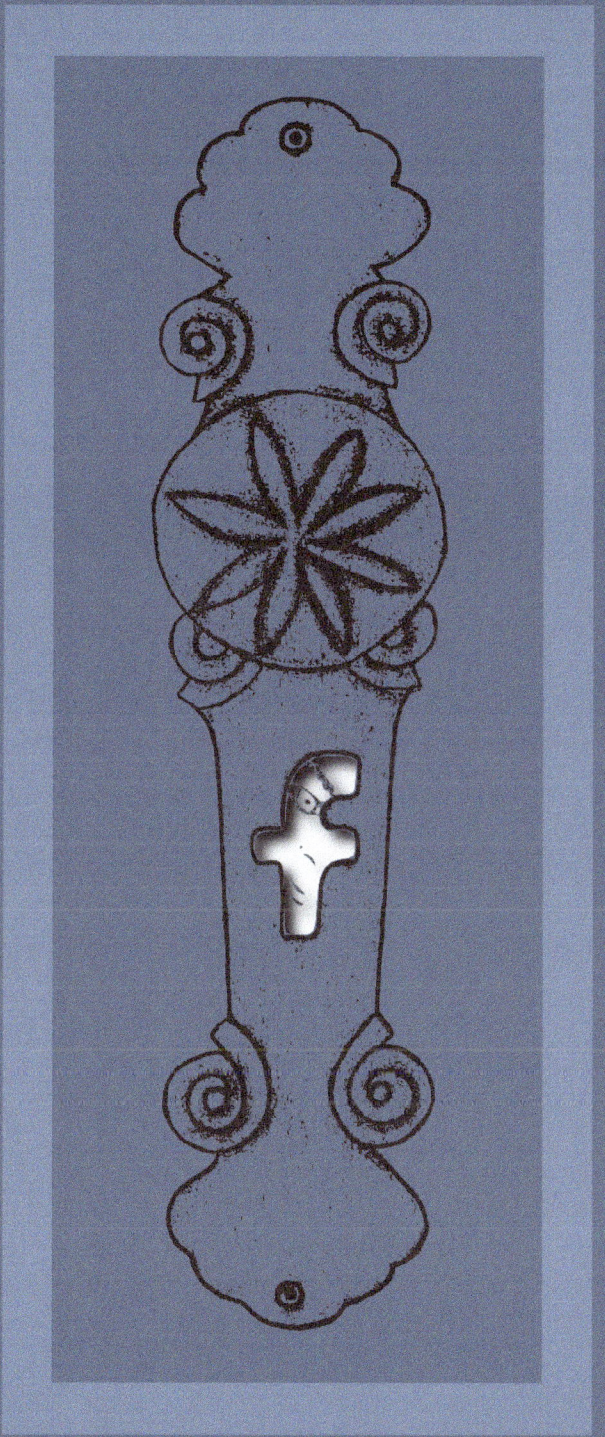

Profile Picture

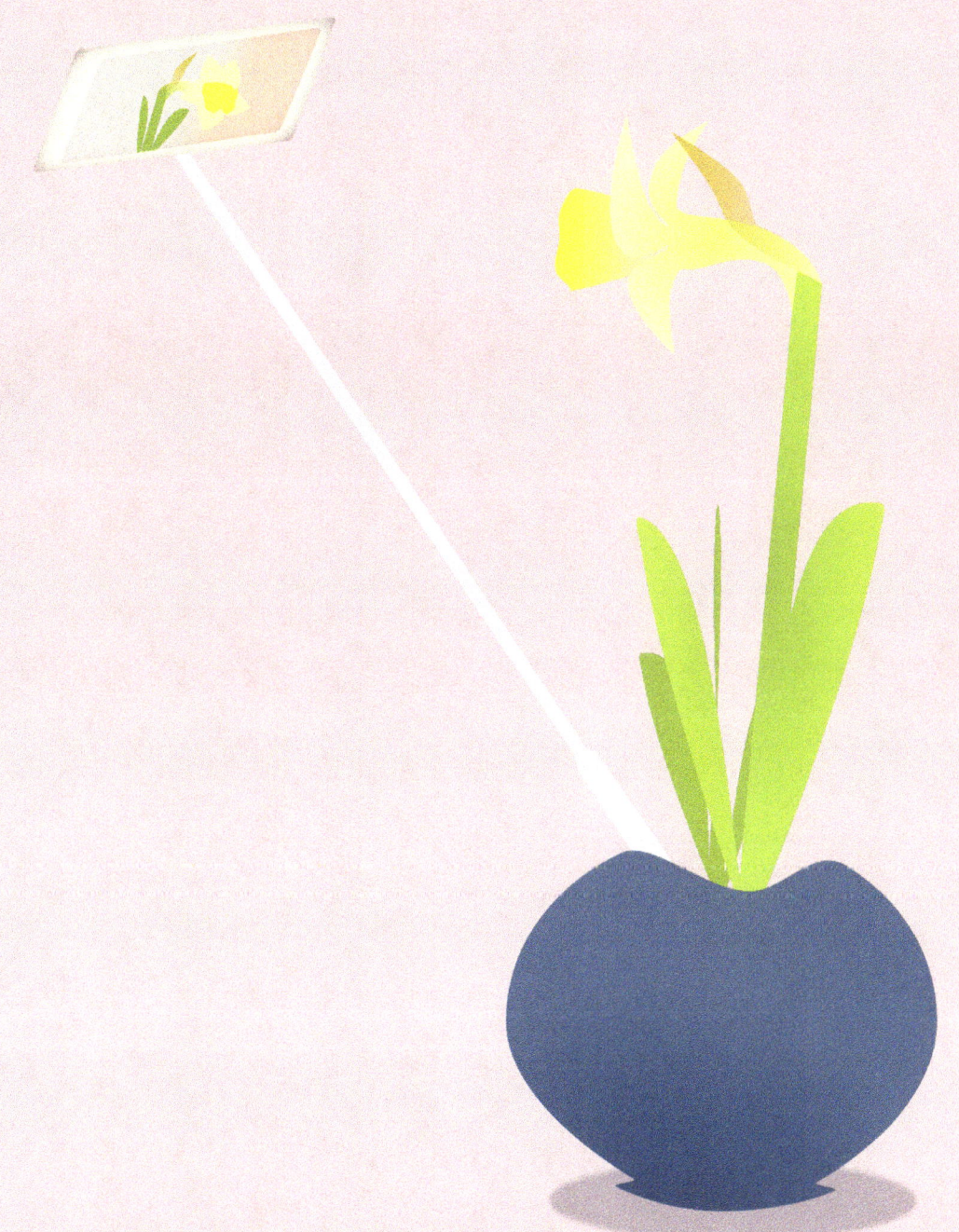

Feed

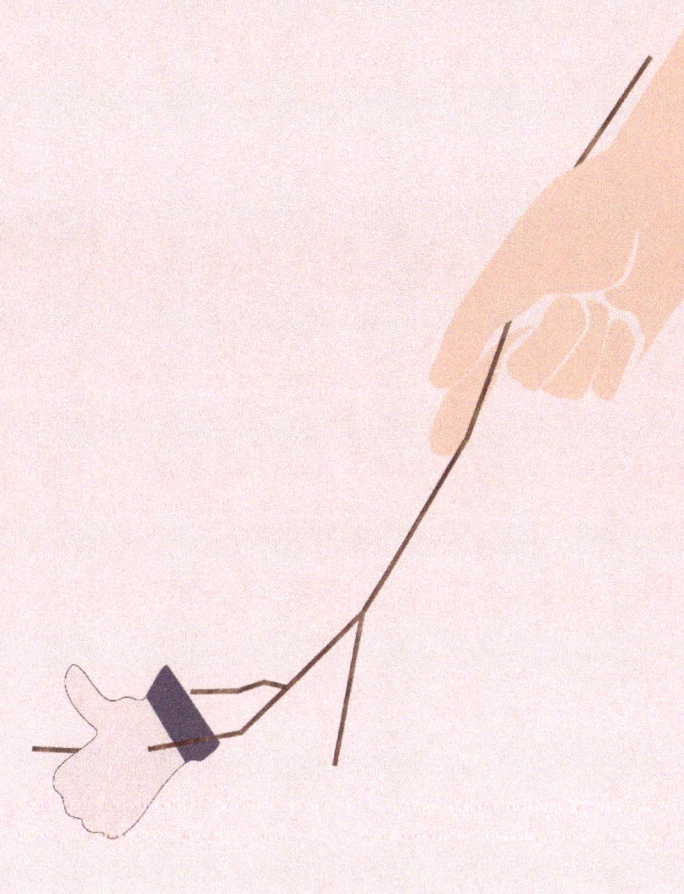
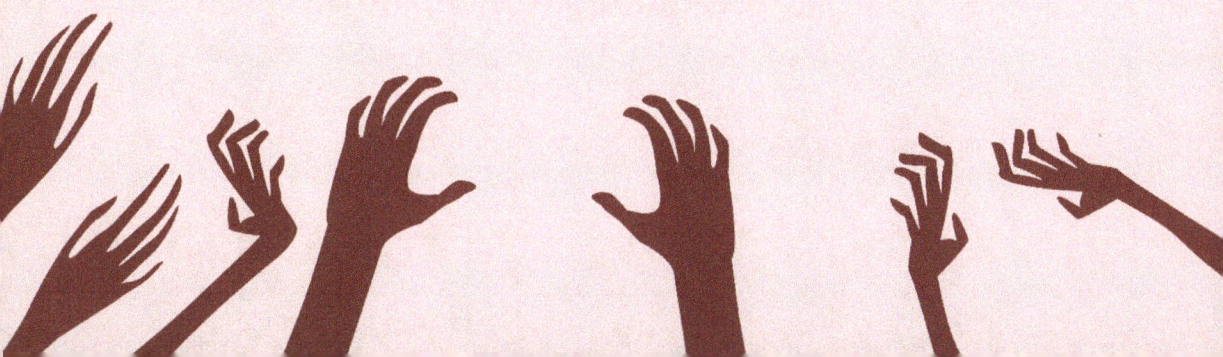

What's on your mind?

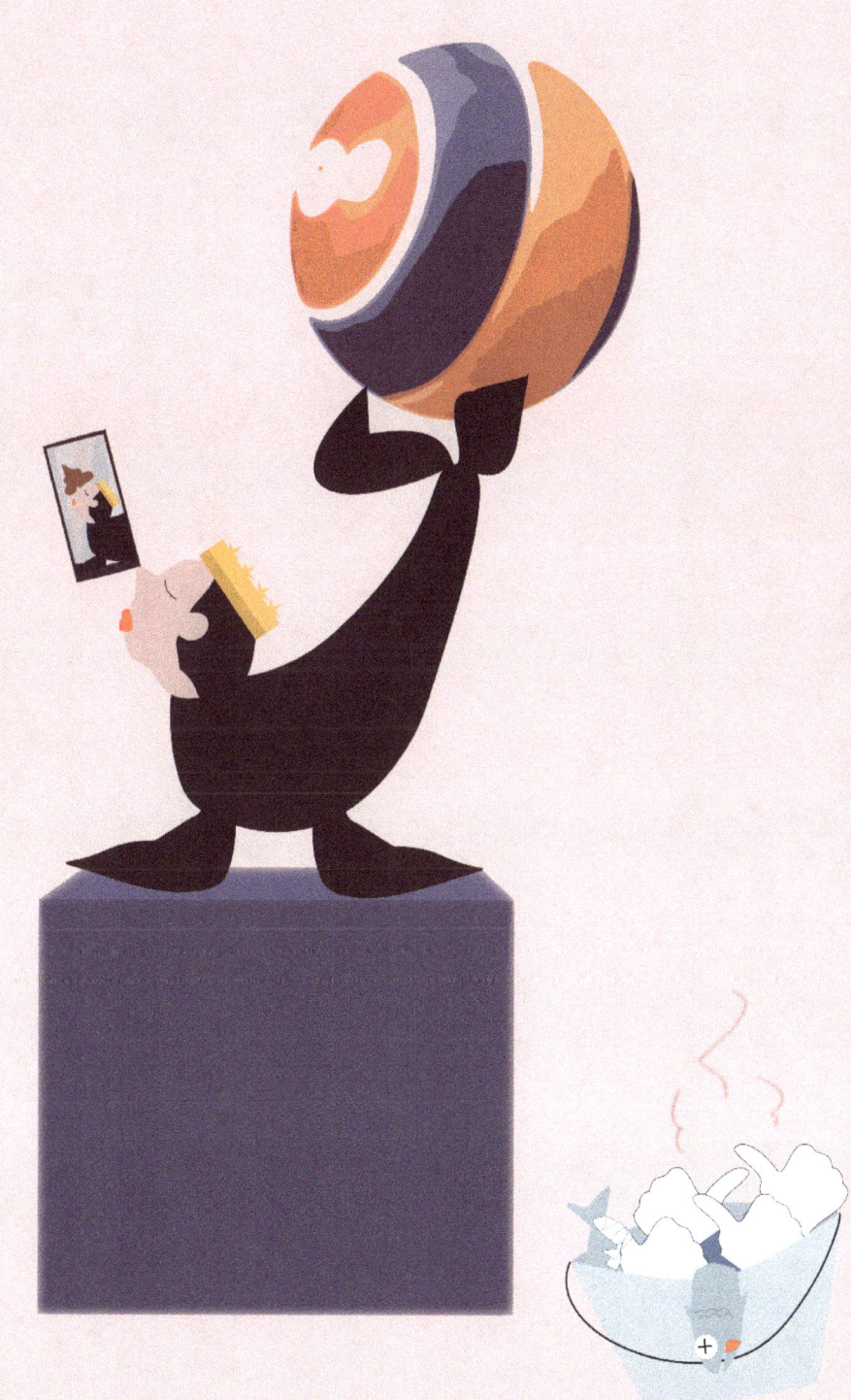

What's on your mind?

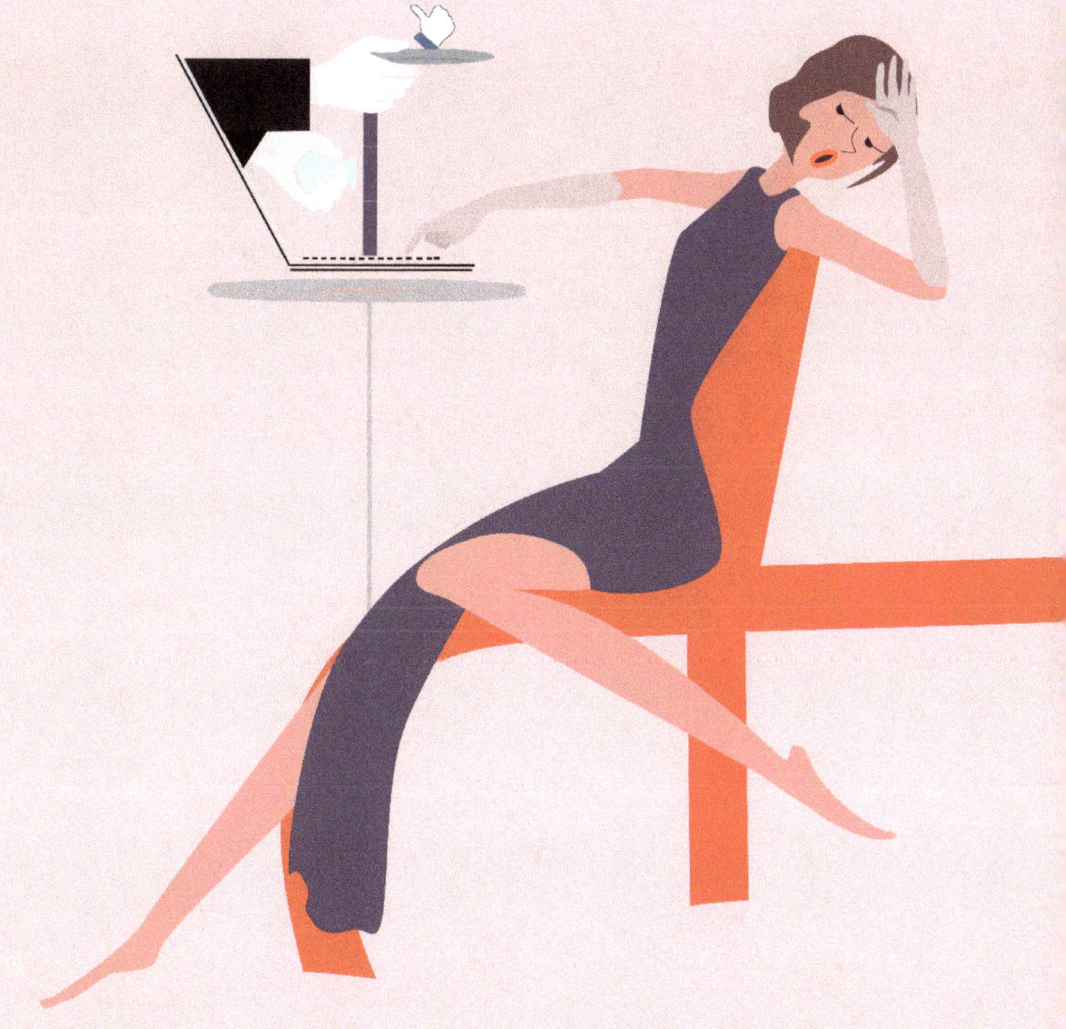

What's on your mind?

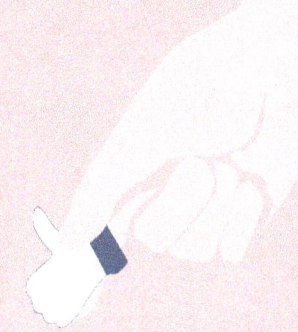

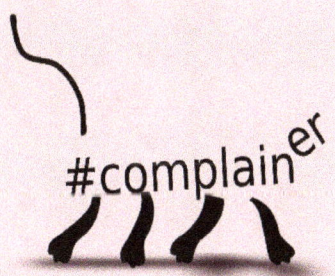

#complainer

M//-L

What's on your mind?

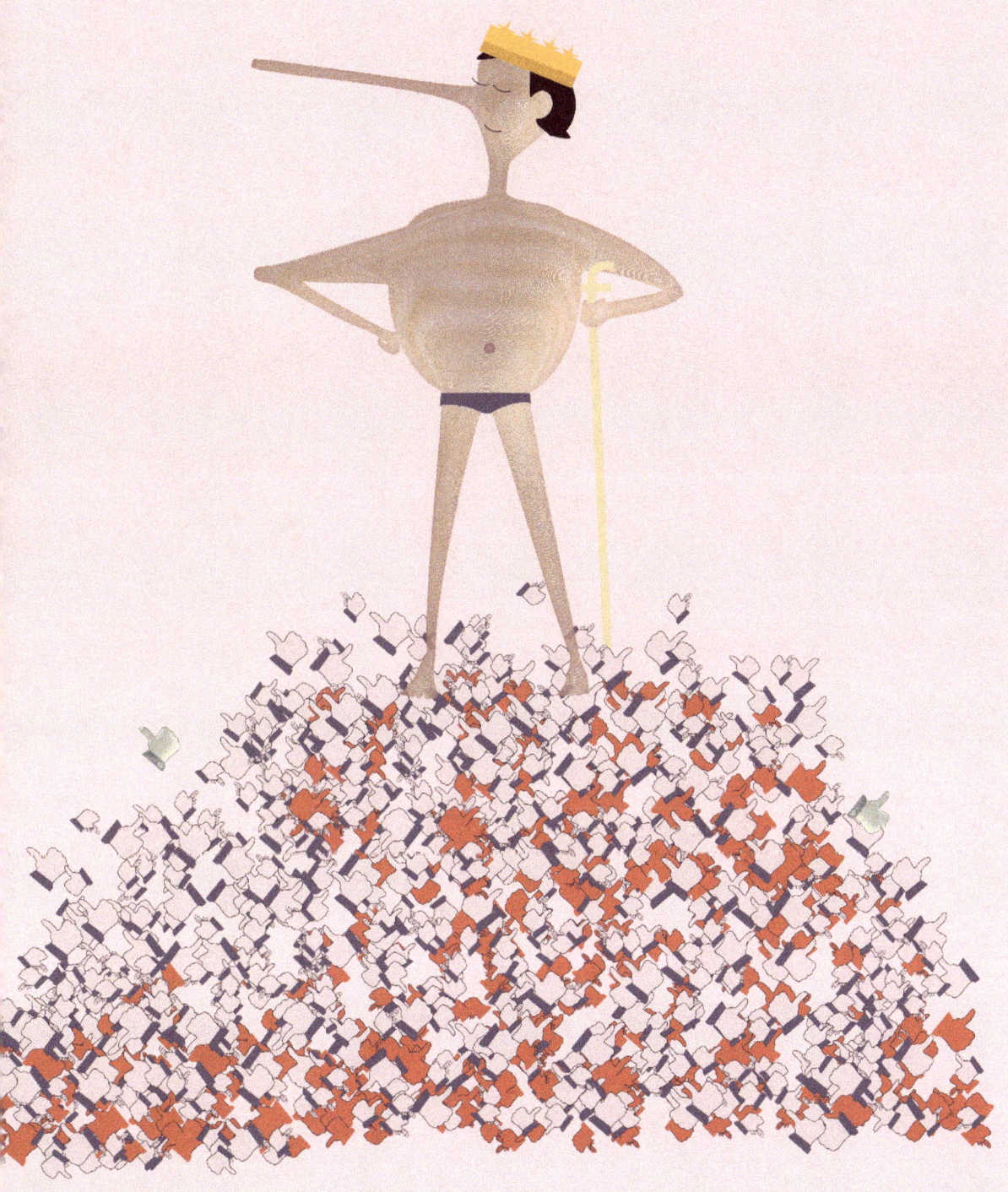

What's on your mind?

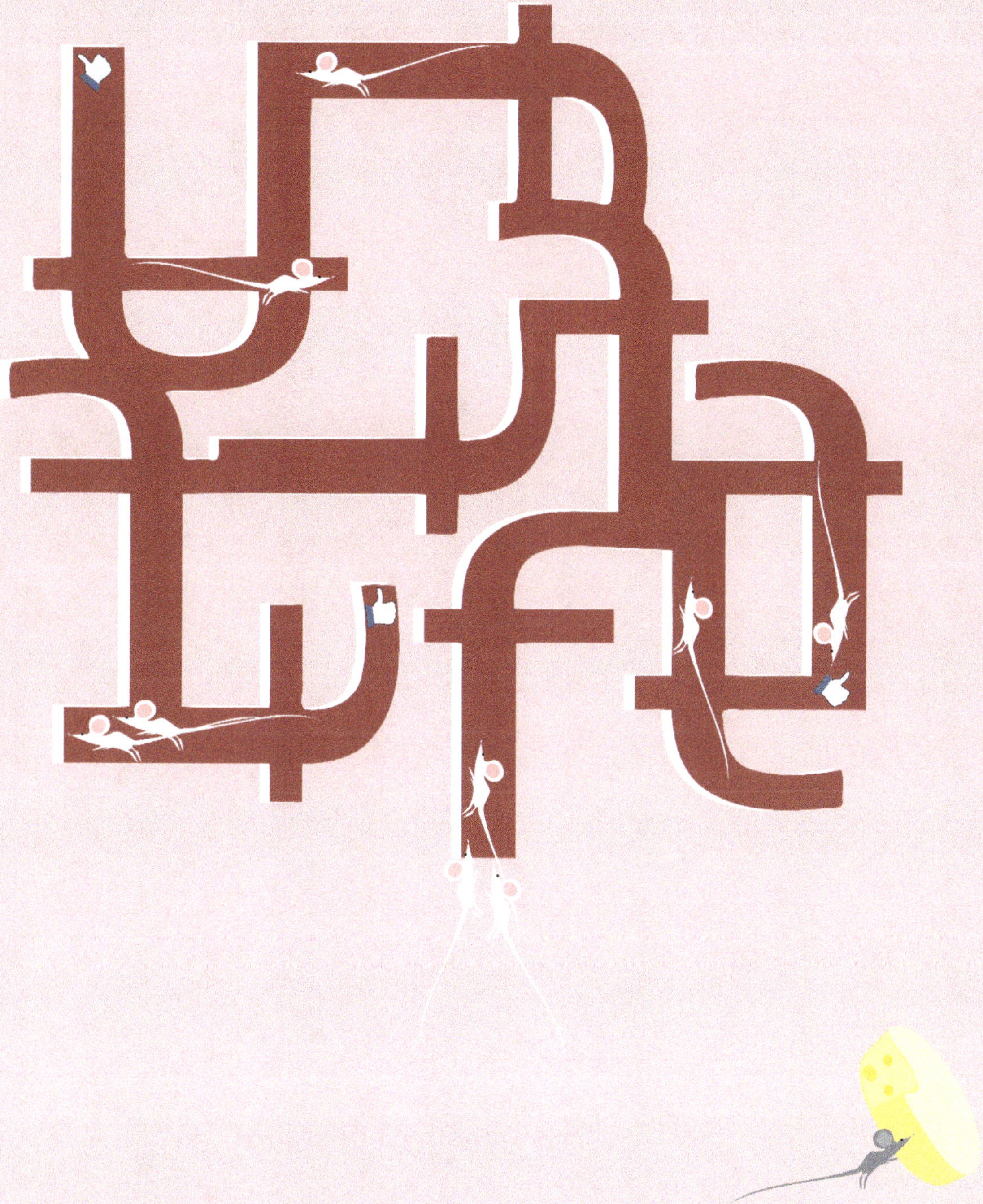

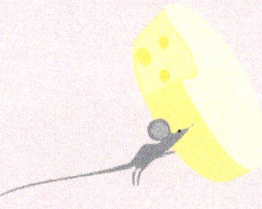

#GOALS

MYA

What's on your mind?

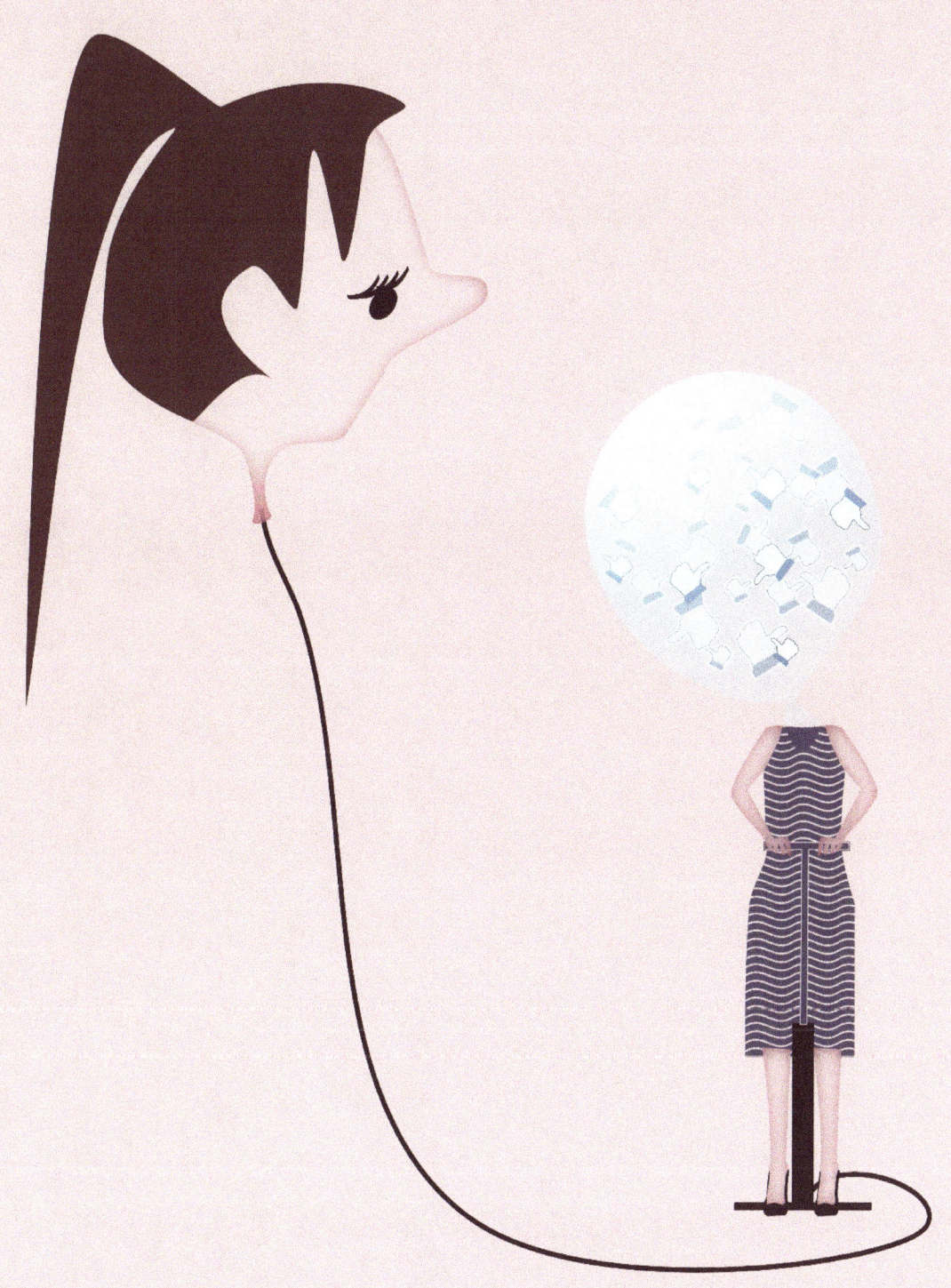

What's on your mind?

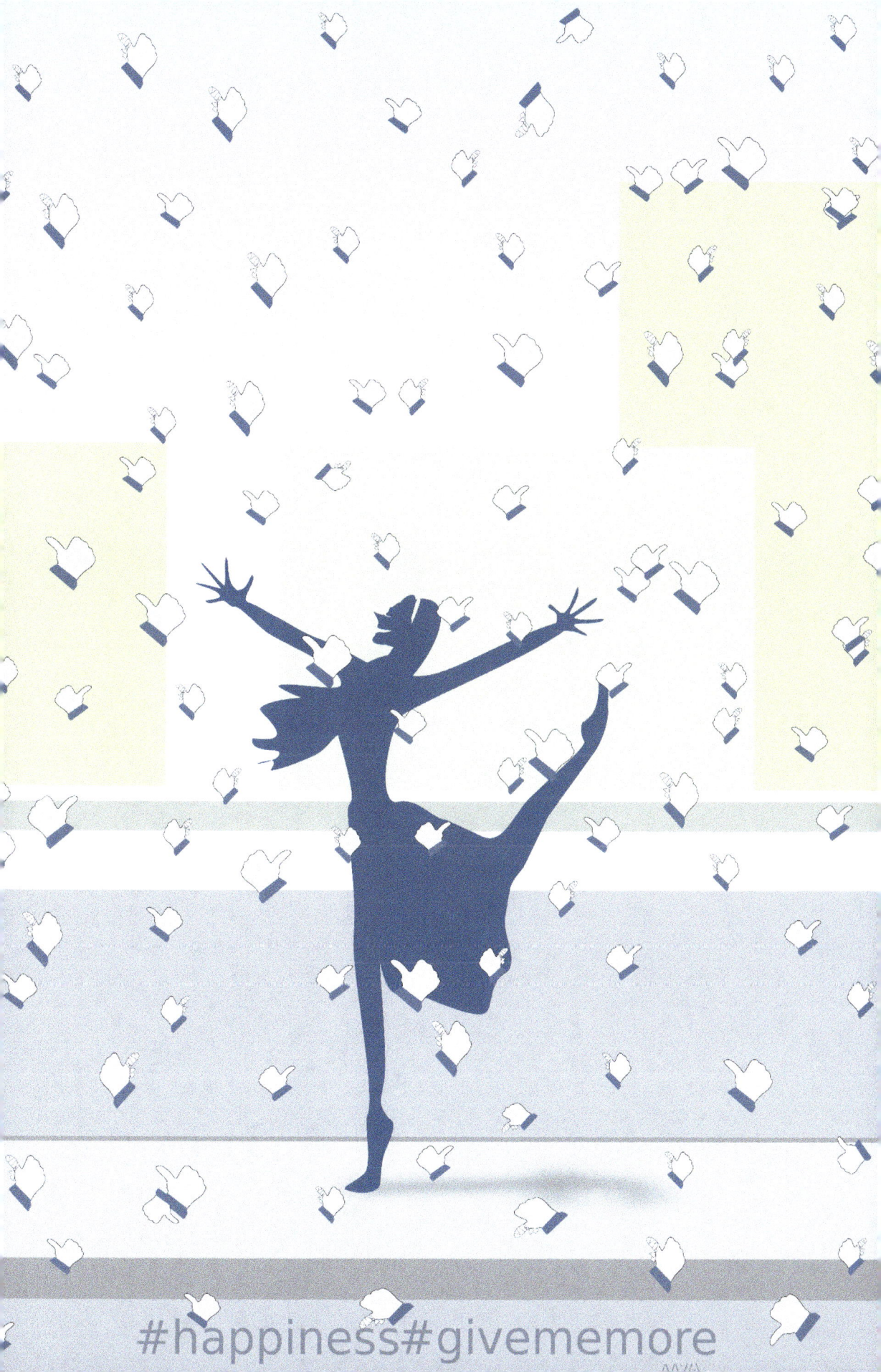
#happiness#givememore

What...

WHAT RULES THE WORLD

IN 2019

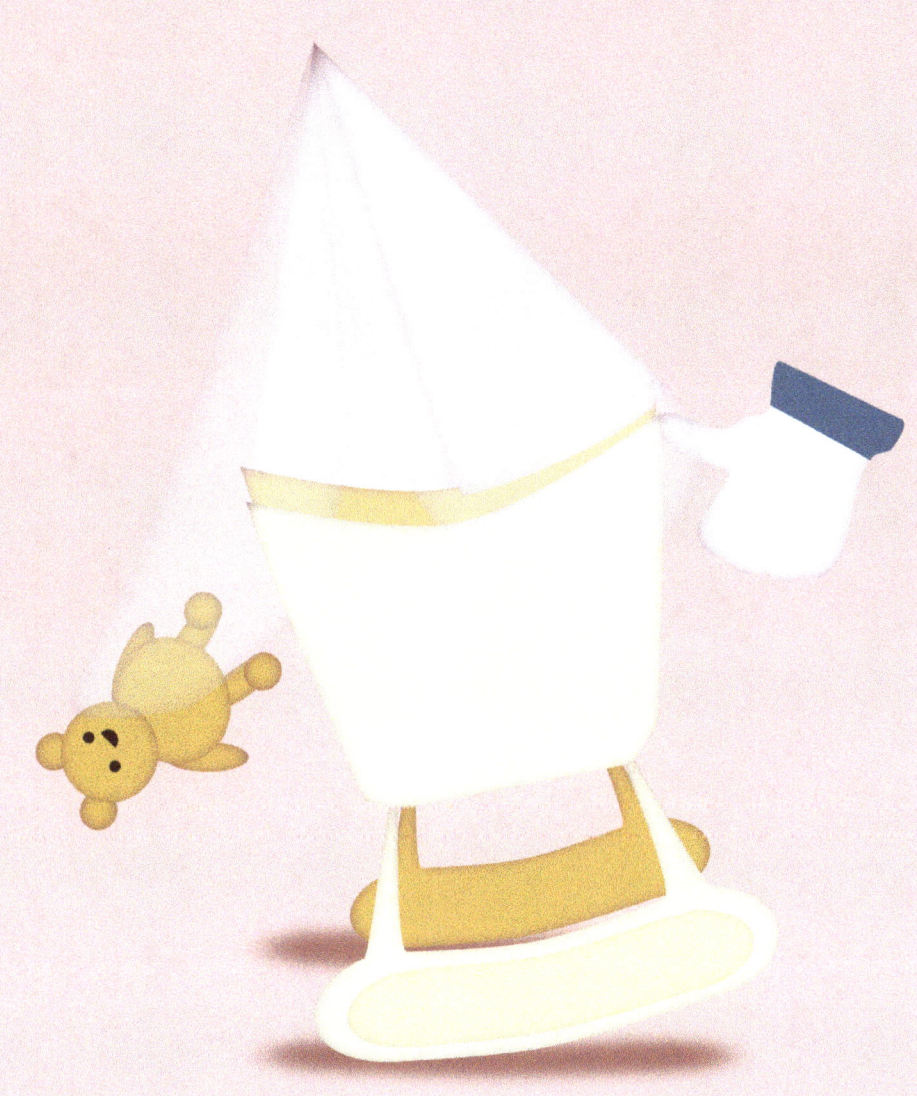

Monkey see, monkey do

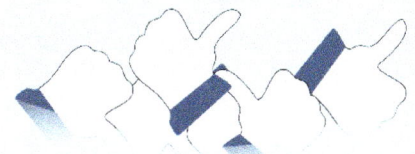

#brain**f**reeze

Monkey do not see, but monkey want to believe

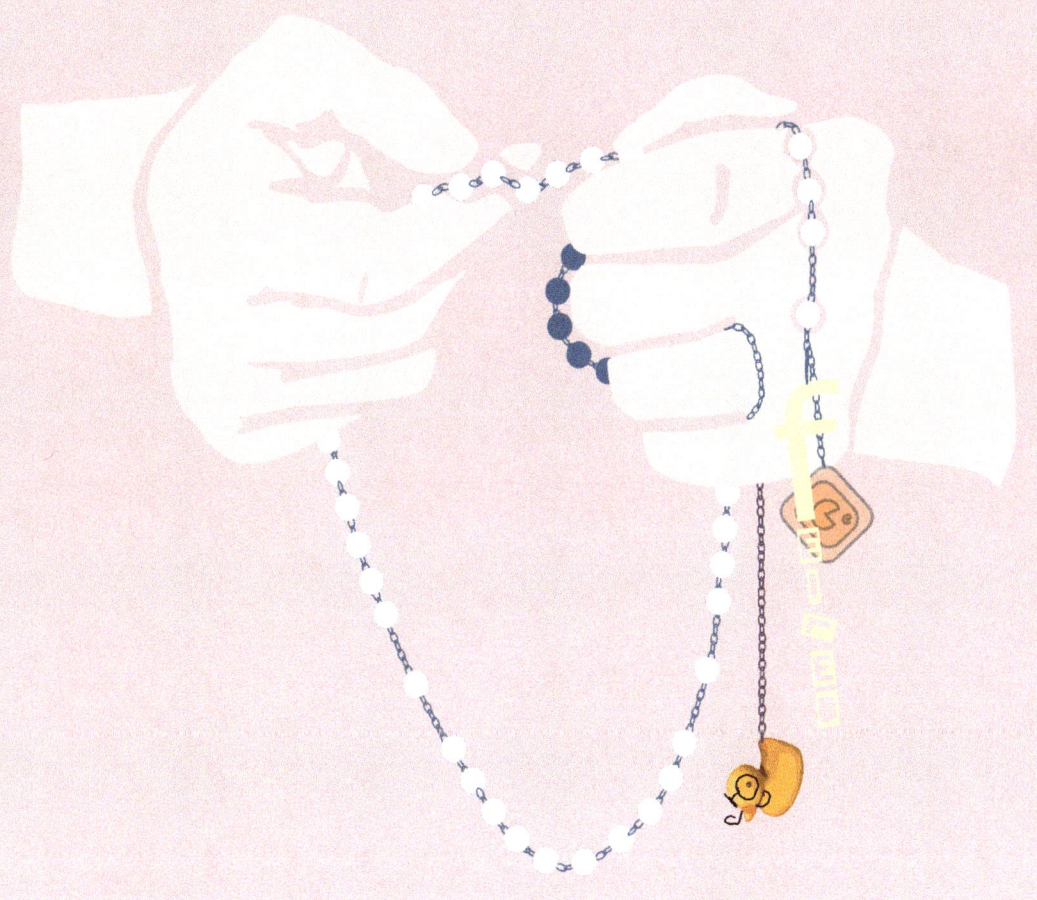

A friend has commented (on) your status

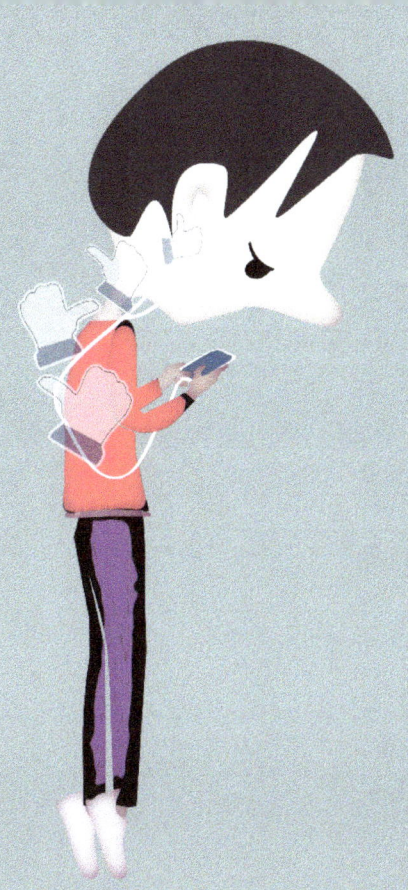
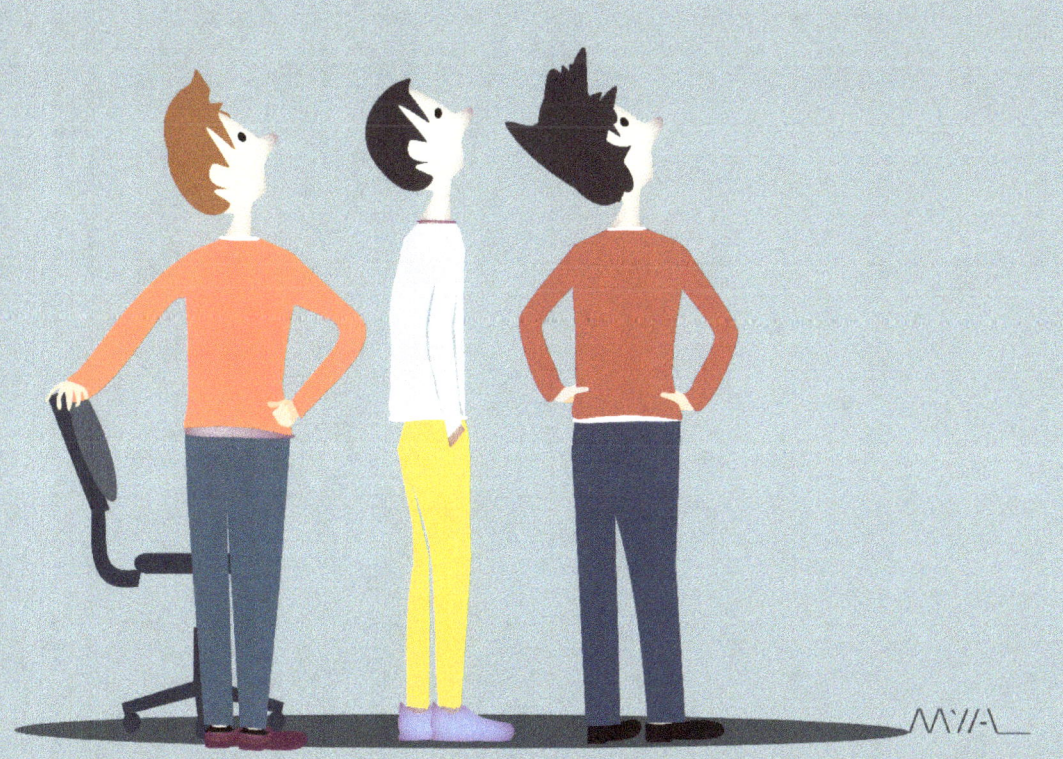

ANOTHER SWELLED HEAD

Find Friends

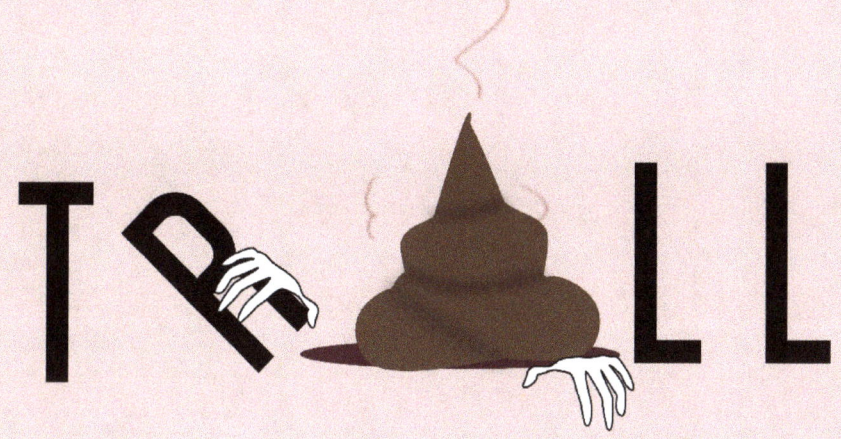

Find Friends

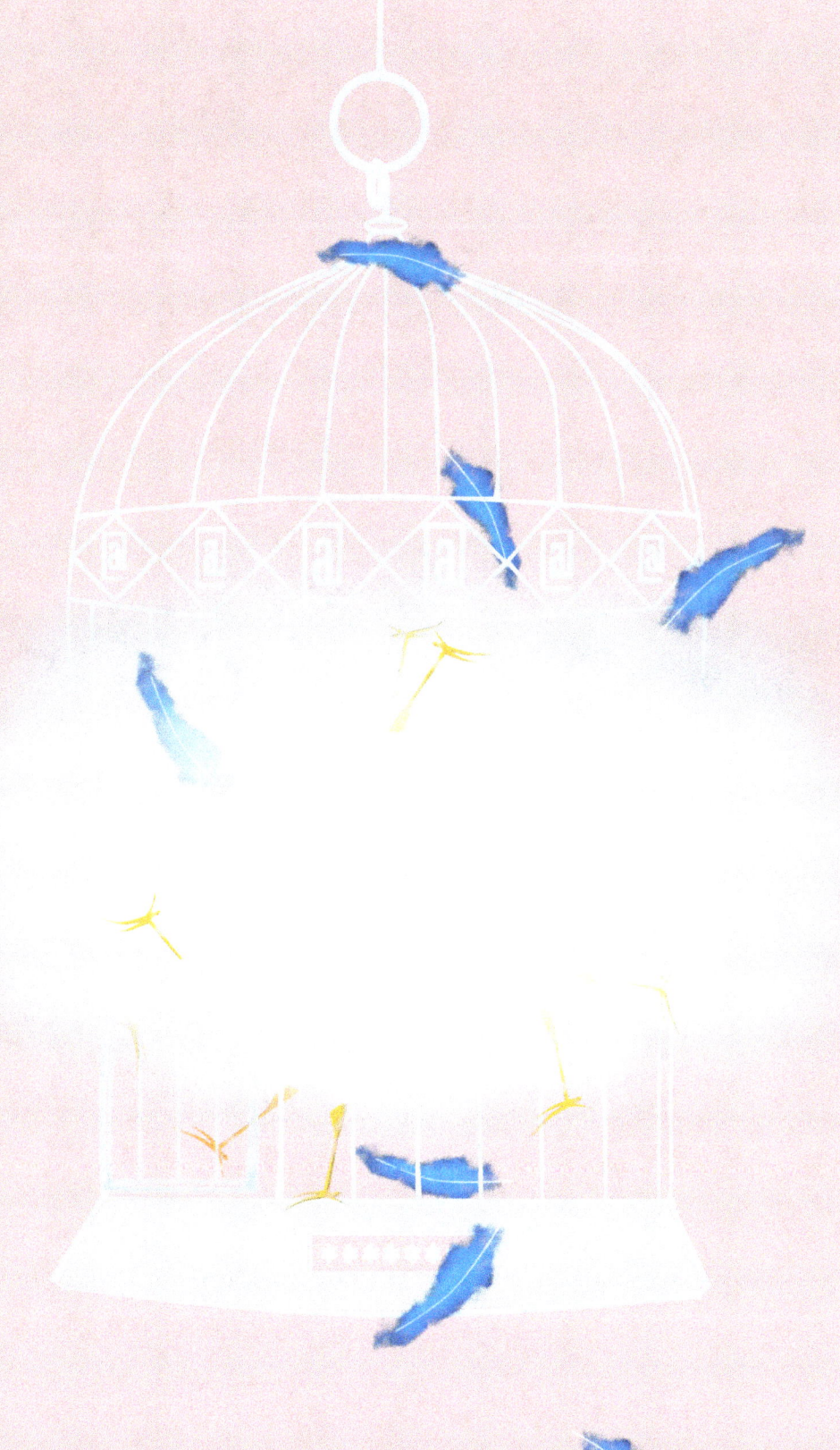

Find Friends

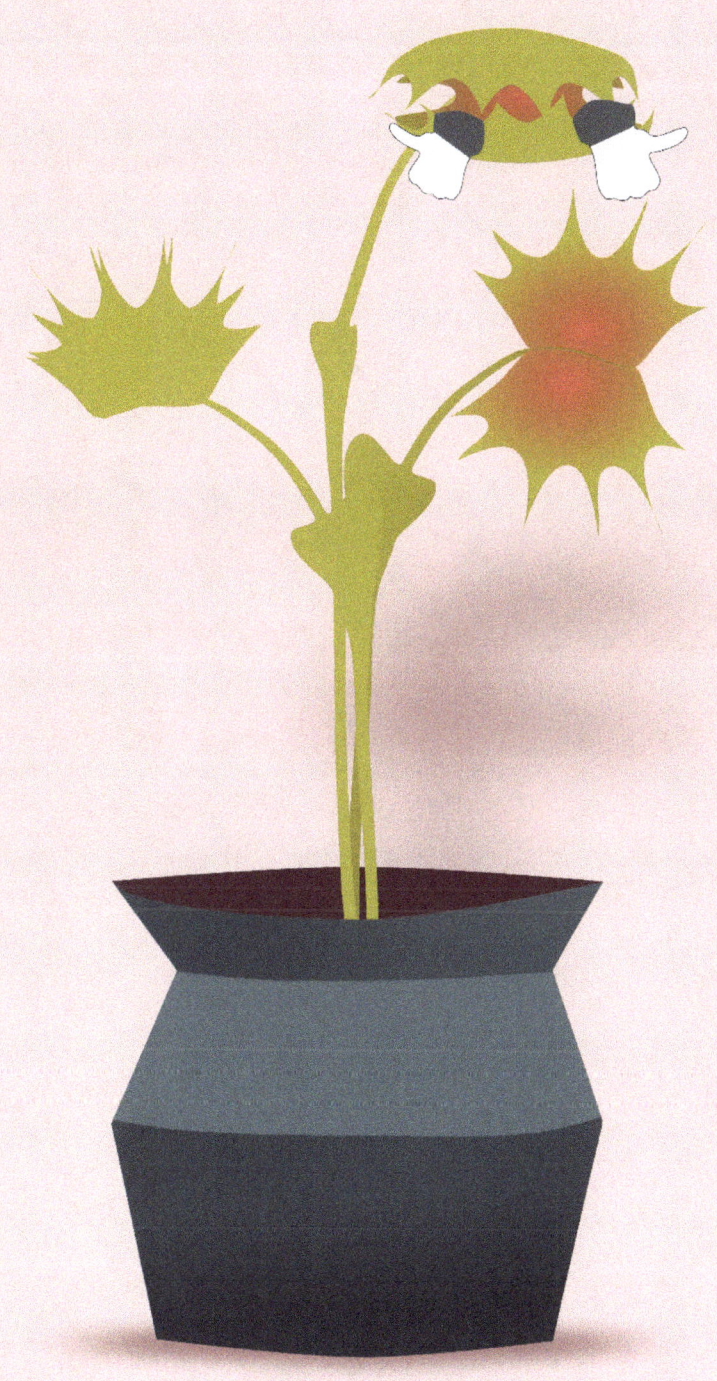

Find Friends

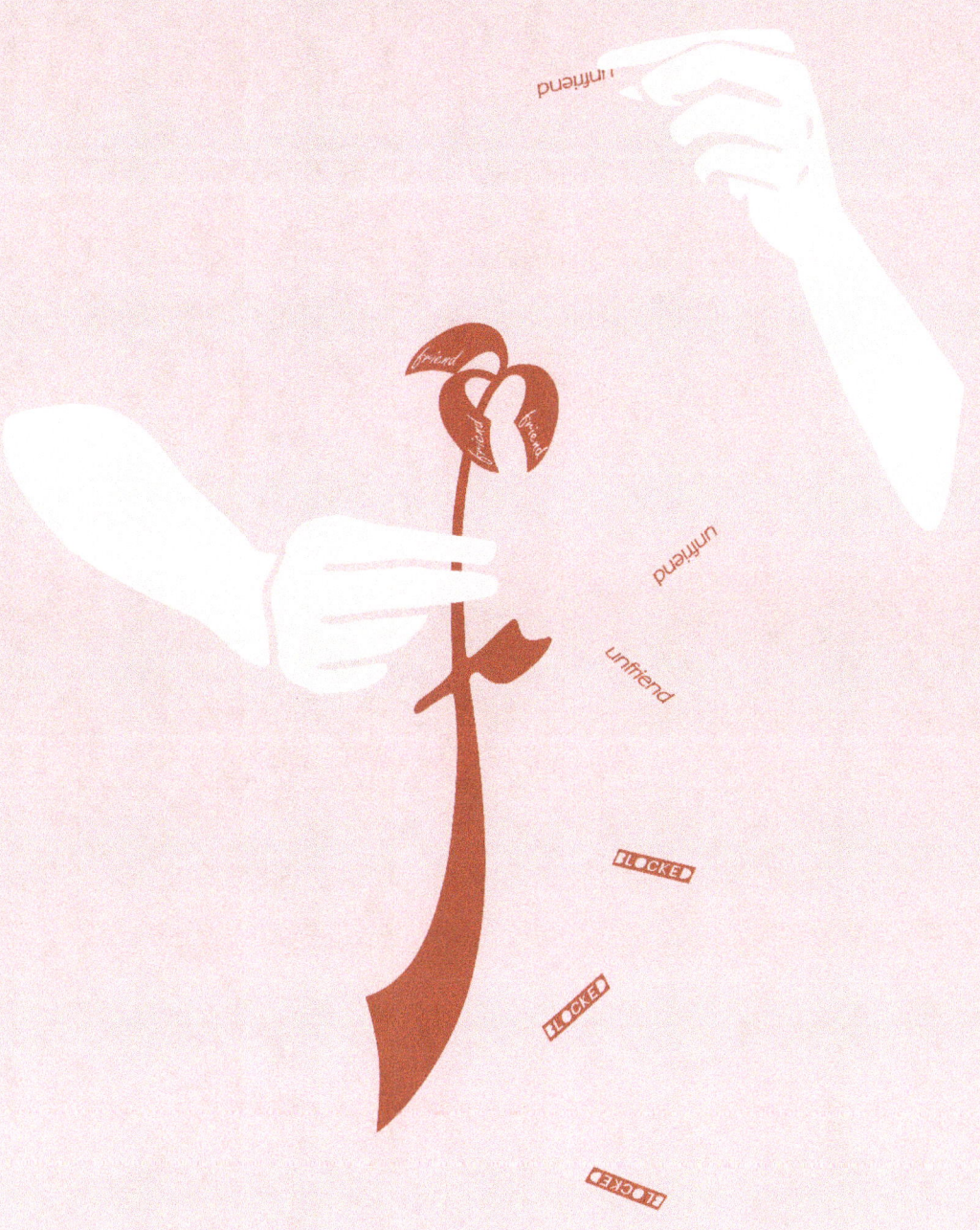

#FILTER
#Ifriendyou IFRIENDYOUNOT

Find Friends

RELATIONSHIPS

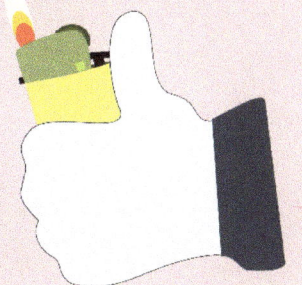

MIA

Messages

$$f + \text{password} + \text{you}$$
$$= f \quad ***** \quad U$$

Messages

SOCIAL

DISTANCING

Log out

Deactivate Account

Delete Account

Tschüss!

MIA

Refresh

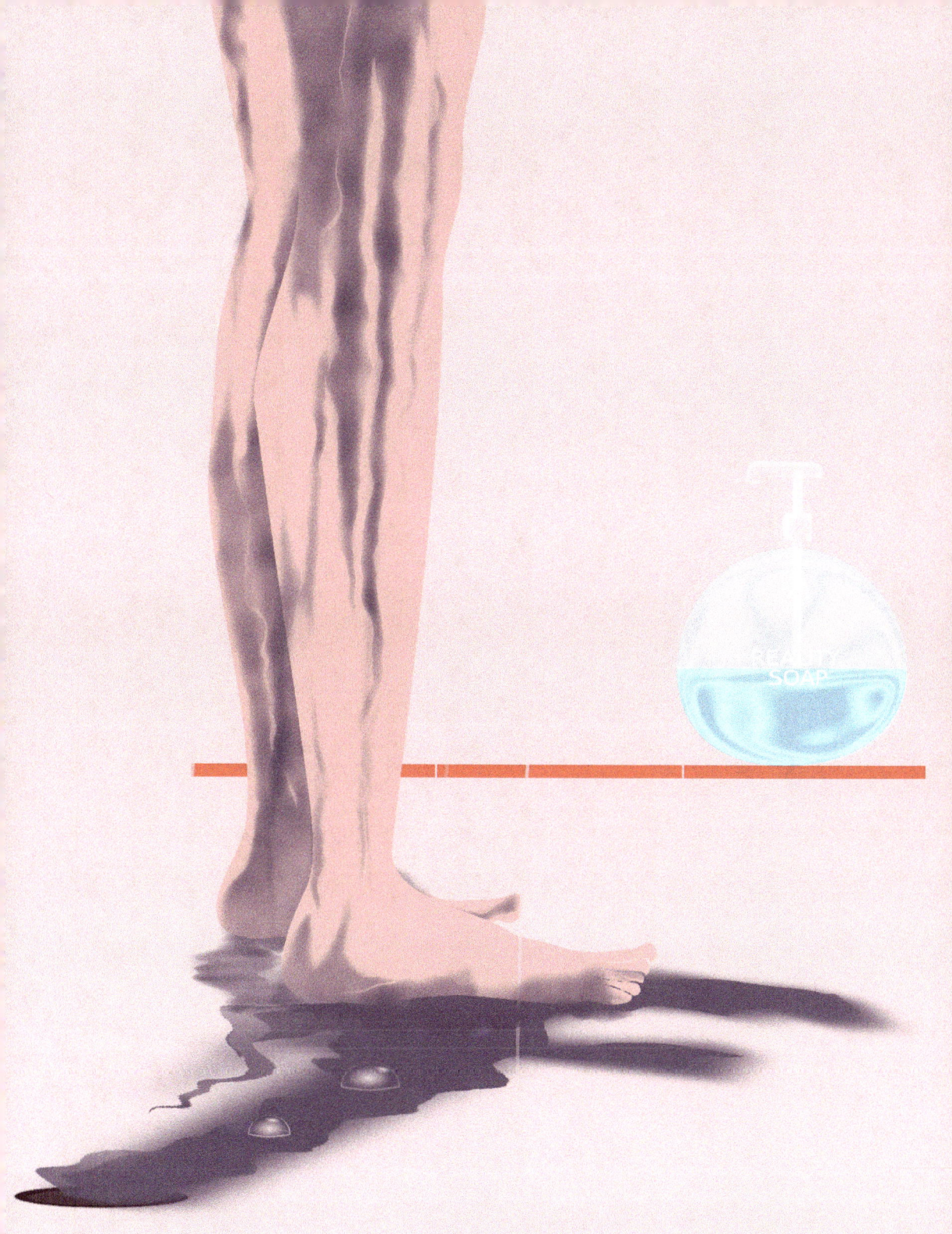

Home

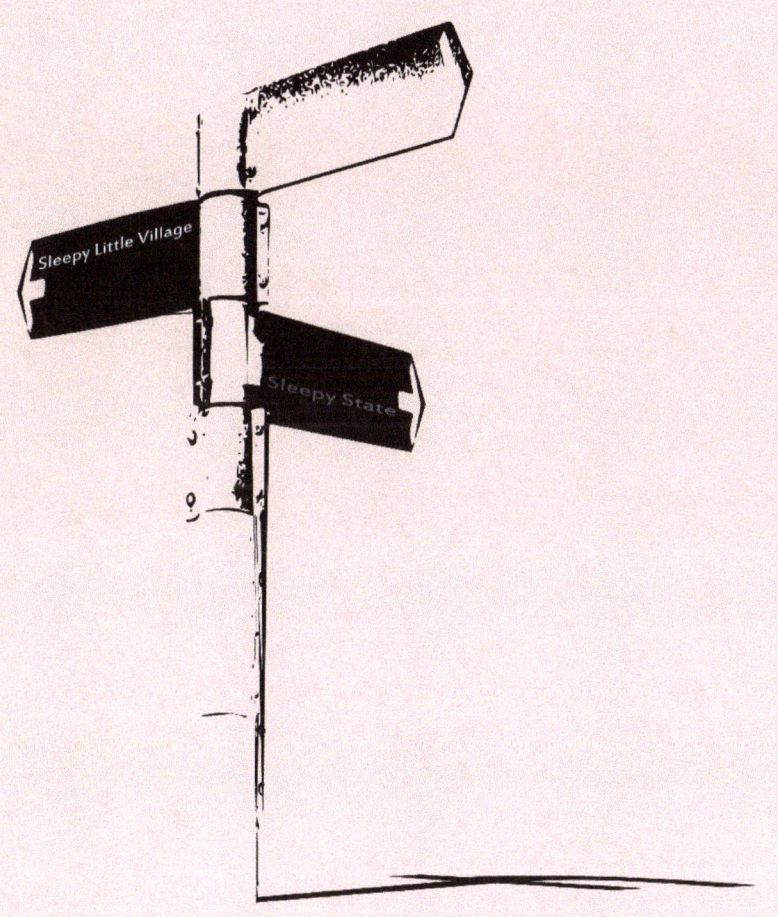

www.ingramcontent.com/pod-product-compliance
Lightning Source LLC
Chambersburg PA
CBHW080422190526
45161CB00004B/253

Biblioteca Angelica ms. 1551

and the Origins of Ethnohistorical Illustration of Asia and the Americas around 1600 in Rome

Barbara C. Anderson

American Philosophical Society Press
Philadelphia

Transactions of the
American Philosophical Society
Held at Philadelphia
for Promoting Useful Knowledge
Volume 109, Part 3

Cover Photo Credits

Figure 1.4 4. Taino figure, identified as Mexican. 5. Hometeotl/Hieitleutli. Rome, Biblioteca Angelica, ms. 1551, section 1, fol. 3. On concession from the Ministry for Arts and Culture and Tourism. All rights reserved.

Figure 2.6 Artist unknown, *Reina de Dialcan (Queen of Dialcan)*, Rome, Biblioteca Angelica ms. 1551, fol. 69. On concession from the Ministry for Arts and Culture and Tourism. All rights reserved.

Figure 3.6 Artist unknown, Maytac Capac. Rome, Biblioteca Angelica ms. 1551, section 3, fol. 74. On concession from the Ministry for Arts and Culture and Tourism. All rights reserved.

ISBN: 978-1-60618-093-8
Ebook ISBN: 978-1-60618-098-3
U.S. ISSN: 0065-9746

Library of Congress Cataloging-in-Publication Data

Names: Anderson, Barbara C., author.
Title: Biblioteca Angelica ms. 1551 and the origins of ethnohistorical
    illustration of Asia and the Americas around 1600 in Rome / Barbara C.
    Anderson.
Description: Philadelphia : American Philosophical Society, [2020] |
    Series: Transactions of the American Philosophical Society, 0065-9746 ;
    volume 109, part 3 | Includes bibliographical references and index. |
    Summary: "An exploration of the classical text, Biblioteca Angelica
    Manuscript 1551, including explanations and theories on how it came to
    be"-- Provided by publisher.
Identifiers: LCCN 2020027248 | ISBN 9781606180938 (paperback) | ISBN
    9781606180983 (epub)
Subjects: LCSH: Anthropological illustration--Europe--History. | Watercolor
    painting, European--Themes, motives. | Biblioteca angelica (Rome,
    Italy). Manuscript. 1551--Illustrations. | Indigenous peoples in art.
Classification: LCC ND2192.E85 A53 2020 | DDC 758/.994--dc23
LC record available at https://lccn.loc.gov/2020027248

Also available as an ebook.

Contents

Acknowledgments

My deepest gratitude goes to the Getty Research Institute for supporting an initial consultation of Biblioteca Angelica ms. 1551 in Rome in 1995, and to the American Philosophical Society for awarding a Franklin Research Grant for a lengthier examination in 2016, as well as support for Latin translations and photographs. Warmest thanks go to the staff of the Biblioteca Angelica and photographer Mario Setter for their cordial reception and patient assistance to an investigator with highly imperfect Italian.

Interpretation of each section of ms. 1551 often required the expertise of generous scholars in fields outside my own. For section 1, I am especially grateful to Barbara Mundy, whose explanation for one cryptic and seemingly concocted Nahuatl word turned out to be key to the understanding of the drawings and their cognates. Section 2's Latin inscriptions were translated by Eduardo Engelsing, Antoine Haacker, and Burt Westermeier, who shared my fascination with the material and showed me the nuances of early modern language hidden in plain sight in the texts. Cristin Sethi McKnight forwarded my questions about papermaking in 16th-century Asia to her colleagues, whose perspectives and knowledge were indispensable. For the third section, I benefitted enormously from long discussions over several years on Inca history and material culture with Thomas B.F. Cummins, Juan Ossio, Elena Phipps, Nancy Turner, Karen Trentelman, Rolena Adorno, Ivan Boserup, and Emily Engel. Alexander Nagel's careful reading of and thoughtful comments on the whole manuscript were invaluable. I am greatly indebted to all who enriched my knowledge of such diverse areas, but solely responsible for any and all failings in this work.

List of Illustrations

Chapter 1

1.1 Recreation of intended screenfold arrangement (Anderson diagram).

1.2 8. Image identified as Mexican, but actually Japanese. Rome, Biblioteca Angelica, ms. 1551, section 1, fol. 4v. On concession from the Ministry for Arts and Culture and Tourism. All rights reserved.

1.3 2. Images identified as Mexican, but actually the Roman gods Mercury and Jupiter. Rome, Biblioteca Angelica, ms. 1551, section 1, fol. 2. On concession from the Ministry for Arts and Culture and Tourism. All rights reserved.

1.4 4. Taino figure, identified as Mexican. 5. Hometeotl/Hieitleutli. Rome, Biblioteca Angelica, ms. 1551, section 1, fol. 3. On concession from the Ministry for Arts and Culture and Tourism. All rights reserved.

1.5 Cesare Malfatti, *Quetzalcoatl* from *Codex Ríos*, based on drawing by Philips de Winghe, Cartari/Pignoria 1626, p. 550.

1.6 Alfonso Chacón (Ciacconius) or Philips de Winghe, *Homehuic and Entipalcoatl from codex in Vatican attributed to Pedro de los Ríos*, 1592. Rome, Biblioteca Angelica ms. 1564, fol. 57. On concession from the Ministry for Arts and Culture and Tourism. All rights reserved.

1.7 Pedro de los Ríos, *Homoyoca, Codex Ríos*, Vatican, Biblioteca Apostolica, Vat.lat.3738, fol. 1v. Reproduced by permission of Biblioteca Apostolica Vaticana, with all rights reserved.

1.8 Alfonso Chacón (Ciacconius) and workshop artists, copy of manuscript page from book in the Vatican. Rome, Biblioteca Angelica ms. 1564, fol. 5. On concession from the Ministry for Arts and Culture and Tourism. All rights reserved.

1.9 Pedro de los Ríos, *Quetzalcoatl, Codex Ríos*, Vatican, Biblioteca Apostolica, Vat.lat.3738, fol. 37r. On concession from the Ministry for Arts and Culture and Tourism. All rights reserved.

1.10 Alfonso Chacón (Ciacconius) and workshop artists, sketches of Early Christian figures in S. Andrea. Rome, Biblioteca Angelica ms. 1564, fol. 44. On concession from the Ministry for Arts and Culture and Tourism. All rights reserved.

Chapter 2

Chapter 3

Introduction

The Biblioteca Angelica in Rome holds a green leather-bound volume containing three sets of watercolor drawings, each depicting non-European peoples or places. Catalogued as ms. 1551,[1] the volume is part of a large donation made by the ancient and noble Roman Massimo family to the library in the late 19th century and was first identified in the death inventory of the famous collector and antiquarian Camillo Massimo (1620–1677).[2] The first set consists of representations of deities from around the world: Egyptian, East Indian, Japanese, Roman, Mexican, and Taino; the second part, Asian peoples in architectural or landscape settings from Hormuz, India, Indonesia, the Philippines, Pegu, Ceylon, Timor, Japan, and China; and the third, individual Inca kings and one queen from Peru. The first two series are on glossy, translucent Asian papers, either pale or deeper yellow, or dark red, and mounted on European paper with an unidentified watermark.[3] The drawings in the third section are executed directly on the same type of European paper, with unidentified watermark and the same degree and character of foxing and wear.

All three sets are unattributed, out of order as mounted and bound, and either undated or incorrectly dated. Each is the work of a different artist and scribe (or in the case of the Asian section, probably two scribes), but inscriptions on all sheets are in Spanish, with the Asian section also bearing lengthier Latin texts. In addition to the shared Spanish and papers, the only other obvious connection among the three series is date, which, based on previously unexamined artistic and calligraphic style, would fall between the last decades of the sixteenth century and the first decade of the seventeenth. The Inca section would be the latest in execution, as it is made directly on the paper on which the other two sets are mounted, and last bound. Detailed discussions of each folio (fol.) in all sections follow at the end of the chapters on individual sections.

The first and third sections have been subjected to scholarly examination, but only in isolation and with regard to selected elements,[4] and the second section has apparently not been previously investigated.[5] None of the three has been considered in depth in terms of materials or manufacture, possible relations to one another or other contemporaneous illustrations, or role in advancing understanding of the depicted peoples. Nevertheless, clues within the drawings and their style and content suggest not only new interpretations but also specific links between and among them, and likely origins, placing them squarely into the most intense period in the early modern era of European interest in these cultures.

Chroniclers in this moment were recounting and illustrating the histories of lands newly claimed, either physically or spiritually, or opened up to trade with Europeans, particularly in the Americas and Asia, but also Africa. Their efforts often considered these disparate cultures in relation to one another as well as to ancient Greek, Roman, and Egyptian cultures.[6]

Many of these observers of other cultures visited or resided in Rome or sent descriptions back to Rome of the new lands they saw. Michele Mercati (1541–1593) touched on Mexican codices in Rome in *De gli obelischi di Roma,* otherwise focused on Egyptian antiquities in that city, and published in 1589.[7] José de Acosta (1540–1600), a Jesuit who had lived in Peru and Mexico between 1570 and 1587, and in Rome in 1565, 1588, and 1590 to 1592, published his *Historia general y moral de las Indias* in 1590.[8] While concentrating primarily on the peoples of Peru and Mexico, Acosta's book also included a discussion of elements of Chinese culture he had first learned while in Mexico from his fellow Jesuit Alonso Sánchez (1547–1593), whom Acosta met in Mexico in 1585 on his way to Spain from China and the Philippines, and from a number of Chinese men Acosta encountered in Mexico. Acosta's Jesuit colleagues in Asia sent accounts of the people and their customs in letters back to the Gesù, their motherhouse in Rome, beginning with Francis Xavier (1506–1552) in the 1540s. The first known illustrations of the people of Kongo were published in Rome in 1591 by Duarte Lopes.[9] The Paduan antiquarian Lorenzo Pignoria (1571–1631), who visited Rome and had copies made of objects from China, Japan, India, Mexico, and Peru in Roman collections in 1605 and 1607, added a long section on comparative religions of all these areas except Peru to his expansions of Vicenzo Cartari's *Imagini della sposizione degli dei degli antichi* (1556), first issued in 1615 under the title *Le vere e nove imagini de gli dei delli antichi di Vicenzo Cartari.*[10] That ms. 1551 is in Rome is probably not coincidental, and that these three superficially disparate sets of watercolors are bound together suggests a common provenance within that city before Camillo Massimo.

CHAPTER 1:

Gods of Ancient Rome, the East and West Indies, Egypt, China, and Japan

Twenty-four small images are painted in a palette of green, blue, yellow, orange, pink, and red on glossy, translucent pale-yellow Asian paper forming double spreads, some cropped at one or both sides, and at one time folded in half. Spanish inscriptions describe the deities (with Nahuatl identification also used for the Mexican "idols"), without the condescension or disparagement common in such characterizations of this era.

Asian papers were known but evidently not widely used in Italy by the later 16th century. Alessandro Valignano (1539–1606), a Jesuit visitor in India from 1574 and Japan in the 1580s, wrote letters to Rome while in Japan on yellow Japanese paper, according to entries in the Roman Archives of the Society of Jesus.[11] Lorenzo Pignoria's death inventory, compiled in 1631, listed Chinese papers among his holdings.[12] But, although Asian papers were collected, no other artistic use of Asian papers in Italy is known in this period, so it possible that these are the only surviving examples.[13] This would suggest that the use there of these papers might have been confined in this period to antiquarians in contact with missionaries, likely Jesuits, who had recently established missions in Asia, and brought or sent the papers from Asia to Rome.

The images, painted on both sides of each sheet, are numbered 1 to 24 but are out of order as bound. Nevertheless, an intended order and format may be discerned: the unbound numerical sequence may be reconstructed by imagining each sheet folded in half and connected at each side, accordion or screenfold style, an arrangement that seems to have been implemented, and then undone, as several sheets have been cut and parts of words lost (**fig. 1.1**). One slight deviation from the simple accordion fold is in the middle, where a single sheet (numbers 6, 7, and 8, respectively) would take the place of a folded one. Numbers 1–14 would run consecutively on one side, left to right, and 15–24 on the reverse, also left to right.

In this numerical ordering, there is no consistent grouping of deities by region, but the sequencing seems deliberate because number 1 is on the same side of a sheet as number 24 and the reverse of 2 and 3, folding over so that 1 begins the screenfold, while the adjacent number 24 ends it. This would imply that the numbering was inserted after the screenfold was formed. Why the sheet numbered 6, 7, 8, and 21 was not attached like the others is unclear but seems to suggest an error in the numbering before the actual assembly of the sheets.

**Screenfold arrangement
sheets and image**

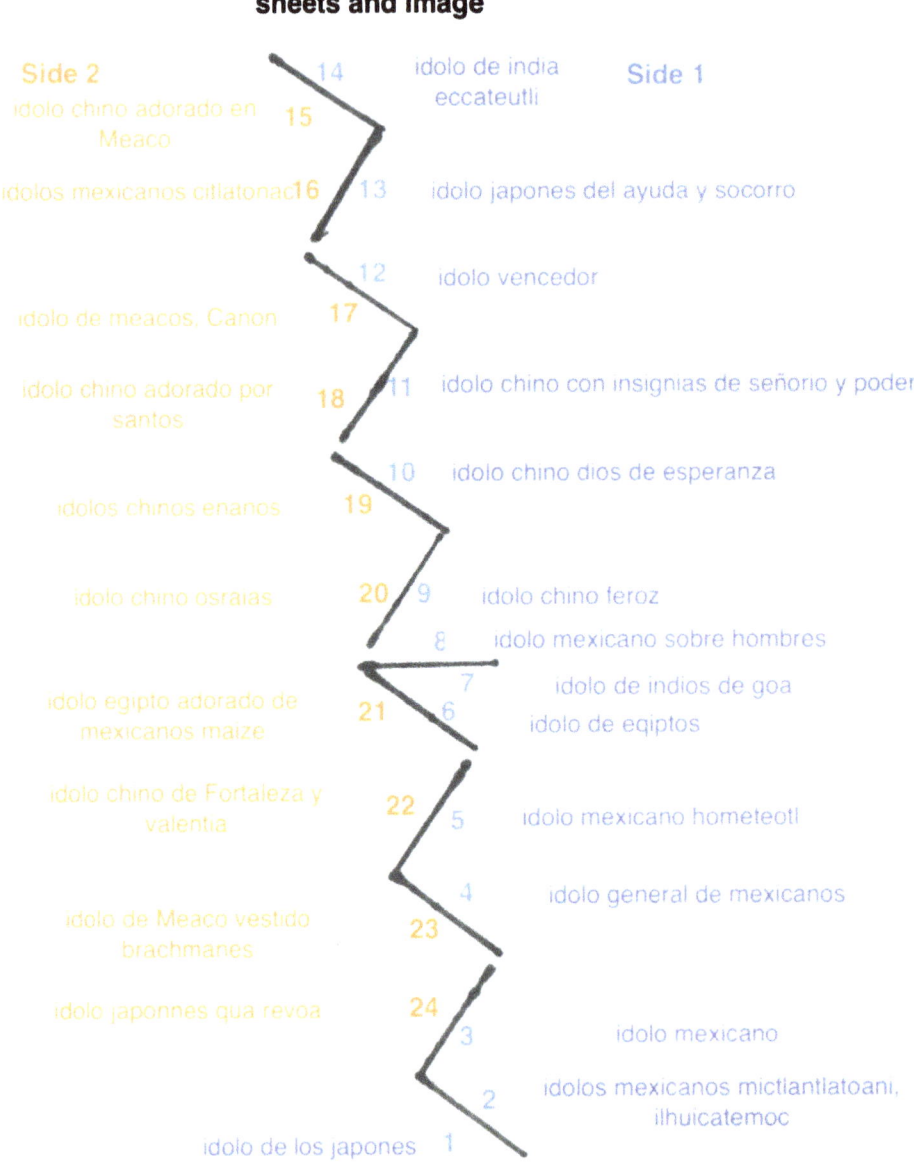

Side 2

idolo chino adorado en Meaco

idolos mexicanos citlatonac

idolo de meacos, Canon

idolo chino adorado por santos

idolos chinos enanos

idolo chino osraias

idolo egipto adorado de mexicanos maize

idolo chino de Fortaleza y valentia

idolo de Meaco vestido brachmanes

idolo japonnes qua revoa

idolo de los japones

idolo de india eccateutli

Side 1

idolo japones del ayuda y socorro

idolo vencedor

idolo chino con insignias de señorio y poder

idolo chino dios de esperanza

idolo chino feroz

idolo mexicano sobre hombres

idolo de indios de goa

idolo de eqiptos

idolo mexicano hometeotl

idolo general de mexicanos

idolo mexicano

idolos mexicanos mictlantlatoani, ilhuicatemoc

Figure 1.1   Recreation of intended screenfold arrangement (Anderson diagram).

The twenty-four images of gods, some misidentified, include: two Roman or Egyptian (although identified in the inscription as Mexican); four Mexican, one now understood as Taino but believed at the time to be Mexican; two Egyptian; one East Indian; and sixteen Japanese, ten of which are erroneously called Chinese. In addition to the Japanese images mistaken for Chinese, other interesting errors of identification appear in the descriptive texts written in Spanish below the images. A few are incorrect as to specific deity or country but still understood correctly as Asian or American, such as the figure now known to be Taino (number 4).[14] In number 14, the figure is Mexican, imprecisely and oddly identified only as "Indian," as it comes from the same source as the images specified as Mexican, as shall be discussed below. In number 8, the figure is Japanese, not Mexican **(fig 1.2)**.

Other apparent errors, however, may actually be implicit but garbled cultural comparisons. In number 2, for example, the two illustrated figures are described in the text of ms. 1551 as the Mexican "idols" Mictlantlatoani and Huitcatemoc. They are probably not Egyptian, as Pignoria indicates,[15] but Roman, specifically Mercury and Jupiter, as they actually appear **(fig 1.3)**, likely alluding to a connection between the Mexican and Roman deities with their common dominion over the sky.

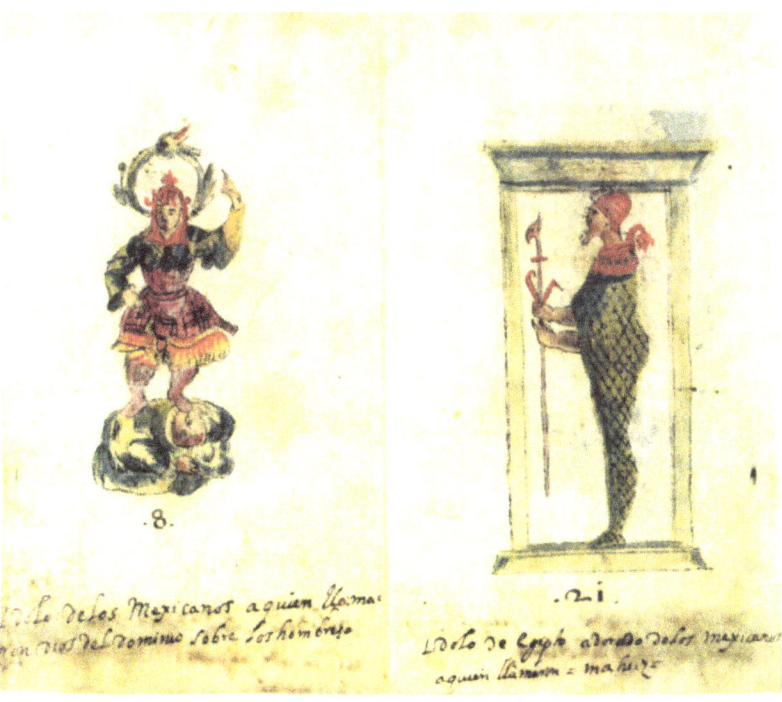

Figure 1.2   8. Image identified as Mexican, but actually Japanese. Rome, Biblioteca Angelica, ms. 1551, section 1, fol. 4v. On concession from the Ministry for Arts and Culture and Tourism. All rights reserved.

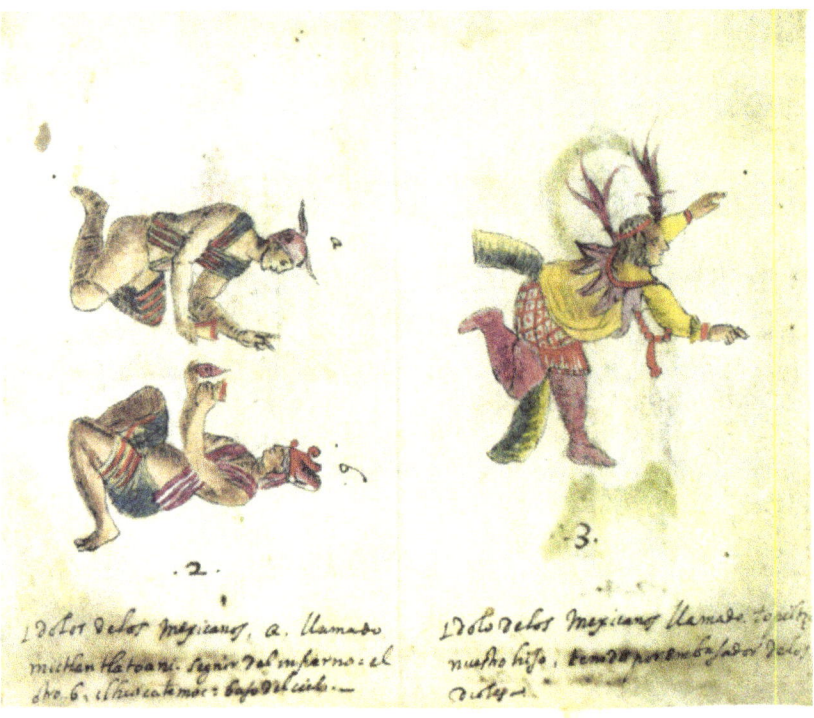

Figure 1.3   2. Images identified as Mexican, but actually the Roman gods Mercury and Jupiter. Rome, Biblioteca Angelica, ms. 1551, section 1, fol. 2. On concession from the Ministry for Arts and Culture and Tourism. All rights reserved.

Biblioteca Angelica mss. 1551 and Related materials in Italy: Biblioteca Angelica ms. 1564, Vaticanus 3738 (*Codex Ríos*), and Lorenzo Pignoria's new editions of Cartari

It has been well understood for many decades that there is a relationship among Biblioteca Angelica ms. 1551 and two images in Biblioteca Angelica ms. 1564, as well as with Codex Vaticanus A (or Vaticanus 3738, commonly known as *Codex Ríos*), Vicenzo Cartari and Lorenzo Pignoria's *Le Vere e nove imagini* (hereafter Cartari/Pignoria 1615), and Pignoria's revised second edition of 1626 (hereafter Cartari/Pignoria 1626).[16] The exact nature of those relationships, however, has been and continues to be debated.

One question concerns the sources of these images in Pignoria and ms. 1551. All the drawings in ms. 1551, section 1, appeared in print in Cartari/Pignoria 1615, in which gods from Mexico, Egypt, India, and Japan were added to the original discussions and illustrations of ancient Roman deities. Pignoria credited his immediate sources, but often ambiguously enough that his words have caused considerable confusion.

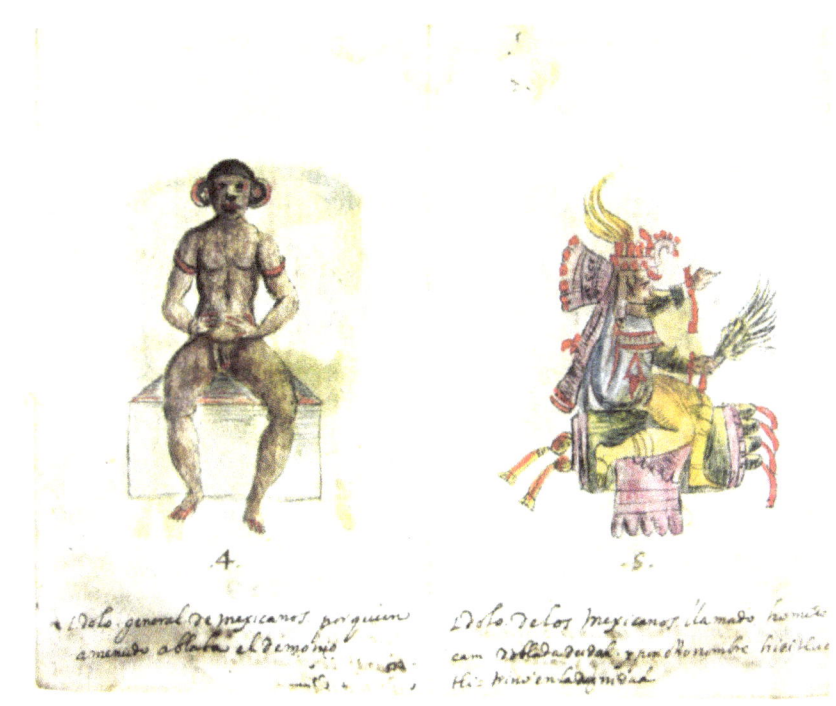

Figure 1.4 4. Taino figure, identified as Mexican. 5. Hometeotl/ Hieitleutli. Rome, Biblioteca Angelica, ms. 1551, section 1, fol. 3. On concession from the Ministry for Arts and Culture and Tourism. All rights reserved.

An example is the Taino deity identified as Mexican (**fig. 1.4**). Pignoria claimed it was based on a drawing of an object in the Munich *kunstkammer* belonging to Albrecht V, Duke of Bavaria (1528–1579), sent to him by Georg Herwart (1563–1622), who explained that the figure had been in the possession of Francisco Ximenez de Cisneros. Cisneros (1436–1517), archbishop of Toledo from 1495 to 1517, was involved in Caribbean affairs as an overseer when Columbus was deemed unfit to govern, so it is plausible that Cisneros was in possession of a Caribbean object. But, as Cisneros died in Spain in 1517, if it did belong to him there must have been at least one intermediate owner in Europe between Cisneros and Albrecht, and the object must have been in Rome, as several were known to be, at some point during that interval, including several *cemis*, or Taino figures of worship, accompanying a letter from Alessandro Geraldini (1455–1525), first bishop of Santo Domingo, to Pope Leo X (Giovanni Lorenzo de' Medici) in 1519 or 1520.[17] It could not have been among the gifts given to Albrecht in 1572 by Francesco de' Medici (1541–1587) if, as Francesco said in his letter to Albrecht in May of that year, the objects in the gift had recently arrived in Livorno from Mexico.[18] Lia Markey suggested, based on the Spanish prohibition against Italian shipping directly from the New World to an Italian port without first stopping in Seville, that the gift from Francesco de' Medici was not comprised of objects recently brought to Italy from Mexico but, rather, collected by Francesco over time, with some items perhaps obtained from his brother Ferdinando (1549–1609) in Rome.[19]

Pignoria's description alludes to this drawing by attributing its identification as Mexican to a "brief comment in Spanish."[20]

In the 1615 edition, Pignoria claimed that the source images for the other Mexican "idols" came from Cardinal Amulio (1506–1572) by way of Ottaviano Malipiero (father active 1560 as canon of Padua Cathedral, son Ottaviano, 1598–1660),[21] and in the 1626 edition Pignoria tells us that he saw the images made by Philips de Winghe of Tournay (1560–1592) from a large book in the Vatican Library compiled by Pedro de Ríos (d. 1563–1565).[22] This is the Mexican manuscript Vaticanus 3738, known as Vaticanus A or *Codex Ríos*, a sixteenth-century copy of images from a now lost pre-contact Aztec manuscript made by Ríos, a Dominican friar born in Mexico. *Codex Ríos* was first recorded as being in the Vatican in 1589 by Mercati.[23] If Pignoria's reference in 1615 to Amulio as the original source for his Mexican images is correct, then the book was in Rome by 1567, Amulio's last year as Vatican librarian and the year of his death.[24]

The Mexican image added to Cartari/Pignoria 1626 and attributed to Winghe (**fig. 1.5**) is very like that of a vivid watercolor drawing, likewise identified, although in Latin, as from a book in the Vatican Library by Pedro de Ríos (**fig. 1.6**). The watercolor is in a sketchbook mostly of Roman and Egyptian antiquities, as well as a few early Christian murals, all in Rome, and a European manuscript illumination in the Vatican. The sketchbook, ms. 1564 in Biblioteca Angelica and, like ms. 1551, once in the Massimo collection, is attributed to Alfonso Chacón (1530–1599), a Spanish Dominican called to Rome in 1567 to succeed Amulio as Vatican librarian, a post Chacón held until his death in 1599.[25] While Vatican librarian, Chacón directed groundbreaking visual documentation projects related to ancient Roman and early Christian sites around the city, the best known being the Catacombs and the Column of Trajan.[26] For these projects, he enlisted the aid of several artists and scribes, including Winghe (in Rome from 1589 into 1592), Jean l'Heureux (also known as Maccarius, 1540–1614),[27] Alonso Sánchez (whom Chacón suggested paying in 1589),[28] and others with discernible styles, but still unidentified.

The Ríos image in ms. 1564, dated 1592 on the same folio, differs in style from the images in ms. 1551, but the two manuscripts share a palette with the same pink, soft green, and yellow in some of the images in mss. 1564 (**fig. 1.8**) and 1551 (**fig 1.4**) that echo those in *Codex Ríos* (**fig. 1.7**), and brilliant reds and blues in others from a different part of *Codex Ríos* (**fig. 1.9**). The common palette of ms. 1551 and ms. 1564 confirms their execution in the same workshop in Rome, and close in time, that is, around 1592, the date of the image in ms. 1564, and the year that Winghe left Rome for Florence, where he died.

The palette of ms. 1551, section 1 is the same throughout, for Mexican as well as Asian deities. It uses more vivid hues, and while sharing some colors, especially green and pink, deviates in significant areas from that used in *Codex Ríos*, as well as from Pignoria's descriptions of color. These, provided for the images of Asian objects, according to Pignoria, by Girolamo Aleandro the Younger (1574–1629),[29] are detailed, suggesting that the source drawings supplied by Aleandro were executed in black and white, perhaps based on ms. 1551, but included some errors. For example, the Japanese figure XLII of Cartari/Pignoria 1615 is the same as that in ms. 1551, number 8, but Pignoria's description of color differs in the manuscript, as in the stockings, which he calls blue,[30] but are pink in ms. 1551 (**fig. 1.2**). This is also one of the misidentified images in 1551, where it is characterized as Mexican.

The Mexican gods and rulers identified in ms. 1551 and in Cartari/Pignoria 1615, all taken from the first section of *Codex Ríos*,[31] are: (no. 2) Mictlantlaoani,

Parte Seconda

550

VN'altra Imagine di Homopoca, o di simile deità mi è venuta per le mani, la quale però altri chiamano di Quetzalcoatl, & s'è hauuta fuora di certi fogli, che furono di Filippo Vinghernio da Tornay, dottissimo giouane, & esso asseriua d'hauerla cauata da vn Libro grande, ch'è nella Libreria Vaticana, compilato da F. Pietro de los Rios.

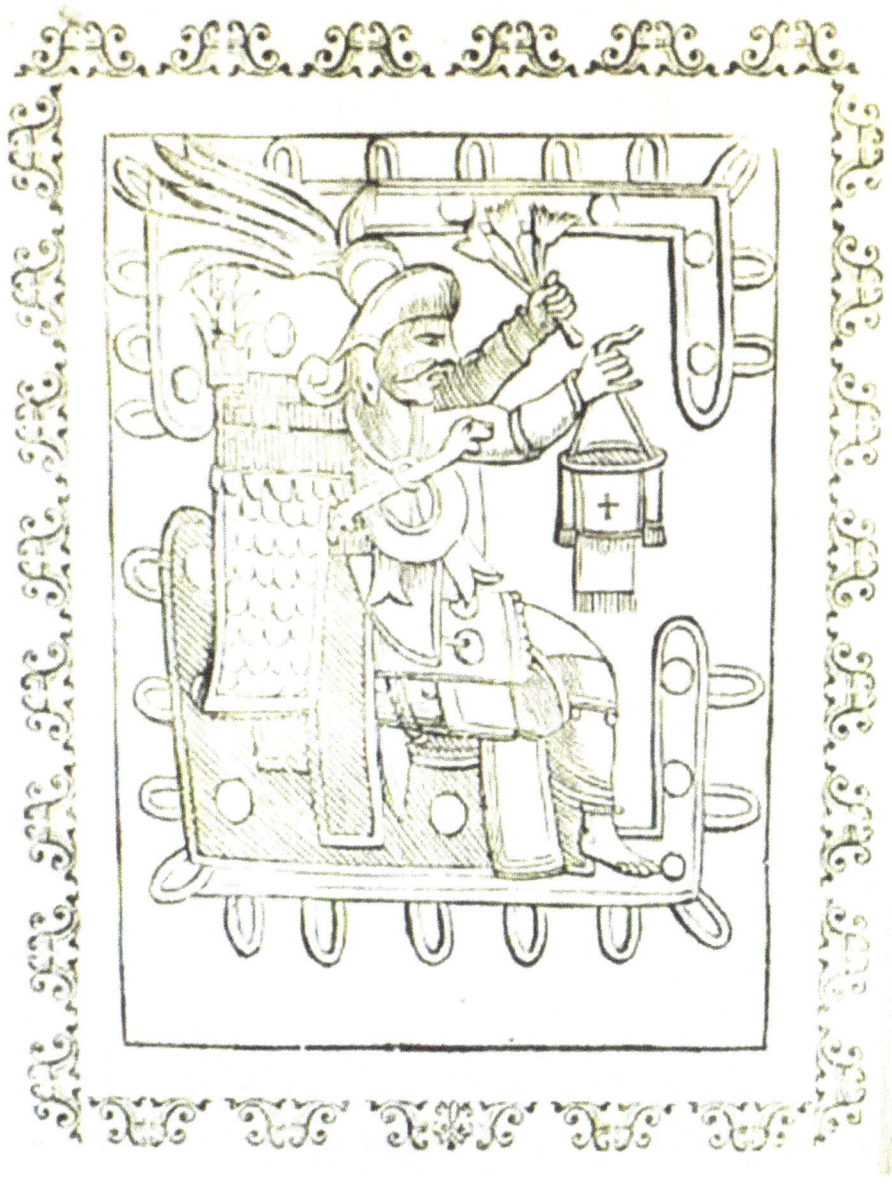

Figure 1.5 Cesare Malfatti, *Quetzalcoatl* from *Codex Ríos*, based on drawing by Philips de Winghe, Cartari/Pignoria 1626, p. 550.

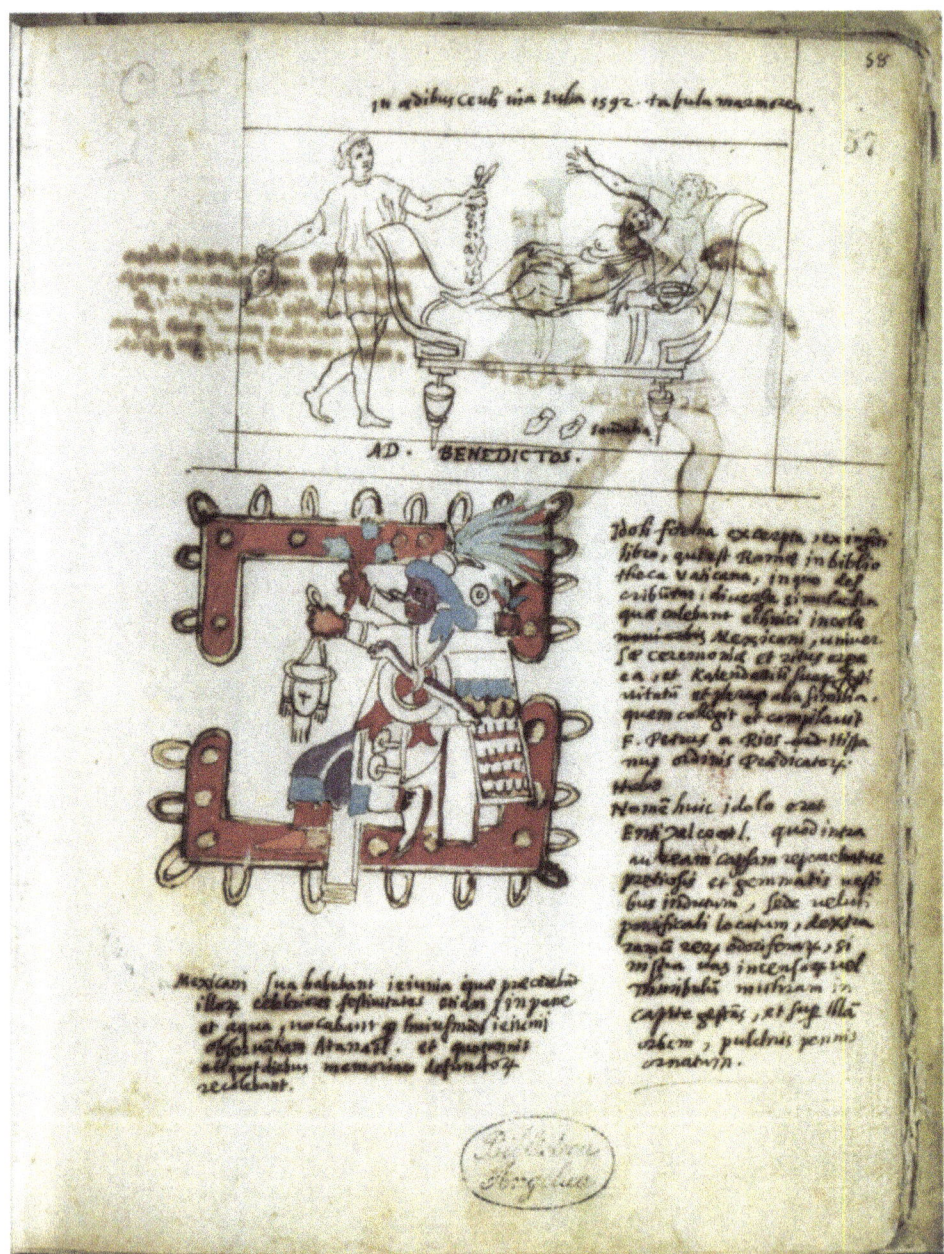

Figure 1.6   Alfonso Chacón (Ciacconius) or Philips de Winghe, *Homehuic and Entipalcoatl from codex in Vatican attributed to Pedro de los Ríos*, 1592. Rome, Biblioteca Angelica ms. 1564, fol. 57. On concession from the Ministry for Arts and Culture and Tourism. All rights reserved.

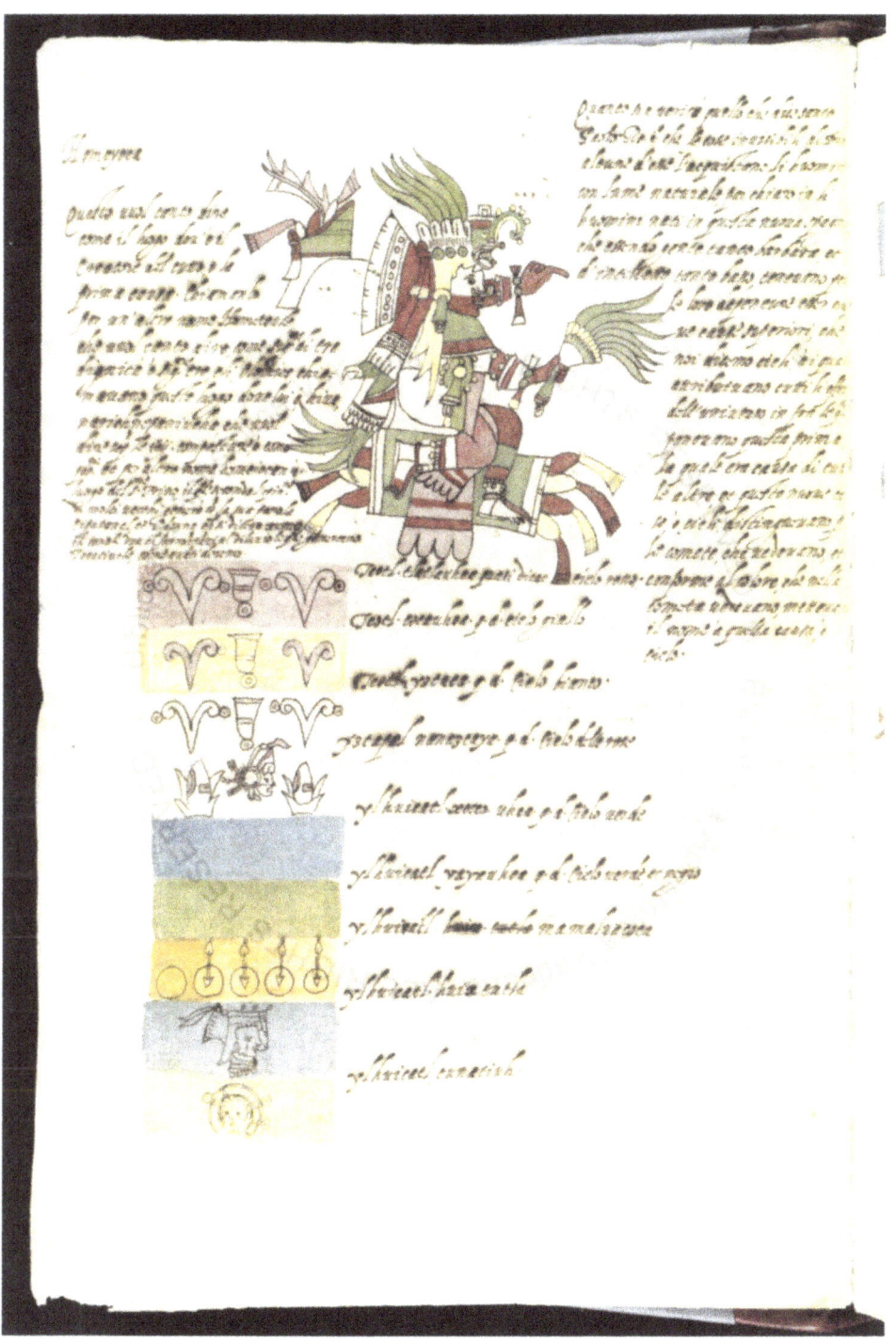

Figure 1.7   Pedro de los Ríos, *Homoyoca, Codex Ríos*, Vatican, Biblioteca Apostolica, Vat.lat.3738, fol. 1v. Reproduced by permission of Biblioteca Apostolica Vaticana, with all rights reserved.

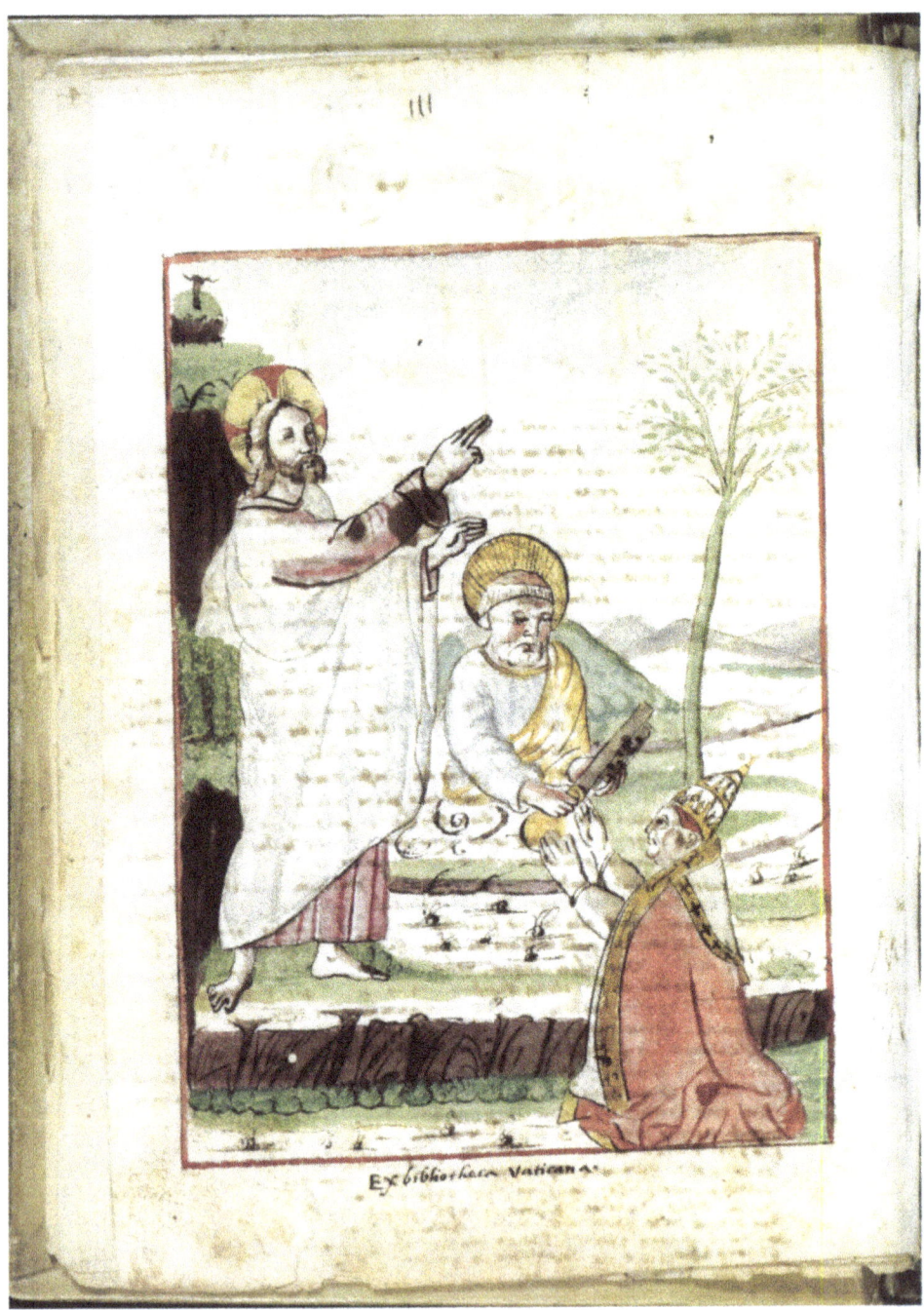

Figure 1.8 Alfonso Chacón (Ciacconius) and workshop artists, copy of manuscript page from book in the Vatican. Rome, Biblioteca Angelica ms. 1564, fol. 5. On concession from the Ministry for Arts and Culture and Tourism.

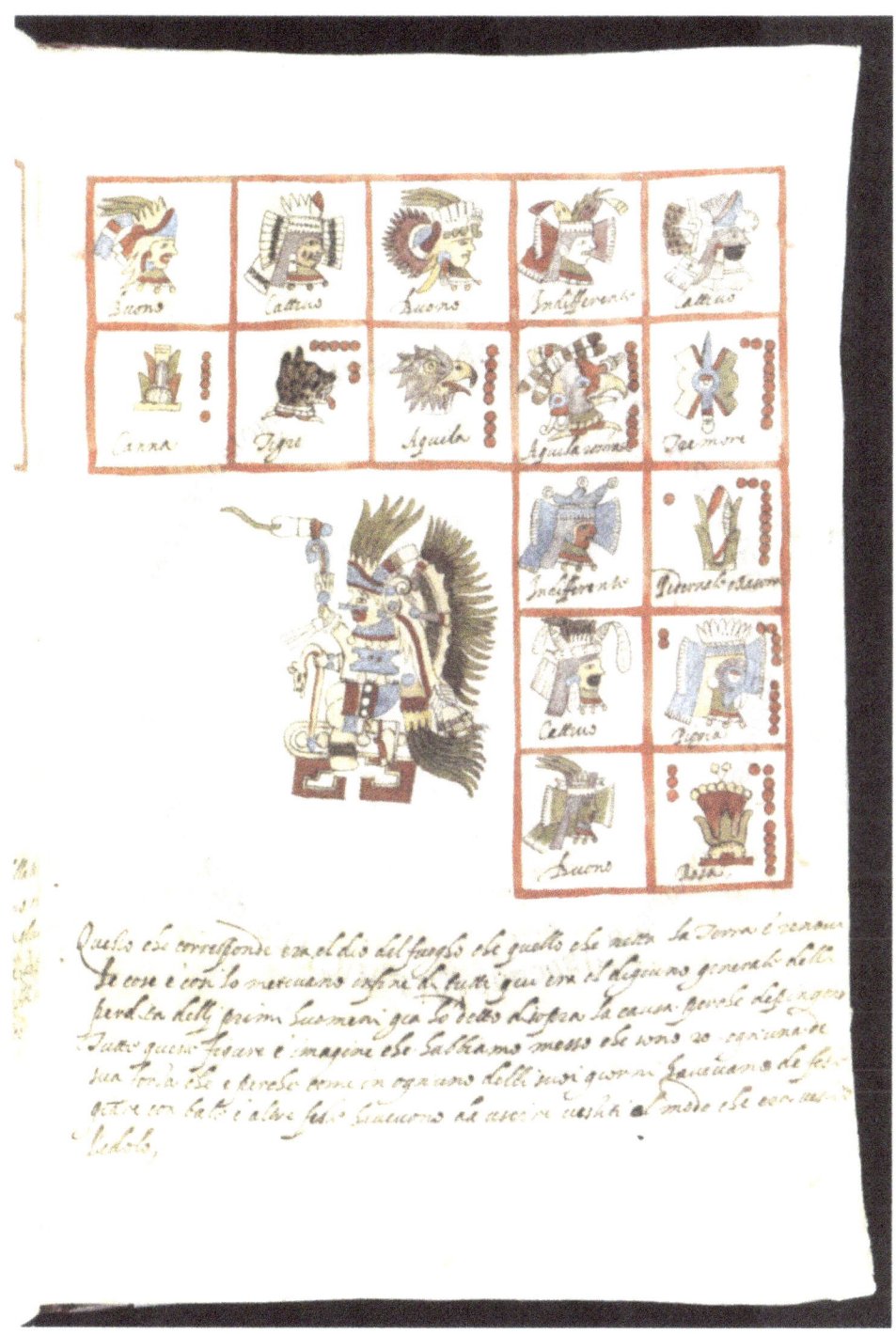

Figure 1.9 Pedro de los Ríos, *Quetzalcoatl, Codex Ríos*, Vatican, Biblioteca Apostolica, Vat.lat.3738, fol. 37r. On concession from the Ministry for Arts and Culture and Tourism. All rights reserved.

rulers of the underworld, below the sky, both in the text only—the images are actually Roman, as noted above; (no. 3) Topiltzin, here, as in other 16th-century interpretations, confused with Quetzalcoatl,[32] which he is named in the almost identical depiction in the closely related *Codex Telleriano-Remensis*; (no. 5) Hometeotl, god of duality also called Hieitleutl here; (no. 14) Eccateutli, god of wind, associated with Quetzalcoatl (more commonly Ehecatl), and; (no. 16) Citlatonac, god of the Milky Way. In 1551, as in Cartari/Pignoria 1615, those Mexican deities considered primary by their Aztec worshippers, such as Huitzilopochtli, Texcatlipoca, and Tonatiuh, are not represented, although they do figure in *Codex Ríos.*

There are a number of discrepancies among the images of the various versions, particularly in style and identification of gods. In terms of orthography and language, Codex Ríos and Pignoria are generally similar, even when Pignoria misidentifies a figure with a place name near the image, such as Homoyoca (p. V), rather than the god Ometeotl named in Ríos (1v) as residing in Homoyoca (**fig. 1.7**). The same god is identified in ms. 1551 with the alternate name and spelling "Hometeo[tl]cam" (**fig. 1.4**). In other words, Pignoria or his source chose the wrong name on the correct folio in *Codex Ríos*, while ms. 1551 chose the correct god on the same folio in *Codex Ríos* but with the addition of a European "H" in his name, a style employed consistently, for example, by José de Acosta in his annual letters to Rome while in Peru.[33] The orthographic differences in ms. 1551 might support Eloise Quiñones Keber's suspicion of a lost intermediary stage of *Codex Ríos* written in Spanish as a basis for the Italian version.[34]

The Mexican images in ms. 1551 called Hometeo[tl]cam (**fig. 1.4**), Homoyoca in *Codex Ríos* (**fig. 1.7**) and Cartari/Pignoria 1615,[35] and in ms. 1564 called Entipalcoatl (**fig. 1.6**), Homopoca in Cartari/Pignoria 1626 where it is attributed to Winghe,[36] and Quetzalcoatl in *Codex Ríos* (**fig. 1.9**), while similar in composition and pose, are different in style and palette.[37] The figure in ms. 1551 (**fig. 1.4**) is in a European style, with the soft green, yellow ochre, and pale blue of *Codex Ríos* enhanced by shading in parallel lines, a hint of musculature and naturalism in the hands and face. In contrast, the figure in ms. 1564, folio 57 (**fig. 1.6**), also imitating but intensifying the colors used in *Codex Ríos*, is entirely flat, with bold areas of saturated turquoise and red, plus a second blue and mauve, also based on but more intense than the original.

As mentioned previously, other images in 1551 use the identical palette as Quetzalcoatl in ms. 1564. Because Pignoria specifies Winghe as the artist only in his discussion of the Homopoca in the 1626 edition, the artist of 1551 may not be Winghe. But as the two manuscripts must have been executed in the same workshop and around the same time, ms. 1551, section 1 was probably produced by another of the several artists known to have worked with Chacón at this time.[38] It may be worth reiterating that the drawings of Mexican deities in ms. 1551 all derive from the first section of *Codex Ríos*, while the two in ms. 1564 come from the tonalamatal, or calendar, in the second section of *Codex Ríos*, suggesting that the latter might have been done by a second artist after those in ms. 1551.

Not all of the printed images of Mexican deities in Pignoria appear in the drawings of mss. 1551 and 1564. The few images in Cartari/Pignoria 1615 but not among the drawings of 1551 include the Roman figures (except the two facing seated ones that were labeled as Mexican and obviously intended to be from *Codex Ríos* and compared with the Roman figures Mercury and Jupiter) and the three facing and seated Ríos images, one of which was undoubtedly meant to be where those seated and facing Roman figures were inserted incorrectly. At that stage, perhaps the additional seated Ríos figures were considered redundant and either not drawn at all for ms. 1551 or discarded when the remainder were numbered and assembled into the screenfold.

All of Pignoria's Mexican images are from *Codex Ríos,* which was based on a pre-Hispanic Aztec manuscript and produced in Mexico before 1565, probably arriving in Rome shortly thereafter, as mentioned previously. The manuscript's presence in Rome was noted by Michele Mercati in *De gli Obelischi di Roma* in 1589;[39] José de Acosta in *Historia moral y natural de las Indias*, published in 1590;[40] Chacón or Winghe, who inserted the date of 1592 into ms. 1564 on f. 57 bearing the Mexican image; and the French antiquarian Nicolas-Claude Fabri de Peiresc (1580–1637) in a letter to Pignoria dated 1616, after seeing Cartari/Pignoria 1615 and informing Pignoria that he (Peiresc) was in possession of images copied from the book, which Pignoria had reproduced without attribution to *Codex Ríos*, as well as several Japanese images.[41]

Authorship of *Codex Ríos* and ms. 1551, Section 1

How did ms. 1551 come to be a seemingly complete set of selected images from a larger number in the book, considering that Pignoria said that he obtained his Mexican and Asian images from two different sources, Amulio via Malipiero, and Aleandro? Why are the inscriptions in ms. 1551 in Spanish, not Italian, as in *Codex Ríos* and Pignoria? And what about the use of an Asian paper?

Codex Ríos

Some scholars have posited that the Italian texts and European paper in *Codex Ríos* indicate either that Italy was its intended destination, even while being produced in Mexico,[42] or possibly its place of manufacture.[43] Neither seems likely: Italian paper was already regularly exported to Spain and its colonies in this era,[44] and Italians were eager recipients of a number of Mexican manuscripts with Spanish texts as well as other objects coming from New Spain around this time, usually via Spain. As Ferdinand Anders, Maarten Jansens, and Luís Reyes García noted, moreover, two hands in Italian in *Codex Ríos* may have been native Spanish speakers who wrote in imperfect Italian, employing Spanish orthography, and even more telling, referring to "our Spain" ("nra Spagna").[45] One of them identified himself as a priest who knew Oaxaca.[46] If so, who might such Spanish speakers with familiarity with Mexico and with knowledge of Italian have been, and could they also have been responsible for the Spanish texts of section 1 of ms. 1551?

José de Acosta explained that the history of the Aztecs

> "is depicted in the Annals of Mexico, the book of which is in Rome; and it is located in the Holy Library or Vatican book repository, where a father of our society who had come from Mexico saw it and the other histories and explained them to His Holiness's librarian, who was extremely happy to understand that book, which he had never been able to comprehend before."[47]

The passage implies that the book was not yet annotated before the Jesuit father explained it to the Vatican librarian, otherwise the librarian would have been able to understand it without the Jesuit's help. That likelihood calls into question Pignoria's recollection of Amulio's drawings "with explanations,"[48] which were almost certainly not added to any drawings in or based on *Codex Ríos* as early as Amulio's tenure, which ended in 1567, before any known Jesuit was in Rome after having been in Mexico and studying the ancient texts there.[49] Pignoria must have meant that he saw the codex that had arrived in Rome during Amulio's tenure, with the explainations that he, Pignoria, did not know were later additions.

The textual and orthographic relationships among *Codex Ríos*, ms. 1551, and Cartari/Pignoria are complex. Pignoria hewed closely to the text of *Codex Ríos* in most of his descriptions of "idols," but in this instance describes a comparison, that of the Holy Trinity, which is referred to in *Codex Ríos* as "tre dignità" in conjunction with this image in fol. 1r, and identifies the same image in ms. 1551, but with a word that did not actually exist in that language or culture but was fabricated for this purpose from Nahuatl components to convey the idea of the trinity (see discussion under fol. 5, below).

Who was the Jesuit father who came to Rome from Mexico and explained the book and other histories to the Vatican librarian? Acosta was one of three Jesuits known to have been in Rome after time in Mexico and one of two to also have spent time in Oaxaca,[50] but the only one of the three with direct and intimate knowledge of Mexican codices.[51] While residing in Mexico from 1585 to 1587, Acosta was in contact with Juan de Tovar (1543–1623), a fellow Jesuit who sent his manuscript copy of the Aztec calendar, now in the J. Carter Brown Library, ms. 6579,[52] to Acosta, who used its information and referred to its images, as well as those of Diego Durán, in his own unillustrated work, signaling an early appreciation of the importance of pictorial sources.[53]

Beyond the orthographic clue in the addition of an "H" by Acosta to words in ms. 1551 that begin with a vowel, as mentioned previously, there is also a scribal link between the hand of ms. 1551, section 1 and that of Acosta in various areas of the Tovar manuscript: strikingly in a probable copy of a letter from Acosta to Juan de Tovar, in the marginal notations throughout, and in the more carelessly calligraphed portions of the chapter on gods and ceremonies (see, for example, fol. 79) in the Tovar manuscript.[54] Jacques LaFaye attributed the marginal notations in the Tovar manuscript to Acosta based on strong similarities between the notations and Acosta's letters in the Archivum Historicum Societis Iesu (ARSI).[55]

Acosta concerned himself in *Historia natural y moral de las Indias* with religious comparisons with Mexican gods and practices also found in ms. 1551, for example, Osiris (no. 20); Mercury and Jupiter (no. 2); and various Indian, Japanese, and Chinese gods and observances he knew from the Jesuit letters.[56] Thus, it seems certain that Acosta was observing a literary convention by employing the third person to refer to himself in *Historia natural y moral de las Indias* as the Jesuit who enlightened the Vatican librarian. This would not be the only such usage by Acosta, who, in an annual letter from Peru in 1577, referred to himself, writing, "from Father Joseph to Father doctor Plaza."[57]

The Vatican librarian to whom Acosta refers is surely not Amulio, who held the post during Acosta's first stay there in 1565, but before the Jesuit had been in Peru and Mexico and exposed to indigenous history in the New World. Rather, the librarian must have been Chacón, who held that post during Acosta's second and third stays in Rome in 1588 and 1592–1594, when Acosta was assigned to the Jesuit confessors at St. Peter's in close proximity to the library.[58] In a collection of manuscript leaves in the Getty Research Institute attributed to Chacón and dated 1578–1589[59] is an essay on giants in the ancient Old World, from the Bible, Babylonia, Egypt, and Greece. Is it a coincidence that *Codex Ríos* folio 4v contains an image and roughly contemporary discussion of giants in ancient Mexico?

It would seem inescapable, therefore, that Acosta and Chacón are the authors of the *Codex Ríos* texts and that Pignoria saw annotated drawings in *Codex Ríos*, probably during his stay in Rome between 1605 and 1607, and made or commissioned copies of the drawings and texts. This would explain the imperfect Italian and the reference to "our Spain" in *Codex Ríos*, particularly because Chacón was a self-proclaimed proud Spaniard whose work on Roman antiquities, including that on Trajan's Column, was often in pursuit of the promotion of Spanish Roman achievements.[60] It would also account for a copy of selected images from *Codex Ríos* with Spanish, rather than Italian, texts in ms. 1551.[61] One seeming lapse in ms. 1551 into Italian, in the inscription on folio 2, "segnor dal," rather than "señor del," would suggest either Acosta or Chacón in the original text or an Italian copyist's mistake in transcribing those originals.[62]

Finally, it would explain the use of the screenfold arrangement of this section of ms. 1551, a format not known to have been used in European manuscripts but characteristic of pre-Columbian Mexican ones. Only Acosta, among contemporaneous Rome residents or visitors, would have known this format firsthand, either from his time in Mexico or perhaps as close at hand as *Codex Vaticanus B* (Vat. Lat. 3773), the arrival of which in the Vatican Library is undocumented but may be the same as that referred to by Mercati in 1589 as one of two there.[63]

Chacón, Winghe, Acosta, Peiresc, and the Asian Connections

And how to account for the source of the sixteen drawings of Asian objects in ms. 1551, section 1? Pignoria tells us that he obtained for his book 15 of the 20 drawings of East Indian, Chinese, and Japanese objects, one in the Gesù, from Girolamo Aleandro the Younger.[64] For Cartari/Pignoria 1626, Pignoria clearly had access either to the drawing in Biblioteca ms. 1564 or some other version of it. Pignoria was in Rome in 1605 and 1607, and he wrote to Galileo in 1612 that he had visited various princely collections there, including the pope's, and, given his Jesuit education and connections, possibly that of the Jesuits in the Gesù, making or commissioning copies of drawings of the cultures of the East and West Indies, including India, China, Japan, Egypt, Mexico, and Peru, the same regions minus Peru (although see Chapter 3) as in ms. 1551, section 1.[65]

In the aforementioned letter to Pignoria of 1616, Peiresc says that he has in his possession drawings that Pignoria had reproduced in 1615, perhaps from Aleandro, which come from *Codex Ríos*. Peiresc's mention of Aleandro as a possible source raises the possibility that ms. 1551 was Aleandro's source for his Japanese images, which Aleandro could have reproduced in black and white, but with texts explaining the colors based on ms. 1551, as Pignoria included in his text. Peiresc also mentions a drawing of Quetzalcoatl and several drawings of Japanese subjects as well as his ownership of a nude ivory figure,[66] which is similar to a drawing in one of Chacón's sketchbooks in the Vatican.[67] These drawings in Peiresc's possession in 1616 found their way into Cartari/Pignoria 1626. Peiresc had borrowed materials by Philips de

Winghe in 1612 from Winghe's brother Hieronymus, suggesting that among those materials could have been mss. 1551 and 1564, or other now-lost copies by Winghe of those drawings.[68] Pignoria, in turn, mentioned in a letter to Peiresc in 1623 his intention to include Winghe's drawings in his expanded edition of 1626.[69]

Chacón's ms. 1564 includes a sketch of an Egyptian statue from the Quirinale hill,[70] and the manuscript attributed to Chacón and now in the Getty Research Institute contains a Chinese alphabet based on a book then in the Vatican Library.[71] Two of the drawings in ms. 1551 of standing Asian deities, no. 7 Ganesha and no. 17 idol from Miyako,[72] are posed similarly to the Roman and early Christian statues and relief sculptures documented by Chacón and his artists in sketchbooks ms. 1564 in the Biblioteca Angelica (**fig. 1.10**), and Vatican Library ms. Vat. Lat. 5409 and 10545 in the Vatican Library. It does not seem unreasonable to credit Chacón with interest in the Asian objects in Roman collections, especially those in the gallery of Pope Clement VIII or those in the Gesù at this time.

Likewise, Acosta, who mentioned Chinese men he met in Mexico and was the first to suggest the Asian origin of indigenous Americans, in his chapter on China in *Historia moral y natural de las Indias*, would also have seen the objects in his mother church in Rome. As Walter Mignolo observed,

> "Acosta is unique in his efforts to draw the peoples of the East Indies into a comparison and classification with the Inca and the Aztecs. His information on China and Japan likely came from his association, in Mexico, en route to Spain, and in Rome, with Alonso Sánchez, a fellow Jesuit, who was a missionary in the Philippines,"[73]

and who also spent time in China before being recalled, and passed through Mexico in 1587. Sánchez, whose unpublished writings on China were influential to Acosta and other Jesuit authors on China, such as Luis de Guzmán, had traveled to Spain with Acosta, was in Rome at the same time as Acosta, and could be the same Alonso Sánchez who worked under Chacón in Rome in 1589, along with Winghe. Just as Acosta seems to have worked alongside Chacón on *Codex Ríos*, he might well have discussed Chinese characters with the Vatican librarian and with Sánchez.

Philips de Winghe visited the Vatican collections and saw the *byobu*, or folding screen, sent by the Jesuit Alessandro Valignano with his Japanese ambassadors to Rome in 1585 as gifts for Pope Gregory XIII.[74] Pignoria mentions in his 1626 edition that Winghe's drawing of Azuchi was based on this gift from the Japanese ambassadors.[75] One wonders whether the screenfold arrangement of these drawings might have been intended to make its own connection between Mexican codices and Japanese screens, another possible clue to Winghe or Chacón's involvement in the drawings of ms. 1551. Other Japanese objects then in the Gesù came to Pignoria's attention thanks to a drawing sent him by Girolamo Aleandro the Younger for the 1615 edition and were published in the same edition.[76]

Jesuit missionaries stationed in Asia were responsible for many of the Asian objects that reached Rome in this period.[77] Acosta, like his contemporaries Winghe and Aleandro, both of whom, like Pignoria, had close Jesuit contacts, would likely have known them and might have had access to the Asian papers that, like Asian objects, were reaching Italy in this period largely through Jesuits either returning or sending them back.[78] Although the scribe obviously had access to the Asian objects, he did not identify them as precisely as he did the Mexican manuscript figures, perhaps betraying a deeper familiarity with the latter.

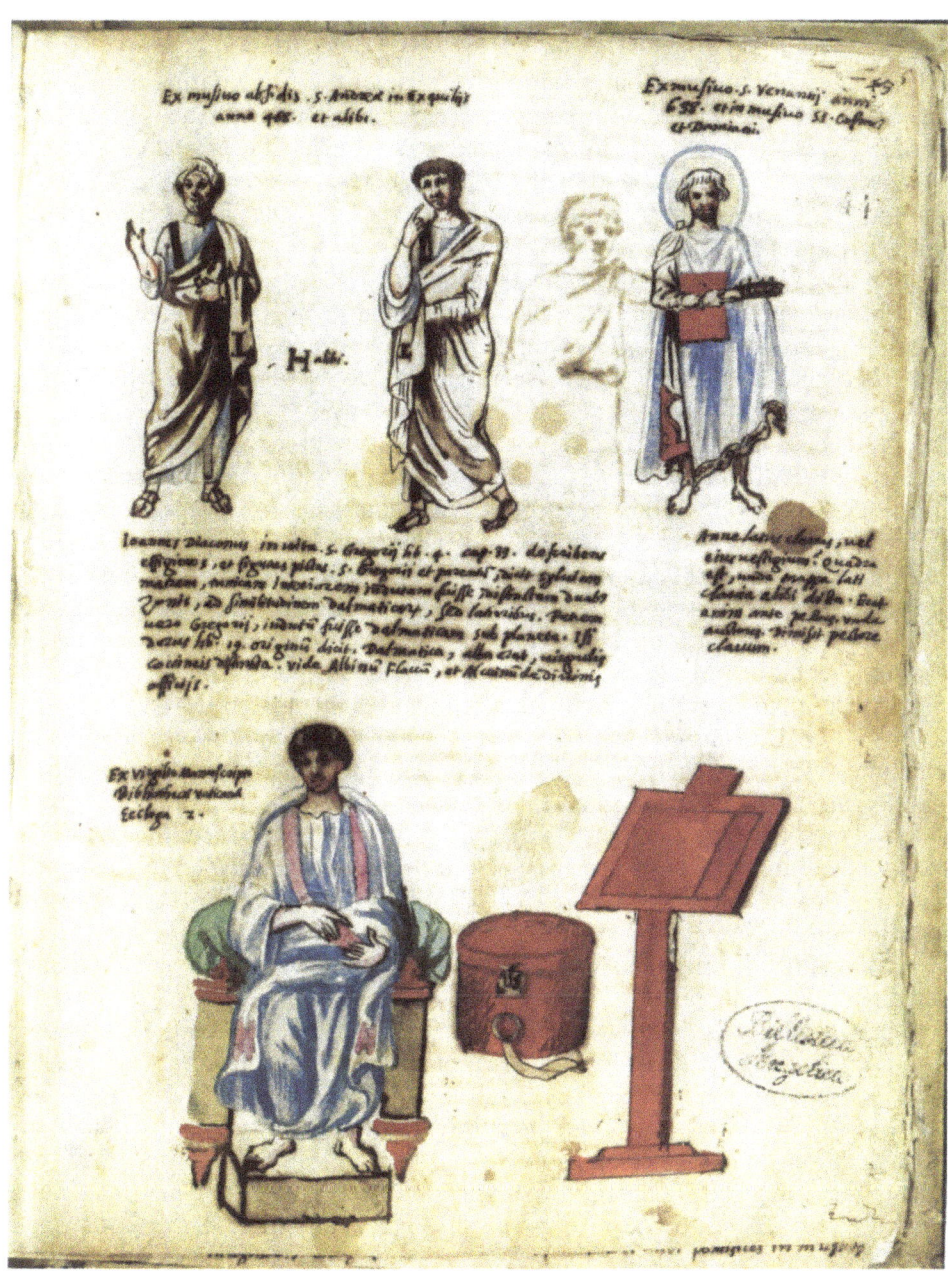

Figure 1.10 Alfonso Chacón (Ciacconius) and workshop artists (?), sketches of Early Christian figures in S. Andrea. Rome, Biblioteca Angelica ms. 1564, fol. 44. On concession from the Ministry for Arts and Culture and Tourism. All rights reserved.

The Paths to Pignoria and Massimo

For a number of reasons, but primarily because of the likely dating of ms. 1551 between 1589 and 1592; and the complex relationship among the texts of Cartari/ Pignoria 1615, *Codex Ríos*, and ms. 1551 discussed next; it seems clear that ms. 1551, section 1 is not a copy after the printed images, as Sonia Maffei argued.[79] Rather, ms. 1551 was, at least indirectly, a source for Pignoria. But how did the manuscripts reach him?

Peiresc was not the source of ms. 1551 for Pignoria, who had already published the images by the time of Peiresc's letter, but he does suppose Aleandro to be a possible source for Pignoria's drawings from *Codex Ríos*, as well his Japanese images. But Peiresc could have been referring in that letter to ms. 1551, which might have been among the papers of Winghe lent to Peiresc by Winghe's brother. Or ms. 1551 could have been acquired by Peiresc from Chacón's estate, from which he also obtained an ancient weight in 1600.[80] Another possibility is that Peiresc acquired the drawings from Aleandro, from whom he obtained other drawings. Caterina Volpi refers intriguingly, but only in passing, to Winghe having been one of Pignoria's correspondents and a visitor to Pignoria's friend Pinelli in Padua.[81] If true, his brother (active 1609) might have shown or lent these drawings directly to Pignoria or one of his other correspondents, including Malipiero, the Venetian senator Pignoria named as the transmitter of Amulio's drawings. Part of the complexity of unraveling the origins of ms. 1551 involves the numerous red herrings in early sources. Drawing conclusions in many instances depends upon examination, and often rejection, of original statements of contemporaneous writings and documents, such as Medici and Pignoria.

It does seem clear that Acosta and Chacón supplied the texts in *Codex Ríos* between 1588 and 1590, when Acosta's book was published. Between 1590 and 1592, they and Chacón's artists copied selected drawings from *Codex Ríos* and drawings of Asian objects they could see in Rome, with further comparative interpretations. From there, ms. 1551 appears to have been copied or traced, the original perhaps making its way to Peiresc via Hieronymus de Winghe or Chacón's estate, a copy to Pignoria. From Peiresc, ms. 1551 and possibly ms. 1564 passed to Camillo Massimo.[82]

Despite a lack of evidence of interest in either the ancient Americas or Asia, Camillo Massimo was fascinated by the Roman and Egyptian antiquities in his native Rome and could have acquired these drawings because they included depictions of such objects.[83] Regardless of their journey around Italy and Provence, it is apparent that it was during the brief catalytic moment between 1589 and 1592 when José de Acosta, Alfonso Chacón, Philips de Winghe, and the other artists around Chacón forged a pioneering investigation into comparative religions through imagery, a quarter century before Pignoria's publications were inspired by them.

The folios arranged by illustration numbers, as in screenfold (entries followed by folio numbers as in ms. 1551)

1. idolo de los Japones el qual daba respuesta y era su oraculo. Cartari/Pignoria 1615, XXXVIII.

Idol of the Japanese who gave answers and was their oracle.

Lightbown identifies as Kwannon.[84] (fol. 2v)

2. idolos mexicanos: a. llamado mictlan tlatoani, segnor dal infierno = el otro. b. ilhuicatemoc = bajo del cielo. (fol. 2r, **fig. 1.3**)

Mexican idols: a. called mictlan tlatoani, lord of the inferno = the other. b. ilhuacatemoc = below the sky.

Cartari/Pignoria 1615, VII, refers to this image as Egyptian, but the figures are Roman; that is, Mercury and Jupiter. (Reference to Mexican gods Miquitlantecatli as Lucifer and Contemoque as Heaven, is depicted in Cartari/Pignoria 1615, IX.) *Codex Ríos* 2v, top left, is the same god as in the inscription, but depicted figures in 1551, no. 2 are facing Romans, not Mexicans. Ilhuicatemoc is explained as "descends from the sky," a variant of the incantation "ilhuicatl" that appears on *Codex Ríos* folio 1v, below the image of Hometeotl, also depicted in ms. 1551, no. 5. Mercury, as the messenger who flies across the sky, and Jupiter, god of the sky, would make apt comparisons to the Mexicans.

3. idolo de los mexicanos llamado topiltzi [n cropped] nuestro hijo tenido por embajador de los dioses. (fol. 2r, **fig. 1.3**)

Idol of the Mexicans called topiltzin, our son taken for ambassador of the gods.

Cartari/Pignoria 1615, XIV, as Topiltzin in text, p. XV. *Codex Ríos*, 7r.

4. idolo general de mexicanos por quien a menudo ablaba el demonio.

General idol of Mexicans of whom the demon often spoke.

Cartari/Pignoria 1615, VI. The figure is Taino, not Mexican. (fol. 3, **fig. 1.4**)

5. Idolo de los mexicanos llamado homete[otl]cam doblada a deidad y por dho nombre tleutli = dvino en la dignidad. (fol. 3, **fig. 1.4**)

Idol of the Mexicans called Ometeotl double deity and by this name hieiteutl = divine in dignity.

Codex Ríos 1v: as Hometeutl in Homeyoca. Pignoria 1615, XXVI, as Homoyoca. Barbara Mundy convincingly suggests that "hieitleutl" might be "Yei teuctli," translating as "Three God," adding that although there is no such Mexican god, this is probably a reference to the Christian Trinity,[85] which, in fact, is mentioned in *Codex Ríos* 1v as "sig.^{re} di tre dignità, o sig.^{re} tre." Acosta ponders the apparently diabolical transformation of a notion of the trinity into idolatry in Peruvian religion in *Historia natural y moral de las Indias*.[86] Pignoria calls out the Trinity, but without the particular Nahuatl translation.[87] The addition of "hieitleutli" to further explain hometeotl might be understood as the ms. 1551 scribe's demonstration of his familiarity with the Nahuatl language and complexities of the god.

6. idolo de los egiptos, dios de las letras, adorado de los indios del oriente.

Idol of the Egyptians, god of letters, adored by the East Indians.

Cartari/Pignoria 1615, XXXVI. (fol. 4)

7. idolo de los indios de goa en la india tal llamado pagode con tres cabessas, tres brac, y tres piernas. (fol. 4).

Idol of the Indians of Goa in India, so-called pagoda with three heads, three arms and three legs.

Cartari/Pignoria 1615, XXVIII. According to Peter Mason, this image is a composite based on a report by an anonymous Jesuit of the Shiva Maneśamūrti at Elephanta and the account of Ganesha by Luis Froís.[88]

8. idolo de los mexicanos aquien llamaron dios del dominio sobre los hombres. (fol. 4v, **fig. 1.2**)

Idol of the Mexicans whom they called god of dominion over men.

Cartari/Pignoria 1615, XLII. Japanese, not Mexican. Lightbown identifies as Bishamon.[89]

9. idolo de los chinos, feroz, enojado por senal de su Fortaleza y por esto tiene debaxo de sus pies un h^e hollado y pissado. (fol. 5r)

Idol of the Chinese, ferocious, angered as a sign of his fortitude and for this he has beneath his feet a trampled and downtrodden man.

Cartari/Pignoria 1615, LVI. Lightbown identifies as Bishamon.[90]

Another example of a Japanese object identified as Chinese.

10. idolo de los chinos. Llamado segnor o dios de la esperanzas. (fol. 5r)

Idol of the Chinese. Called lord or god of hopes.

Cartari/Pignoria 1615, LII. Lightbown identifies as Japanese, not Chinese.[91]

11. idolo de los chinos con insignas de señorio y poder. (fol. 6r)

Idol of the Chinese with insignias of lordship and power

Japanese, Bishamon.

Cartari/Pignoria 1615, LVII.

12. idolo llamado vencedor. (fol. 6r)

Idol called conqueror.

Japanese, Bishamon.

Cartari/Pignoria 1615, LX.

13. idolo de los Japones llamado dios del ayuda y del Socorro. (fol. 7r)

Idol of the Japanese called god of aid and succor.

Cartari/Pignoria 1615, LXII. Lightbown identifies as Monju Bosatsu.[92]

14. idolo de la india llamado dios del viento eccateutli. (fol. 7r)

Idol of Indies called god of wind, eccateutli.

Codex Ríos 7v, as Quetzalcohuatl. Pignoria 1615, XVII, as Quetzalcoatl. Eccateutli
   is probably the same as the more commonly spelled "Ehecatl," god of the
   wind and associated with Quetzalcoatl.

15. idolo de los chinos adorado en meaco lla = mado amidas, puesto sobre una
   rossa. (fol. 7v)

Idol of the Chinese adored in Miyako called Amidas, placed on a rose.

Cartari/Pignoria 1615, XXXII.

16. idolos de los mexicanos llamado citlatonac = estrella de alumbrea como el sol.
   En qe s . . . una embajada de sus dioses a una doncella.

Codex Ríos 2v in reverse, as Yxpuzteque and Hexoxochl, star demons known as
   tzitzimime. (fol. 7v)

Idols of the Mexicans called citlatonac = star of light like the sun on which is an
   embassy of its gods to a virgin.

Cargtari/Pignoria 1615, XII (image) and IX (text), as Yzpuzteque and XIII as Citlatonac.

17. idolo de los meacos, llamado canon hijo de amidas. (fol. 6v)

Idol of the Miyakoans called Cannon, son of Amidas.

Cartari/Pignoria 1615, XXX. Lightbown identifies as Jū-ichi-men Kwannon.[93]

18. idolos de los chinos a quien adoraron po[r] sanctos. (fol. 6v)

Idols of the Chinese whom they adored as saints.

Cartari/Pignoria 1615, LVIII. Lightbown identifies as Fudō Myō-ō and a nobleman.[94]

19. idolos de los chinos en forma de enanos a los quales tenian por intercessors
   para con sus dioses. (fol. 5v)

Idols of the Chinese in the form of dwarfs, whom they had as intercessors with the
   gods.

Cartari/Pignoria 1615, XLVII. Lightbown identifies as the Japanese idols Daikoku
   and possibly Yebisu.[95]

20. idolo [word added above = osraias, meaning "Osiris"?] de los chinos echo de
   madera por el que los engannaba el demonio como lo haze siempre. (fol. 5v)

Idol [Osiris] of the Chinese made of wood for he who deceives the demon as he
   always does.

Cartari/Pignoria 1615, XL.

21. Idolo de egipto adorado de los mexicanos a quien llamaron; maheiz.

Idol of Egypt adored by the Mexicans, whom they called maize. (fol. 4v, **fig. 1.2**)

Cartari/Pignoria 1615, XXIV–XXV.

This is a depiction of an Egyptian god making a connection with the Mexican worship of the corn god (likely Centeotl).

22. idolo de los chinos. Con cinco braços a quien atribuieron la Fortaleza y valentia. (fol. 3v)

Idol of the Chinese with five arms, to whom they attributed fortitude and valor.

Cartari/Pignoria 1615, L. Lightbown identifies as Marishi-ten.[96]

23. idolo de los meacos vestido como los brachmanes, con guarda de soldados y una echiçera a le assistia. (fol. 3v)

Idol of the Miyakoans, clothed like the Brahmins, with soldier guards and a witch who attended him.

Cartari/Pignoria 1615, XXXIV.

24. idolo Japones, a quien llamaron qua = reuoà [?], a quien atribuieron la piedad. (fol. 2v)

Japanese idol, whom they called qua = revoa, to whom they attributed piety.

Cartari/Pignoria 1615, LIV. Ronald Lightbown identifies the figure as Kwannon.[97]

CHAPTER 2:
Asian Peoples and Places

The second section contains thirty-three scenes, mostly of people, from Hormuz, India, Ceylon, Timor, the Philippines, Java, Burma, Japan, and China. The greatest number, eighteen, depict inhabitants and locations in India; and the second largest, six, peoples of the Philippines. One artist executed the drawings in a simple figural style, with faces often expressive and deftly delineated with only a few strokes.

The sheets, which at one time were folded in half, are drawn in black ink and washes on translucent Asian papers with a satiny sheen, some the same pale yellow (**fig. 2.1**) as those of the first section of ms. 1551 (**fig. 1.4**), others a darker golden (**fig. 2.2**) or a deep red (**fig. 2.3**). Some of the sheets are backed with the same type of glossy Asian paper of similar, but not identical, color. All are mounted onto the same larger European sheets as the other two sections. Those drawings on the pale yellow paper are set in landscapes indicated by swaths of green mounds, sometimes with mountains in the distance, and their palette consists of several colors, including blue, red, orange, deep yellow, and green. In contrast, the red and gold-colored papers depict interiors or no defined settings. In the red and gold papers, all but the depiction of two Tartar men in orange costumes are drawn in black contours, with either white or dark gray pigmented skin color (**fig. 2.4**).

All have Spanish captions briefly identifying the elements in the composition, executed in black ink and a thick pen nib by one hand in a late 16th-century style and orthography occasionally interspersed with Portuguese.[98] Two black ink line drawings of boats, folios 17 (**fig. 2.5**) and 57, may also have been executed with the same ink and nib. Each also bears a longer Latin text in a second hand from the same period, smaller and more regular, using a thin nib, and in some cases, a faded or different dark ink.[99] In at least one folio, 17, depicting the people of Bisayas, the Latin text explains the Spanish word "virrei" and the boat beside it as the type of the boat (**fig. 2.5**).[100] Folio 71, on the Queen of Ceylon, inserts the Spanish word "pico" into the Latin text, as though an unconscious lapse by a native Spanish speaker. Some parts of the Latin text in other folios are written on top of the drawings, indicating that they were added after the drawings and Spanish labels.

The drawings are not numbered or mounted in any discernible groupings by geographical region or color of paper, and although multiple scenes are devoted to some cultures, others have only one. That the set is incomplete may be inferred by this imbalance and by references in some Latin texts. In the first sheet as bound, folio 9, the Tartars are described as "also known to the ancients," as though a now missing sheet originally meant to precede this one described another people or place known to the ancients. In folio 35, the inhabitants of Sogau are called "eastern peoples as the aforementioned," but no eastern peoples are called out before

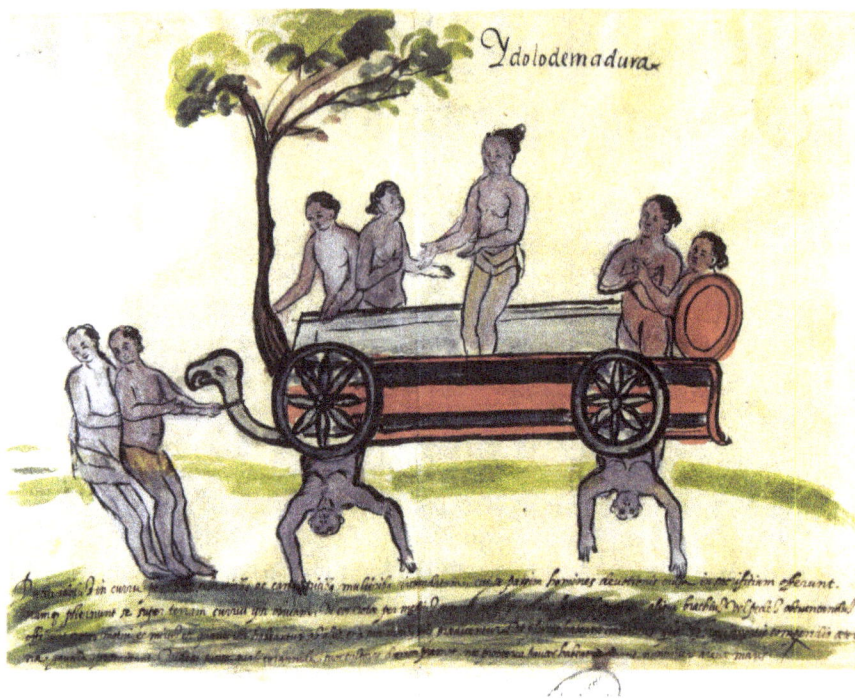

Figure 2.1   Artist unknown, *Ydolo de Madura*, (*Idol of Madura*), Rome, Biblioteca Angelica ms. 1551, fol. 27. On concession from the Ministry for Arts and Culture and Tourism.

this folio, and the only other eastern peoples so-called are the Brahmins in folio 41, "this people" who "also comes from the East."

The subjects of the complex compositions include typical inhabitants, royalty and their entourages, warriors, priests, a few figures in European costume, two boats (one Portuguese *nao* and the virrei), one scene of a temple, sculptures and religious figures, and one unpopulated landscape. Many simply show figures, usually standing, but also on horseback; carried on a litter or seated on a chair or throne; wearing local costume and gear, such as weaponry, against a limited background of landscape or interior furniture. Two treat Indian queens from Cochin and Dialcan almost identically, with the queens seated on a backless chair or low table, flanked by two attendants (**fig. 2.6**). They, like the other queens of Mogor and Hormuz, are described perfunctorily in the Latin texts, as though of lesser interest than kings. Other scenes are more narrative, depicting religious or other cultural practices: the Indian custom of sati, festival processional carts trampling observers (**fig. 2.1**), male fornication rituals, or jousting.

Most scenes are identified in Spanish concerning culture, custom, and location, although the Brahmins (fol. 41) are not located geographically. The temple scene (**fig. 2.3**) is identified only with regard to specific figural elements in the Spanish but has been cut at the bottom and top, where a location might once have been written, as it is in the other sheets. The Latin inscription refers to East India, apparently to distinguish the Asian from the American Indies, not to pinpoint the

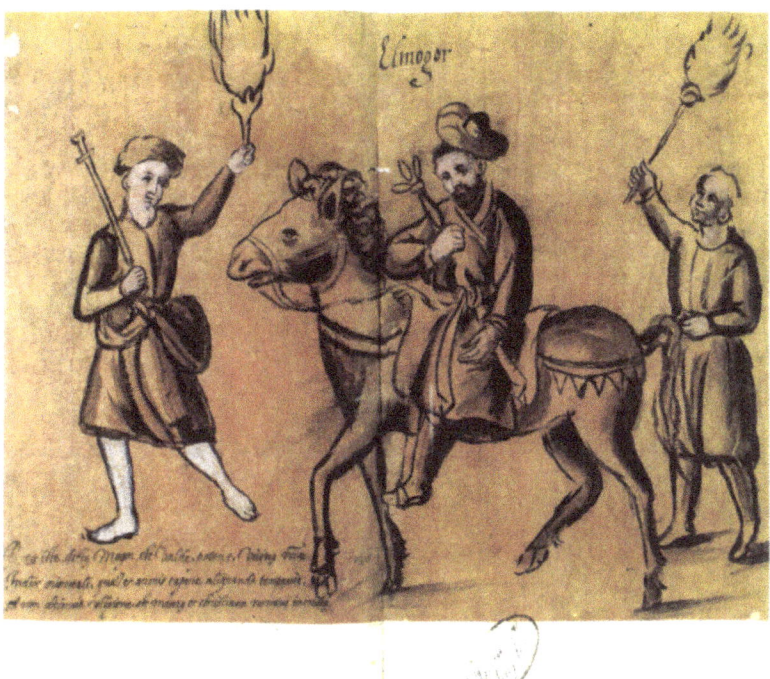

Figure 2.2 Artist unknown, El Mogor *(The Mughal)*, Rome, Biblioteca Angelica ms. 1551, fol. 29. On concession from the Ministry for Arts and Culture and Tourism.

region in India, which in this case would likely be western, not eastern. More extensive discussions of the subjects of each folio, with historical and literary context where known, follow at the end of this overview.

The Latin inscriptions generally expand upon the images and the brief Spanish captions, usually to provide additional description of what is pictured, for example, in folio 17 (**fig. 2.5**), where the word "virrei" seemingly required further clarification. In some instances, they provide completely unrelated information, such as that relating to the Malabars (fol. 53). Likewise, the text referring to the king of Cochin (fol. 49), in addition to a characterization of the king and his followers, also contains a lengthy Latin text that does not pertain to the drawing but refers to the troubles "a few years back,"[101] between the Archbishop Aleixo de Meneses of Goa (1559–1617) and the St. Thomas Christians. Aleixo served between 1595 and 1599 when he declared the St. Thomas Christians, formerly independent and considered unorthodox, subject to the religious jurisdiction of Rome. This would suggest a *terminus post quem* of around 1597 for the Latin texts, perhaps earlier for the drawings and Spanish glosses.

While the Spanish captions are brief and purely descriptive, a number of the lengthy Latin texts not surprisingly include harshly critical comments on the subjects' customs, especially their idolatry. Singled out for their barbarism are the people of Mongau (fol. 23); Sogau (fol. 25); Nicuban, "the most barbaric" (fol. 47);

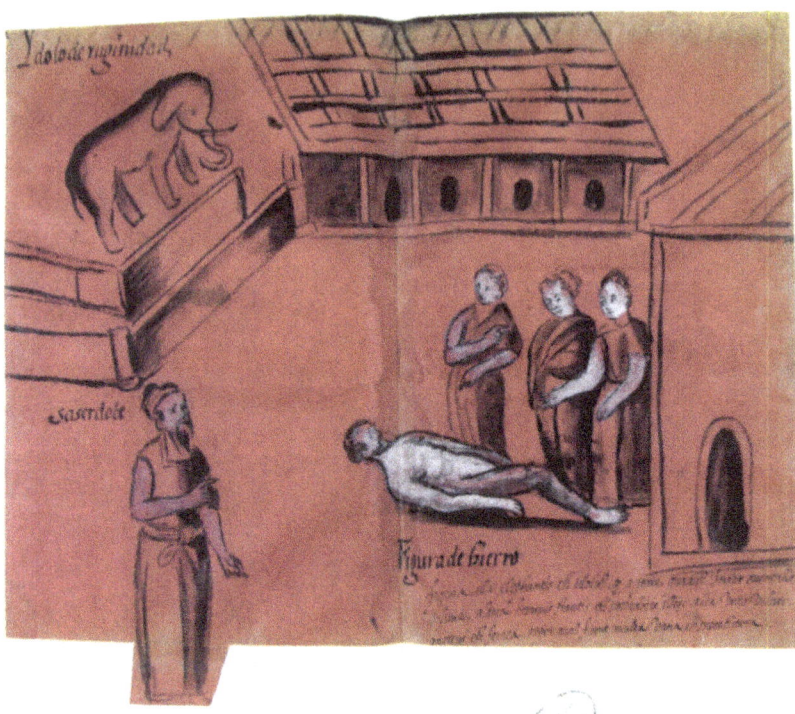

Figure 2.3 Artist unknown, *Ydolo de Virginidad, sacerdote, figura de hierro (Idol of Virginity, priests, iron figure)*. Rome, Biblioteca Angelica ms. 1551, fol. 45. On concession from the Ministry for Arts and Culture and Tourism. All rights reserved.

and Pegu, "gloomy hypocrites" (fol. 37). The King of Bisnaga (fol. 65) is smugly admonished that although he lives in a hot climate, "he will be castigated in hell, which is hotter." The Zambales (fol. 13) and Visaias (fol. 17) are, on the other hand, praised for their acceptance of Christianity and its resultant bestowal of civilization on them.

16th-Century European Accounts of Asian Peoples

Of the numerous accounts by Europeans in Asia in the late 16th century, none contain all the peoples and places identified and pictured by the unknown artist of section 2 of ms. 1551, and only four surviving examples are illustrated, including ms. 1551. None of the known 16th-century chronicles is an obvious source for the Latin texts of ms. 1551, which do not copy or translate verbatim or paraphrase these accounts, although they sometimes incorporate similar information.

The Portuguese provided the earliest detailed written and illustrated descriptions of Asia in the 16th century, whereas authors writing in Spanish predominated later in that century. At least one extensive series of watercolor drawings glossed in Portuguese is dated tentatively to the middle of the century and now known as ms. 1889 in the Biblioteca Casatense in Rome. All the Portuguese accounts deal mainly

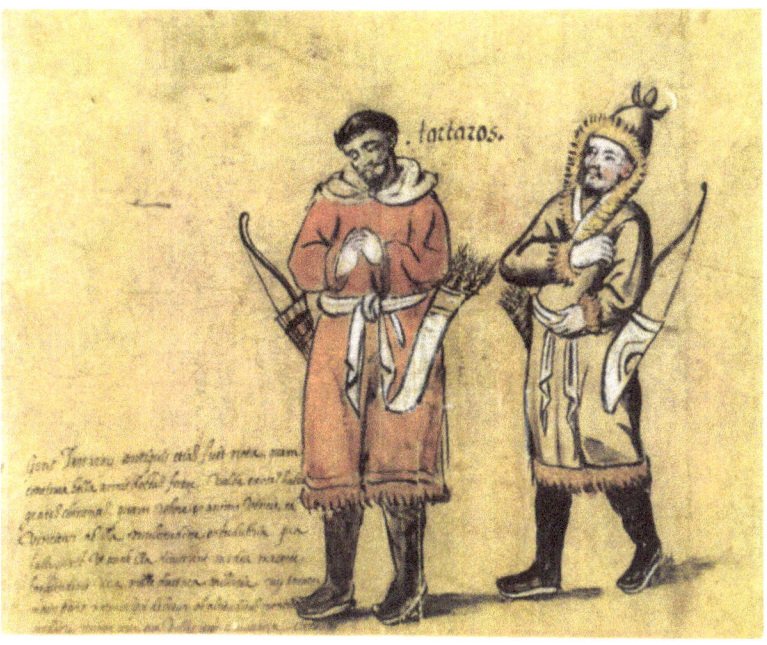

Figure 2.4 Artist unknown, *Tartaros (Tartars)*, Rome, Biblioteca Angelica ms. 1551, fol. 9. On concession from the Ministry for Arts and Culture and Tourism.

with the coastal cultures, as the Portuguese maritime traders did not generally venture far inland.[102] A later manuscript, the so-called *Boxer Codex* in the Lilly Library at the University of Indiana,[103] is lavishly illustrated with pairs of figures identified by captions and a long descriptive narrative in Spanish dated to around 1590–1595.

The illustrations by Jan Huyghen van Linschoten (1563–1611), printed from now-lost drawings to accompany his *Itinerario: Voyage oft schipvaert van Jan Huygen van Linschoten* of 1596,[104] and shortly thereafter in Johann Theodor and Johann Israel de Bry's *Petits Voyages*, parts two through four (with additional plates), published from 1599 to 1601.[105] Donald Lach called Linschoten's illustrations "a watershed in Europe's pictorial impression of Asia," as the first printed book to show the peoples and cultural traits of South Asia.[106] As important as these printed illustrations undoubtedly were, they were probably not all based on the author's firsthand observation, as he was only in a few locations in India, never in China or other Asian regions depicted in the illustrations, and is known to have derived much of his information on those locations from merchants and written chronicles, as well as local Dutch friends and associates. His information on China came from the Augustinian Juan González de Mendoza, whose book Linschoten translated and mentioned in his own text.[107] Linschoten noted the appearance in Goa of Alessandro Valignano's Japanese delegation on their way to and from Europe in 1584 and 1587, respectively,[108] and was likely engaged with the Jesuits as part of his work with his employer, Archbishop Fonseca.

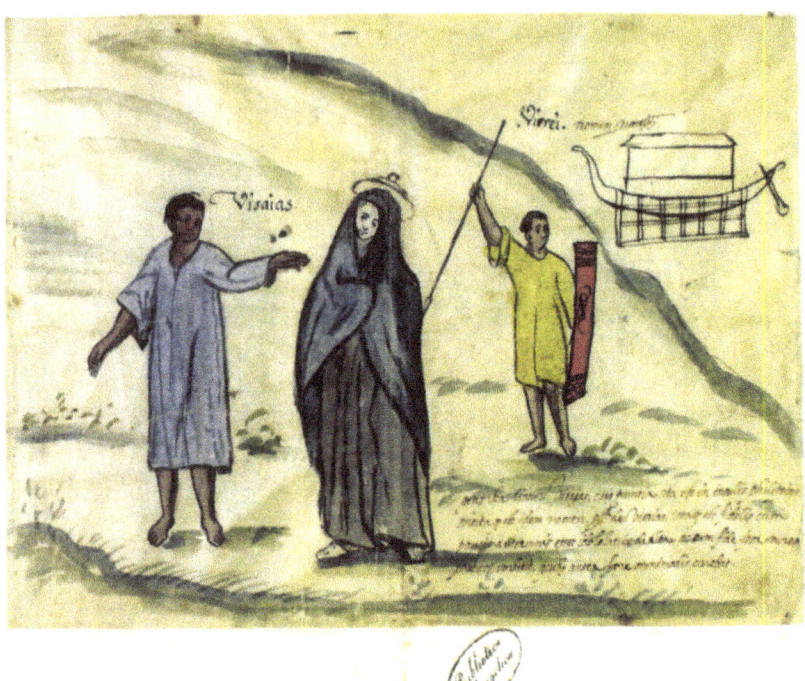

Figure 2.5 Artist unknown, *Visaias, virrei (Bisayas, viceroy)*, Rome, Biblioteca Angelica ms. 1551, fol. 17. On concession from the Ministry for Arts and Culture and Tourism.

A few subjects in de Bry's editions are also treated, although much more summarily in ms. 1551, including the king of Cochin and his entourage, and a chariot procession in Narsinga (specified as Madura in ms. 1551) in which the wagon crushes figures who lie in its path (**figs. 2.1** and **2.7**). Linschoten's organization of images, as noted by Ernst van den Boogaart, focuses on couples, processions, boat types, and natural resources.[109] Ms. 1551 also includes depictions of couples, processions, and two boats, but not in a systematic arrangement. The people of Pegu (fol. 43) are more simply rendered, but similar to the illustration of Gottard Arthus in de Bry's *Indiae orientalis pars septima* of 1601.[110]

According to an inscription in the volume, ms. Casanatense 1889, possibly the earliest of the three chronicles based on style and subjects, was owned early, but not necessarily originally, by a novice in the Jesuit College of St. Paul in Goa, Joaõ da Costa, who sent it to Lisbon in 1627. The volume's journey ended in Rome in Dominican hands in the library established by Girolamo Casanate at his death in 1700. In addition to their common final resting place in Rome, Casanatense and ms. 1551 consist of colored drawings (142 in Casanatense), mostly of multi-figured scenes of Indian peoples and Europeans, with short identifying captions, in the case of Casanatense, in Portuguese.[111] While ms. 1551 is different in style and, with one exception (fol. 15) absent depictions of Europeans, in focus on India and in format it is similar to Casanatense, with some overlap in the places represented, including Hormuz, Cambaya, and Java. Only one scene, however, that of the festival

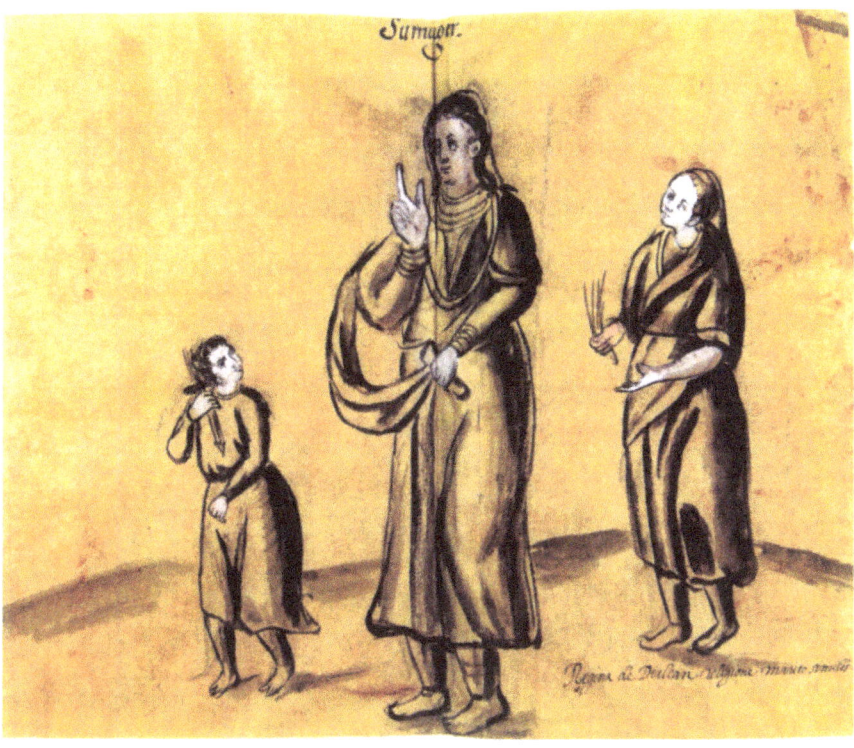

Figure 2.6 Artist unknown, *Reina de Dialcan (Queen of Dialcan)*, Rome, Biblioteca Angelica ms. 1551, fol. 69. On concession from the Ministry for Arts and Culture and Tourism.

cart in Madura (**fig. 2.8**), is depicted in both manuscripts as it is in Linschoten.[112] The king of Cambaya wears a similarly wrapped bodice in Casanatense (fol. 49) and ms. 1551 (fol. 39).

The *Boxer Codex*, written and illuminated on Chinese paper[113] and bound at the Spanish court after 1614,[114] consists of 97 lavish illustrations by an Asian artist, primarily of pairs of figures, male and female, with captions and extensive narrative descriptions in Spanish for each, plus a long historical text (the latest date in which is 1590) compiled from several sources, probably by a secular official in Manila in two 16th-century scribal hands.[115] The places represented include India, the Philippines and nearby islands, Japan, and China, and it shares with ms. 1551 depictions of Zambales, Bisayas, Malucos, Moors in Manila, Javanese in Malaca, Japan, and the Tartars. According to George Bryan Souza and colleagues, "Most of the drawings appear to have been copied or adapted from materials brought to the Philippines from China by Martín de Rada and other sources."[116] The male Tartar figures in both Boxer folio 198 and ms. 1551 (**fig. 2.4**) wear a very similar fur-trimmed two-piece costume and identical knee-length dark boots with light soles.

While the information within this section of ms. 1551 is not entirely unique, it does sometimes provide context that expands on those accounts. For example, several of the unillustrated secular Portuguese and Jesuit descriptions from this period

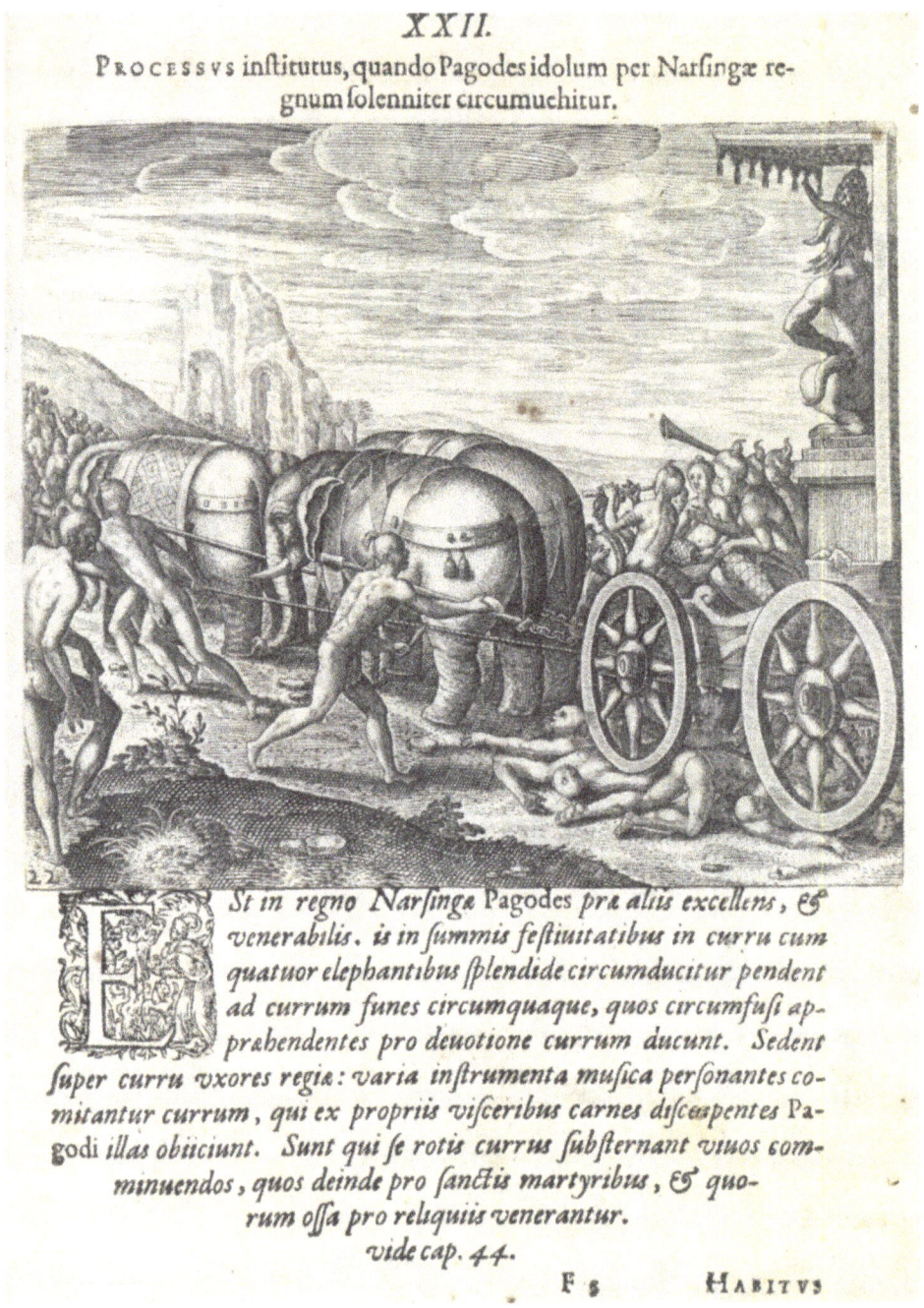

XXII.

Processvs inftitutus, quando Pagodes idolum per Narfingæ regnum folenniter circumuehitur.

St in regno Narfingæ Pagodes præ aliis excellens, &
venerabilis. is in fummis feftiuitatibus in curru cum
quatuor elephantibus fplendide circumducitur pendent
ad currum funes circumquaque, quos circumfufi ap-
præhendentes pro deuotione currum ducunt. Sedent
fuper curru vxores regiæ: varia inftrumenta mufica perfonantes co-
mitantur currum, qui ex propriis vifceribus carnes difcerpentes Pa-
godi illas obiiciunt. Sunt qui fe rotis currus fubfternant viuos com-
minuendos, quos deinde pro fanctis martyribus, & quo-
rum offa pro reliquiis venerantur.
vide cap. 44.

F 3   Habitvs

Figure 2.7   Johann Theodor and Johann Israel de Bry, *Processus insituts,*
quanto Pagodes idolum per Narsinga regnum solenniter circumuehitur,
Linschoten, *Navigatio in Oientem,* in Johann Theodor and Johann Israel
de Bry Pars II: *Indiae Orientalis,* Frankfurt, 1599, plate XXII. General Collection, Beinecke Rare Book and Manuscript Library, Yale University.

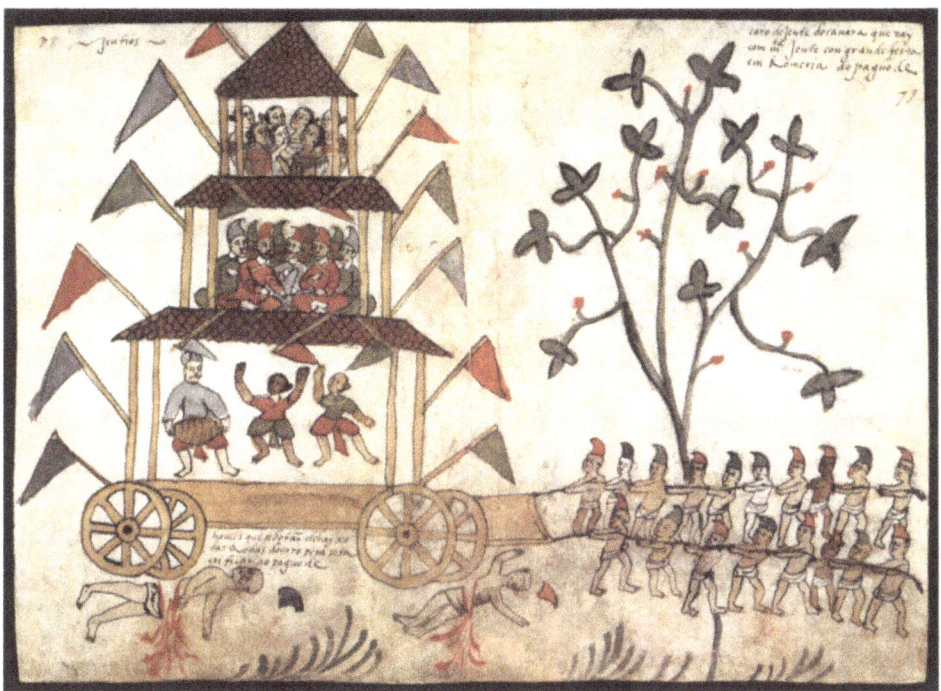

Figure 2.8 Artist unknown, *Caro de Jente do canava que vay com mtq. Jente co grande testa em Romeria do paguode*. Rome, Biblioteca Casanatense ms. 1889, fol. 78. Photo courtesy Biblioteca Casanatense.

include discussions of some of the places depicted in ms. 1551, but none overlap completely or include as many places or subjects as ms. 1551's twenty-three different regions, and none exhibit similar wording.[117] A few Latin inscriptions in ms. 1551 provide historical perspective. These include the text on folio 13 describing the Dominican mission in Zambales, which began in 1581; the king of Cochin and the work of Archbishop Aleixo de Meneses (fol. 49) in the later 1590s; the mission in Ceylon of the Franciscans who arrived in 1543, and the mutilation of Portuguese, undated in the inscription but occurring in 1545 and 1588–1597 (fol. 71). Beyond these examples, however, the Latin inscriptions are primarily ahistorical and descriptive but more general than the 16th-century published accounts.

The extant letters of St. Francis Xavier, whose extensive travels around India, the islands of Indonesia, and Japan are not wholly documented, exhibit familiarity with many of the places depicted in 1551, although not the Mughal empire, as he is not known to have been in contact with it or its ruler, Humayan, during his time in India. While in the islands in 1546, Xavier wrote of a native practice that is not mentioned in other sources but comports closely with the scene labeled as the Nicubar Islands in ms. 1551, folio 47 (**fig. 2.9**).[118]

The large number of published annual letters sent to Rome from Jesuits stationed in India, Japan, and China after 1580 refer to many of the places depicted, but without duplicating precisely either the visual or written details on ms. 1551. The letters written between 1594 and 1597 in particular seem to contain the highest concentration of places and events depicted in ms. 1551, especially new relations with Pegu;[119] the king of Cochin;[120] Aleixo de Meneses, his admiration

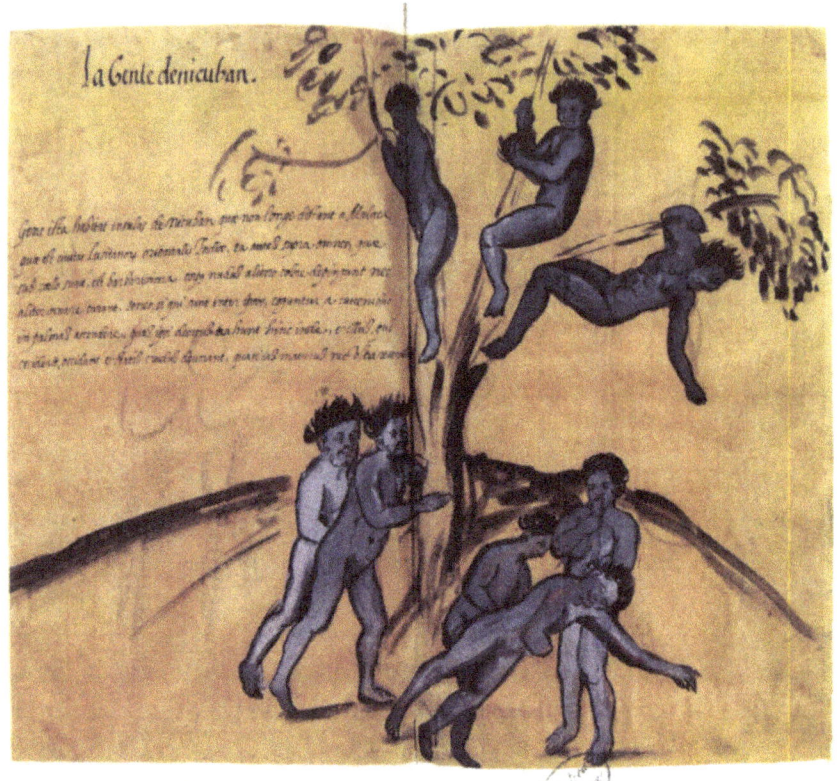

Figure 2.9 Artist unknown, *Gente de Nicuban (People of Nicubar Islands)*, Rome, Biblioteca Angelica ms. 1551, fol. 47. On concession from the Ministry for Arts and Culture and Tourism. All rights reserved.

for the Jesuits,[121] and dealings with the St. Thomas Christians,[122] as in ms. 1551, folio 49; the third mission to the Great Mogor in 1595;[123] good prospects for Christianity in Cambaya;[124] and the Fishery Coast.[125]

Ms. 1551 contains what seems to be the only known texts and illustrations from the 16th or early 17th century specifically describing Mongau, China (**fig. 2.9**) and Sogau, in East Timor (**fig. 2.10**). Other areas are mentioned in contemporaneous written sources, but illustrated only in ms. 1551, including Nicubar (**fig. 2.9**), Malabar (fol. 53), the Comuries (fol. 55), Garcopa (fol. 61), Barcelor (fol. 63), Bisnaga (fol. 65), Dialcan (fols. 67 and 69), and Ceylon (fols. 71 and 73). In all cases, it is the illustrations of ms. 1551 that offer new information, not the texts.

The Jesuit Connections

What inferences may be drawn from the evidence? First, these drawings were likely in Rome by around the same time as section 1 by virtue of the shared Asian paper, which could have reached Rome via Jesuits in Asia as early as 1580, and by virtue of its mounting on the same European paper, as well as the Latin inscriptions probably added in Rome just before or after 1600, looking back upon the tenure of Aleixo de Meneses, archbishop of Goa from 1595–1599. The Portuguese and Spanish were

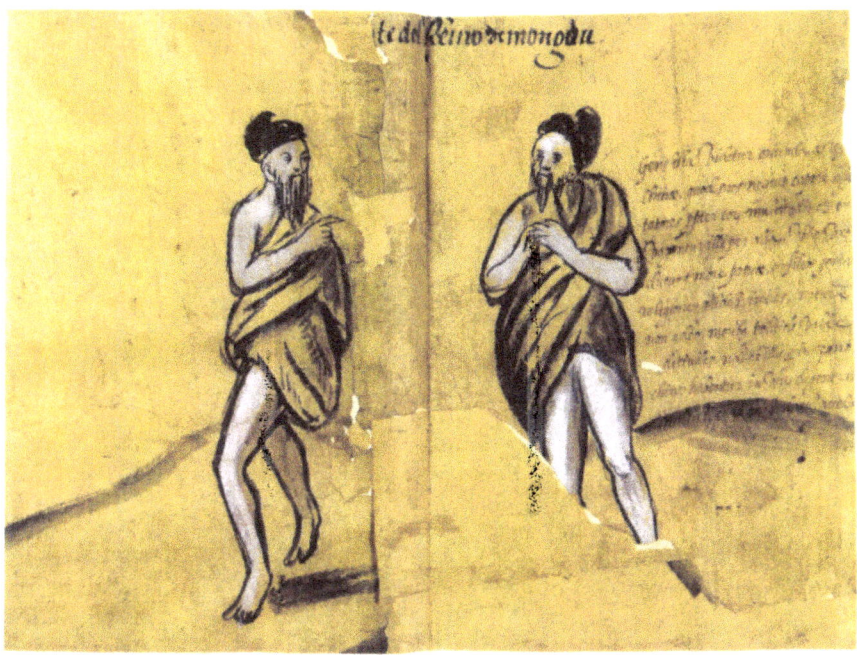

Figure 2.10 Artist unknown, *[torn]te del reino de Mongau (People of the Mangau Kingdom)*. Rome, Biblioteca Angelica ms. 1551, fol. 23. On concession from the Ministry for Arts and Culture and Tourism. All rights reserved.

expelled from Japan in 1610, and the inscription of the Mogor in the present tense would suggest Akbar, who died in 1605, or the young Jahangir, who ruled thereafter, although neither was known to wear a beard, as the Mogor does in ms. 1551 (**fig. 2.2**).

The most likely origins of the drawings are with the Jesuits, who established missions in or visited India, China, and Japan in the last decades of the 16th century, and made a concerted effort to communicate what they encountered to their colleagues in Rome. One clue is that the Latin incorporates words considered to be ecclesiastical, according to the classics scholar Eduardo Engelsing.[126] Jesuits were the first European contacts with Akbar, between 1579 and 1597, and ms. 1551 contains the only European illustrations of the Mogor until de Bry's publication of Robert Coverte's voyage to India in vol. XI of *Petits Voyages,* published in 1619.[127] Casanatense, similar in type although thought to be several decades earlier, was in the Jesuit College of Goa, then that in Lisbon, arriving by an unknown date in Rome. The Jesuit visitor, mainly Valignano, was charged with traveling to other Jesuit stations and twice visited Northern India, as well as Japan, which was closed to foreign missions in 1610.[128] The *Commentaries* of the Jesuit father Antonio Monserrate (1536–1600) are the most detailed descriptions of the Mughal empire of Akbar. But no individual in the period is known to have been in all the places depicted in ms. 1551. Ms. 1551's captions written in Spanish, but with occasional Portuguese orthography, also suggest Jesuit authorship, as the Jesuits in Asia were primarily Portuguese but commonly wrote in Spanish.

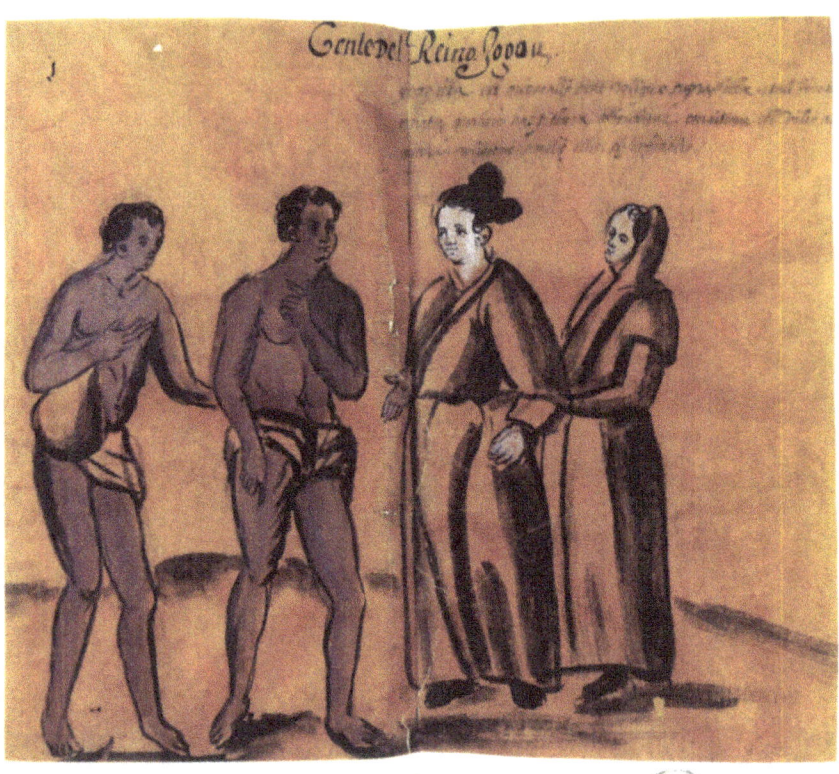

Figure 2.11 Artist unknown, *Gentes del Reino Zogau (People of the Sogau Kingdom)*, Rome, Biblioteca Angelica ms. 1551, fol. 35. On concession from the Ministry for Arts and Culture and Tourism.

Among the Jesuits in Asia who might have commissioned the set, a visitor, whose mission was to know firsthand all areas of Jesuit interest, is the most likely, and in date that would be Alessandro Valignano, who was named the first visitor and in 1574–1577 went to northern India. [129] He was the only Jesuit familiar with the Mughal Empire and Akbar until missions beginning in 1580,[130] as well as the other places depicted in ms. 1551. Valignano, an Italian, wrote primarily in Portuguese and Spanish, rarely in Latin, and as mentioned in the introduction to this volume, he wrote some letters to Rome on yellow Japanese papers.

The Jesuits on their third mission to the Mogor Akbar in 1595–1597 were accompanied by an anonymous Portuguese artist, who also traveled to Japan, the only artist in Jesuit travels known to have been in both places. The style of his surviving works is not similar to that of the artist of ms. 1551, but as the latter are perhaps only quick sketches, one cannot rule out a common authorship.[131]

It seems likely that the drawings were in Jesuit hands in Rome. Perhaps Alonso Sánchez brought them from Asia without the Latin inscriptions, and even Acosta might have had or seen them while there, although that would require that the Latin inscriptions were added after his departure and return to Spain. Pignoria may have seen them when he was in Rome between 1605 and 1607, and it may be worth noting that Peiresc was interested in Mughal India, writing in 1630 for information about it to the jeweler and collector Augustin Herryard, who had been at the Mughal court as of about 1612.[132] So, it is not impossible that these drawings traveled to Rome via Jesuit missionaries, then were gathered together with the other two sections decades before joining the Massimo collection.

The Folios (numbered in brackets in order as bound)

[1] fol. 9: Tartaros. Yellow gold paper. Two standing male figures in orange wash. (**fig. 2.4**)

> Gens Tartarorum antiquis etiam fuit nota quam continua bella armis doc-tam fecere. Valde exosam habet gentem Chinensem, quam robore et animo vincit, sed vincitur ab illa multitudine et industria qua factum est ut se ab illa diviserint media macerie longitudinis ultra mille ducenta miliaria. Cuius tamen maior pars naturae ipsi debetur ob altitudinem montium mediorum, minor arti, qua valles ips<a>s <orna>vere Chinenses.

> Tartars

> The people of Tartary were also known to the ancients. Constant wars made them skilled in fighting. They greatly detest the Chinese people, against whom they are victorious by their strength and bravery, but are defeated by the Chinese's multitude and diligence. Due to their diligence, the Chinese separated themselves from the Tartars by a middle wall whose size reached beyond thousand two hundred miles. However, the bigger part of this wall reaches beyond thousand and two hundred miles. However the bigger part of this wall owes its size to the nature itself due to the height of the inter-mediary mountains, and the smaller part to craftsmanship by which the Chinese equipped/fortified their lowlands. (EE/AH)

The costumes depicted here are very similar to those illustrated in the *Boxer Codex*. The great wall and its purpose were described for European readers as early as 1576 by Francisco de Sande (1540–1602), referring to the Tartars in relation to his account of the Philippines addressed to Philip II.[133]

[2] fol. 11: Gente principal and gente comun de Japon. Pale yellow paper.

> Gens ista Japponensis bel<lica> scien<t>ia viribus ac animosit<ate> pr<a>estat, regulariter duobus ensibus, uno parvo, altero magno, saepe tri-bus (quorum maiori non nisi utraque manu iunctim uti valet) ali quando uno tantum accincta incedit, sed ulterius habet usum lance areus, et b<omb>ardulae etiam. sunt ad bella faciles et ad duella etiam propte<r> honorem, quem vitae praeferunt. sunt idolorum cultores ac ipsis máxime devoti, quorum obsequio deputati sunt plurimi sacerdotes, quos vocant . . . bellica radices aliquas missit?, cui ita devote adhaerent sicut antea idolola-triae; et tam ex corde ut pro ipsa multi animas suas posuerint proxime? in christianae persequ<ti>one tyrannica sacerdotum idolorum suasu suborta.

First-order Citizens/Common Citizens of Japan

This people of Japan stand out for their knowledge of warfare, strength, and boldness. As a rule, they walk equipped with two swords—one small, one big—frequently three (the biggest of those they cannot hold unless they hold it with both hands), but sometimes they walk with only one. The spear-carrier employs the last one and also a small musket. They are ready to war and also to duel on account of the honor, which they held in higher esteem than life. They worship idols and are extremely devoted to them, to whose service many priests are allotted, whom they call [several words unintelligible] of warfare sent some roots, to which/whom they are so devotedly attached as they were previously to idolatry; and they have such an esteem for it that many recently lost their lives in the persecution of Christians, when a tyranny appeared under the advisement of the priests who worship idolatry. (EE/AH)

Two large figures, the "principal" being a woman with long, loose black hair and voluminous red robe with wide sleeves gesture toward a man with two top-knots wearing a calf-length green belted robe with wide sleeves to the elbow and holding a fan in his right hand. In the right background is a group of five tiny standing figures wearing various colored garments and holding what appear to be swords, spears, and other weapons.

[3] fol. 13: Zambales. Pale yellow paper.

> Gens ista habitat provintiam quondam dictam Pangasinam, quae sita est in a<rc>ta insula de Luzon. eius mores primi et novissimi fuere sicuti praecedentis, nam quod ad primos attinet non minus humanum sanguinem sitiebat quam ipsa, quod ad novissimos vero fratrum praedicatorum ministerio non minus exuit barbariemquam illa ac cum fide Christi mansuetudinem induit. adeo autem in fide ipsa profecit ut nullus ferme supersit locus otio ipsorum ministris vacantibus eorum instructioni, confess<i>onum audientiae, et aliorum sacramentorum administrationi. a principio annis quattuor habuere fratres praedicatores ita exossos, ut ipsos fugerent, nec vel uni ipsorum verbo aures praebere vellent. post ipsorum perseverantia ac inculpabili vita convicti ipsis adhaeserunt, dicentes se toto illo tempore expertos illorum innocentiam fuisse, et propterea sibi suasum magistros esse veritatis, quae talis vitae comes esse solet. Post verbum non defluit ab ore ministrorum, sed fuit velut semen cadens in terram bonam. iam nunc Christiane et devote, sed et politice vivunt. Laus deo omnium largitori.

Zambals

This people lives in the province once called Pangasinan, which is located in the high island of Luzon. Both its first and its most recent customs were like the customs of the previous people, for, as regarding its first customs, it was no less thirsty of human blood than the previous people; and, as regarding its most recent customs, through the ministry of the Dominicans, it did not cast off its barbarism less than the other people, and it assumed mildness together with the faith of Christ. It made such progress in faith that there is hardly any place left for their inactivity, as the preachers are devoting themselves to their instruction, the hearing of their confessions, and the administration of other sacraments. At the beginning, for four years, they detested the Dominicans to such a degree that they fled them and did not want to listen to even a single word from them. Afterwards, conquered by the brothers' perseverance and their blameless life, they cleaved to them, saying that they had experienced all that time the brothers' innocence, and were persuaded for this reason that they were teachers of the truth, which is the usual companion for such a life. Afterwards the words proffered by the preachers were not lost, but they were like seeds falling on a fertile soil. Now they live not only as devoted Christians, but also as a civilized people. Praise to the Lord, the source of all goods. (EE/AH)

Four figures stand in a green landscape with a mountain in the background; three wear loincloths in red or pink and bear shields or bow and arrow in red and orange; one central figure in a long black robe holds no weapon. The reference to "previous people" is additional evidence of the disorder of these drawings, the most immediately previous people being the Japanese in folio 11.

Juan de Salcedo (1549–1576) led an expedition that resulted in colonization of the island of Luzon in 1565, a date which provides a *terminus post quem* for these drawings of section 2, although not for the Latin inscriptions, which were added to the drawings no earlier than the very last years of the 16th century, referring back to the tenure of Archbishop Aleixo de Meneses in Goa, which ended in 1599. The mission of the Dominicans began in 1581.

[4] fol. 15: Moros de manila. Pale yellow paper.

Gens ista provin[t]<c>iam quandam habitat Philippinarum, quae est proxima civitati Manilae, quae est illarum metropolis; ipsaque fuit, quae primo Deo per fidem, et Regi Hispaniarum per obedientiam nomen dedit. Vocantur Mauri, quantumvis sint professione Christiani, quia iam apud ipsos cum primum Hispani ad eos appulerunt secta Mauritana per praedicatores suos serpere ut cancer inceperat; sed ab ipsis fugata ministrorum evangelicorum diligentia, alibi non multum longe sedem accepit. adhuc tamen nomen illud perseverat.

Moors of Manila

This people lives in a province of the Philippines, which is very close to the city of Manila, their chief city. Manila was the very one that first enlisted, because of faith, to the service of the first God, and because of obedience to the service of the king of Spain. They are called Moors, although they are declared Christians, because when the Spaniards first arrived, the Muslim religion, due to their preachers, was already spreading among them like a cancer; however, when they themselves sent this religion away due to the diligence of the evangelical priests, it got a place elsewhere not far away. Until now, however, this denomination persists. (EE/AH)

[5] fol. 17: Visaias. Virrei. Pale yellow paper. **(Fig. 2.5)**

Nomen navigii

Gens ista dicitur Visaias, cuius provintia [sic] sita est in insulis Philippinis sortitaque est idem nomen, provintia [sic] de Visaias, totaque est fidelis cum paucis ante annis esset idololatriae dedita, ac cum fide ipsa mores politicos imbuit, quibus antea fere omnimodis carebat.

Visayas. Name of the boat.

This people are called Visayas, whose province is located at the Philippines Islands and obtained the same name, province of Visayas, which is wholly faithful, although a few years ago it was devoted to idolatry. With the faith itself, it gained [some] political practices, which it previously did not have in almost any way. (EE/AH)

A man in knee-length blue robe with elbow-length sleeves gesturing toward a woman in grey robe and blue mantle. A third man at right in knee-length yellow robe, holds a spear and red banner or shield with black motifs. A Philippine outrigger boat, a *virrey,* is drawn in black ink. Landscape with suggestion of mountain in background is depicted in green wash. The garments generally conform to those described by Antonio de Morga in 1609, but he says that the men's bodies are wholly tattooed, not shown in this drawing.[134]

[6] fol. 19: Rei de Ormus. Pale yellow paper.

oromus est insula parva sinui persico proxima, quae quia tota salsa est, ita ut domor(um) etiam parietes salsi sint, nullam omnino habet aguam[135] praeterqua(m) | pluviale(m). ei(us) habitatores sunt mauri p(ro)fessione; sol est in ea popul(us) Lusitano(rum) regi Portugalia subiect(us), mercium multar(um) ac mercato(rum) undiq(ue) ibi confluentiu(m) conspicu(us). tempore | aestatis adeo viget ibi aest(us) ut ei(us) habitatores gaudeant tunc aguis[136] velut pisces.

King of Hormuz

Hormuz is a small island near the Persian Gulf, which, because everything is salty such that even the walls of the houses are salty, has no water whatsoever except for rain. Its inhabitants are avowed Moors; only the population of Portuguese on it is subject to the Portuguese king. One sees there a gathering of many goods and merchants from all over. In the summertime, the tide is active to such a degree that its inhabitants then rejoice at the water as well as fish. (BW)

Four male figures, all with long mustaches and red and white turbans, stand on a green surface. The left figure is in a red robe and dark boots, carrying a sword. The king, in a green belted robe and yellow boots, wearing a holstered sword, stands under a red parasol carried by a figure in a red robe and yellow boots. A shorter figure in a yellow garment and dark boots stands behind and carries a holstered sword and bow.

[7] fol. 21: Reina de ormus, erased letters under an elaborate ligatured combination of letters or perhaps an "R," also in black ink. Pale yellow paper.

Uxor regis de ormis ei(us)dem professionis cum ipso | taliter ornata qualiter hic depicta.

> Queen of Hormuz
>
> The wife of the king of Hormuz, of the same occupation as him, dressed up in such a way as is depicted here. (BW)

Three female figures stand in a green landscape, all wearing wrapped shawls and loose pants tapering at the ankle. The woman on the left wears a yellow mantle and blue pants. The middle woman, presumably the queen, wears an orange and red-brown blouse, red pants, and pale green headscarf. A third woman is in a yellow mantle and red pants.

[8] fol. 23: [torn: gen?]te del reino de Mongau. Pale yellow paper. (**fig. 2.9**)

> Gens ista videtur oriunda a reg<no>chinae, quod suos nequit capere ha<bi>tatores propter eorum multitudinem et vagantur illi per alia; ubi et uxo<rem>ducunt more patriae, et filios gener<rant>religione quidem similes, natura non adeo, moribus politicis valde dissimiles. Nam ab illis qui in regno chinae habentur in usu degeneran[t]multum, et ad barbarismum accedu[nt].

> People of the Kingdom of Mongau
>
> This people seems to come from the kingdom of China, which cannot contain its inhabitants due to their great number. They wander through other kingdoms, and where they take their spouses according to their country's customs, and they have children similar to them certainly on behalf of religion, but not so on behalf of their nature, and very different on behalf of their political customs. They depart a lot from the customs of the kingdom of China and come close to barbarism. (EE/AH)

Two Mongol Chinese men with topknots and beards each wear wrapped mantles over naked bodies. The only added colors are the black outlines and their white skin.

[9] fol. 25: Gente del reino de Madura en la Jaba. Pale yellow paper.

> Incedunt mulieres seminudae soluta caesarie nec ita se hominum presen tari aspectibus verentur. Dominae huic propinat ancilla in canistro herbam quamdam, quam omnes utriusque sexus semper et ubique masticare solent, cuius succo dicunt confortari valde[137] stomachum, quo in eum delibuto? Reliquum proijciunt sed quidquid sit, os ipsum ac dentes reddit valde deformes.

People of the Kingdom of Madura ~~in Java~~

Half-naked women walk with loose hair and do not fear to be shown in this way to the view of other people. The maidservant gives an herbal drink to this lady in a basket, some herb that everyone from both sexes is always chewing everywhere, whose juice they say very much relieves the stomach; *once they have tasted the juice, they throw the rest away*?[138] But in any case, the juice makes the mouth itself and the teeth to become very misshapen. (EE/AH)

As the reference to Java, where one Madura is located, is crossed out, it seems that this is the Madura in South India. Four bare-breasted and barefoot women in yellow and red skirts of different lengths stand in a hilly, green landscape, and one is shown gesturing to another, explained in the Latin text as taking herbs.

[10] fol. 27: Ydolo de Madura. Pale yellow paper. (**fig. 2.1**)

Ducitur idolum in curru per vias saltatricibus ac cantatricibus mulieribus circumdatum, cui se passim homines devotionis causa in sacrificium offerunt. Namque prosternunt se super terram currui ipsi obviam, ut eos rotae per medium seccent. Sunt enim ad hoc bene dispositae. aliqui brachium vel pedem obtruncandum offerunt rotarum motui. Et mirum est quanti isti habeantur ab aliis, et a sacerdotibus suis praedicentur ut plures habeant imitatores. Quibus vim brevi mortis compendio aeterna gaudia promittunt. Videas quaeso quali tyrannide suos cultores daemon praemat, nec propterea paucos habeat. <Aequ>ant enim numerum arenae maris.

Idol of Madura

The idol, surrounded by dancing and singing women, is taken through the streets in a chariot, to which men indiscriminately offer themselves in sacrifice for worship's sake. They throw themselves to the ground to meet the car for the wheels to cut them in the middle. These are well arranged for such a task. Some offer an arm or a foot to be maimed to the motion of the wheels. It is astounding how much these are esteemed by others and how much they are praised by their priests so that they garner many other imitators to whom, by the force of a short economy of a death, they promise eternal happiness. Please see the tyranny by which the devil presses his worshippers, and not for that matter he has few of them. For they equal the number of grains of sand in the sea. (EE/AH)

Two figures in scant loincloths pull a red and black chariot with bird handle and wheels held up by two hanging gray figures. In the chariot are two figures, one naked and the other wearing a loincloth and carrying a round red shield. Behind the chariot by a tree are two naked figures.

The scene is similar to folio 78 in Casanatense (**fig. 2.8**) and to Plate XXII in de Bry's illustration to Linschoten's *Itinerario* in *II Pars. Indiae Orientalis* of 1599 (**fig. 2.7**), in which worshippers are crushed by a chariot in Narsinga, also known as Vijayanagar and next to Madura, which paid tribute to Narsinga and was later under the religious control of the Jesuits. Linschoten wrote that:

> "There they have a Wagon or a Carte, which is so great and heavie, that three or foure Elephants can hardly draw it, and this is Drought foorth at faires, feastes, and processions. At this Carte hang likewise many Cables or Ropes, whereas [also all the countrie people, both] men and women of pure devotion doe pull [and hale]. In the upper part of this Carte standeth a Tabernacle or feaste, wherein sitteth the Idoll, and under it sit the Kings wives, which after their manner play on all instruments, making [a most] sweete melodie, and in that sort is the Carte drawne foorth, with great devotions and processions: there are some of them, that of [great] zeale and pure devotion doe cut peeces of flesh out of their bodies, and throwe them downe before the Pagode: others laye them selves under the wheeles of the Carte, and let the Carte runne over them, whereby they are all crushed to peeces, and pressed to death, and they that thus die, are accounted for holy and [devout] Martyrs, and from that time [forwardes] are kept [and preserved] for great and holy Reliques, besides a thousand other such like beastly superstitions, which they use, as one of my Chamber fellowes that had seene it, shewed me, and it is also wel knowne throughout all India."[139]

[11] fol. 29: El mogor. Gold paper with black ink drawing and whitened faces as the only added color. (**fig. 2.2**)

Rex iste, dictus Mogor, est valde potens, vicinus nostrae Indiae Orientali, quam et armis capere aliquando tentavit sed non obtinuit. Religione est maurus et christiano nomini inimicus.

The Mughal

This king, called Mughal, is very powerful, the neighbor of our Eastern India, which he once tried to conquer by military action ["with his army"] but could not. Regarding religion, he is Muslim and an enemy of the Christian faith. (EE/AH)

This emperor eludes conclusive identification, as elements in the illustration and text conflict with what is known about the Mughal emperors of the 16th and early 17th centuries. First, he is depicted with a beard. Humayun, the second Mughal emperor, who ruled from 1531–1540 and 1555–1556, was the only Mughal depicted as fully bearded until Shah Jahan in the 1620s, despite the fact that beards were the custom in this empire. Humayun was a devoted Muslim who also tried unsuccessfully to conquer eastern provinces of India, as stated in the text. But he had no notable dealings with Europeans.

Akbar, his son, called the great Mogor (1542–1605) and who ruled from 1555 to his death, is described in writing in 1597 by the Italian Jesuit Peruschi, compiling Jesuit sources,[140] especially that of his colleague Monserrate, who wrote in Goa after completing his mission to Akbar in 1590.[141] Akbar is also shown in many

Mughal miniatures, most famously the *Akbarnama*, which he commissioned and was completed around 1589. In Peruschi, Monserrate, and the miniatures of the era, Akbar is described or depicted as clean shaven except for a luxuriant mustache, and he was successful at extending his empire east.[142] Mourning his mother's death in 1604, however, he was said to have shaved his beard, so he may have grown one as an older man.[143] He was also considered hostile to Islam during much of his reign, unlike his devout father. Only one visual clue, provided by Monserrate, points directly and persuasively to Akbar, despite the beard and aversion to Islam. Monserrate said that he "carries his head bent toward the right shoulder,"[144] which is pronounced in this image.

Akbar's son and successor, Jahangir, was portrayed around the time of his becoming the fourth Mughal, with dark stubble over his jaw and cheeks, and a full mustache. Taking into account no other factors in other folios or external evidence, if this depicts Humayun, at least the images would be dated to 1556 or before, as the text is written in the present tense. If Akbar, the beard likely dates to the years after Monserrate and the *Akbarnama*, the illuminated book of Akbar, or between 1590 and 1605.

[12] fol. 31: El mogor va al campo. Red paper.

> Ducitur Rex semicubans lect<icae> sericis ornatae, quae arundini longae et grossae [sic] appensa haeret. Nam arundines recens natae in arun dinetis industria hominum curvantur ad modum arcus, ut post cum creverint abscissae aptae sint huiusmodi lecticis ferendis, quarum in India est ingens copia pro foeminis ac viris etiam nobili<b>us sed quae foeminarum sunt coopertae ducuntur non quae virorum.

The Mogor Goes to the Camp

The King is carried half-lying in the litter, which is decorated with silk that hangs attached to a long and thick reed. The reeds recently born [i.e., still young] in the thickets are bent by men's diligence like a bow in such a way that, after growing, they are cut, suitable to the kind of litters used for transport, which exist in a huge number in India for noble women and also men. The ones that carry women are covered, whereas the ones that carry men are not. (EE/AH)

The Mughal, in red garment and turban, reclines on a bed with short carved legs, carried as a palanquin by two attendants in simple caps and knee-length tunics, also in red, and white gaiters. A third attendant, holding a parasol over the bearded Mogor, wears white. The red is provided by the color of the paper. The only added color is the white of the palanquin's handle and the third attendant's clothing and headgear.

Monserrate accompanied Akbar on his expeditions and described in detail the Mughal's elaborate camps, as well as the European-style palanquin in which he rode on his journeys.[145] But as mentioned above, the Akbar he knew was clean shaven, except for a mustache, at least until the death of his mother, whereas this Mughal is fully bearded.

[13] fol. 33: la reina del mogor. Red paper with paler red back. Three figures, a woman in the center, flanked by two men.

> Regina de Mogor praedicti | regis coniux.
>
> The Queen of the Moghuls
>
> The queen of the Moghuls is the wife of the aforementioned king. (BW)

The only added color, besides the black outline, is whitened skin. The queen's garment is decorated with a series of shallow scalloped bands.

[14] fol. 35: Gentes del Reino Zogau. Red paper backed with gold paper. (**fig. 2.10**)

> Gens ista est orientalis sicut reliquae supradictae, tali inced[unt] ornatu qualis in hac pictura ostenditur. Conditione est vilis a[tque] misera, religione similis illis, scilicet infidelis.

> People of the Kingdom of Sogou [Sogau]
>
> These are eastern people as the other aforementioned; they walk with the clothing such as seen in this picture. They are of a base and miserable condition. Their religion is similar to this condition; that is, they are infidel. (EE/AH)

Four gray-skinned figures, two males with short hair and wearing only loincloths, are posed with hands over bare chest. They face a male with a white face and two topknots wearing a belted long robe and a white-faced woman with a shawl over her head and shoulders and a long dress over a tight-sleeved undershirt.

Sogau, in East Timor, Indonesia, was first seen by Europeans when the Portuguese encountered it in the 16th century. The reference to "eastern people as the other aforementioned" would suggest that other images of nearby peoples preceded this one in the original sequence of existing drawings, or that images are missing.

[15] fol. 37: Hermitanos de Pegu. Deep gold paper with red backs.

> Isti sunt veluti heremitae, qui semper saccis induti et cinere conspe<rso> capite incedunt. dormiunt sub dio et super nudam terram, ac saepe in<cedunt per>medios ignes, quorum ardore torqueantur, poenitentiae causa. quapropter ab <aliis>habentur pro sanctis, cum tamen sint diaboli cultores hypocritae tristes.

> Hermits of Pegu
>
> These are like hermits, who walk around always dressed in sackcloth and with their head covered with ash. They sleep under the open sky and on the bare ground and frequently walk through the fire for repentance so that the heat tortures them. They are considered by others as saints, whereas they are worshippers of the devil—gloomy hypocrites.[146] (EE/AH)

Five male figures wear ragged brown knee-length garments. Two figures on the left have long sleeves and sport small pointed beards and mustaches. Figures in the center and at the inner right have full beards (one in a bare-shoulder garment), and the figure on the right is beardless.

[16] fol. 39: El Rei de Cabaia. Red paper with yellow back.

> Cambaia terra est orientalis Radix omnis bonae texturae generis pannis abundans, quib(us) tota faere In[diae?] | Vestitur e(t) ornatur. e(t) ideo pecuniis mercato(rum) illuc adventantium p(er) illis emendis alioq(ue) deducendis ditescit [m][rest of word cut off] | [another line below is cut off].

The King of Cambaya

Cambaya is a land of the East, the source of all types of good textiles, abounding in cloth, with which nearly all are clothed and dressed up. And for that reason coming there with the money of merchants, through buying these and taking them elsewhere, [subject lost] grows rich . . . (BW)

The only added color is white skin. The bearded king is seated on a throne under a swagged canopy, flanked by five figures, two bearded and three clean shaven, in caps and long robes.

The details of the king's garment—long sleeved, red, with one side wrapping over the other to the waist, and an ornament hanging down the chest—is similar to the depiction of the garb of the same king in Casanatense (fol. 49), the only such similarity between the two manuscripts, despite several other overlapping portrayals of kings, as in Pegu, Hormuz, and Ceylon. The orthography in this folio is closer to Portuguese, whereas that in the Casanatense folio is closer to Spanish, despite its text being predominantly Portuguese.

[17] fol. 41: Los Bramenes. Red paper with paler red back.

> Gens ista etiam est ex orientalibus; bella fugit, pacem diligit adeo ut non solum nulli hominum mortem appetat, sed et animalium etiam vermiculorum. nullum enim animal occidunt, sed nec occisi carnibus ullo modo vescuntur. Aliqu<i> ipsorum sunt philosophiae naturalis ac medicinae gnari vacantque infirmis cur<an> dis propter lucrum; ita ut christicolae etiam ecclesiastici in suis infirmitatibus <se>eorum curae committere non vereantur, propterea quod certi sunt quod eos ultion<e>non occident, id inhibentibus eorum legibus.

The Brahmins

This people also comes from the East; they shun war and are in such degree so fond of peace that they do not seek the death of any man, animal, or even a worm. They do not kill any animal and do not even eat, in any way, the meat of one that has been killed. Some of them are knowledgeable of natural philosophy and medicine and dedicate themselves to the cure of sick people for the sake of profit so that even the Christian clerics do not fear, when they have sickness, to commit themselves to their cure because they are certain that they will not kill them by vengeance, as they are forbidden to do so by their laws. (EE/AH)

The scene is populated with six adult figures: four males and two females. Two clean-shaven men wear wrapped robes exposing one arm; two bearded men are clothed in turbans and sleeved and belted robes; the central figure stands behind a flame, pointing toward one of the bare-armed men, who points back at him. Two women sit in the foreground, one holding a child. This is apparently a representation of the custom of *sati*.

[18] fol. 43: Gentes del Reino de pegu. Yellow paper with red back.

Regnum de Pegu est ditissi<mum> pretiosis abundans gemmis <sed> superstitionibus etiam. Quarum un<a> comburuntur defunctorum <corpora>.

The People of the Kingdom of Pegu

The kingdom of Pegu is very wealthy abounding in precious stones but also in superstitions. One of them is to burn the body of the deceased. (EE/AH)

This is one of the few Latin texts to refer directly to the image. Seven figures kneel around a tripod over a dead man lying suspended over a flame. A more complex scene with similar elements is reproduced in de Bry's Latin edition of Gotthad Arthus, in *Indiae Orientalis Pars Septima*, identified as the burial of the king of Pegu.[147]

[19] fol. 45: Idolo de la virginidad, saserdote, Figura de hierro. Red paper. (**fig. 2.3**)

Figura illa elephantis est idolum quod a gente quadam Indiae orientalis colitur, altera hominis stantis est sacerdotis illius; alia vero veluti mortui est ferrea, super quam fiunt multa vana et superstitiosa.

Idol of Virginity, Priest, Iron Figure

The image of the elephant is an idol that is worshipped by a certain people of East India. The other of a standing man is its priest [i.e., of the elephant]; however, the other figure of someone appearing to be dead is made of iron, on which many empty and superstitious things are being done.[148] (EE/AH)

The text provides brief clarification of the elements in the image. A bearded priest in a turban stands in the lower left, his right arm bent with hand pointing at three Brahmins in wrapped robes exposing one arm, standing to the left of a building and gesturing toward a bearded supine figure identified as iron, clothed in white. At the upper left is an elephant standing on a double platform to the left of a building with a five-columned portico and steep roof. Like the two depictions of the Mogor (**fig. 2.2**), the red paper provides the primary color, the only added hue being the white of the iron figure, suggesting that it belongs with those folios in terms of geography and perhaps timing of execution.

Several ancient temple complexes were known to Portuguese traders and Jesuits in India in the 16th century. This could be a representation of the elephant sculpture (now relocated to a museum) and Buddhist temple caves on the island of Elephanta, near present-day Mumbai. The Portuguese García de Orta (1501–1568) may have been the first non-Indian to see it, in 1534, and his was the first published description in *Coloquio da simples e drogas da India*, of 1563.[149] Several Jesuits, including an anonymous Jesuit in 1553 and Luis Froís (1532–1597) in 1560, referred to Elephanta in letters to Rome, both cited by Pignoria in 1615.[150] It was described in Spanish in a letter posted in Bassein on February 16, 1589, by the Jesuit Fray Pedro Páez to Fray Tomás Iturén.[151] Linschoten's description was first published in 1596 and then in De Bry's *Indiae Orientalis*, volumes II through IV, beginning in 1599.[152] Another possibility is the Ellora complex, also guarded by a life-size sculpture of an elephant in the vicinity of Mumbai and well known to outsiders since its creation around the same time as Elephanta. Although the Latin text refers to this scene as taking place in East India, the likely structures depicted are in western India, so the author is probably making a distinction not to regions within the Asian India, but to the Indies that were also used as the term for the Americas.

The so-called iron figure eludes identification. There seems to be no surviving sculpture or written account of an iron sculpture (which was perhaps more likely bronze), a supine Indian, or a bearded one, from the pre-Portuguese era. This is possibly due to the wholesale destruction of sculptures by 16th-century Europeans because of their heathen subjects. Metal ones were often melted down. Elephanta was especially hard hit in this period, as described by the Jesuit Giovani Pietro Maffei (1533–1603) in 1588.[153] It is possible that such a metal sculpture was intended to stand and had fallen in the period of Portuguese destruction of religious complexes.

[20] fol. 47: La Gente de Nicuban. Gold paper with red back. (**fig. 2.9**)

> Gens ista habitat insulas de Nicuban quae non longe distant a Malaca, quae est civitas Lusitanorum orientalis Indiae. ea autem supra omnes, quae sub caelo sunt, est barbarissima. corpus nudum alieno colore depingunt nec aliter ornare curant. Senes, si qui sunt inter ipsos, coguntur a iuvenibus in palmam ascendere, quam ipsi deorsum trahunt hinc inde, et illum, qui ceciderit, occidunt et statim crudum devorant, quasi iam maturum nec ultra reservan[dum].

The People of Nicubar

> This people inhabits the isles of Nicubar that are situated not far from Malacca, which is a city belonging to the Portuguese of eastern India. This people, however, above all others who are under the sky is the most barbarian. They paint their bodies with a different color and do not care to ornament themselves in another way. They force their elders, if there are some among them, to climb a palm tree, which they drag down from different sides, and they kill the one who falls, immediately devouring him raw, as if already ripe and not to be kept any longer. (EE/AH)

Naked, blue-skinned men are climbing, possibly fornicating, and standing around a tree. One is without a hand, which is being eaten by a man behind him.

While in the islands in 1546, Francis Xavier wrote of a native practice not mentioned in other sources, but comporting closely with this folio:

"There are also some islands in this part of the ocean the people of which eat human flesh, especially the flesh of their enemies who have been killed in battle. If any one of their own people dies by disease, they do not touch the rest of the body, but they cut off the hands and feet, and consider them great delicacies."[154]

[21] fol. 49: Rei de cochin. Pale yellow paper.

Rex iste de cochin est professione idolatra, sed est amicus christi/anorum, immo et maurorum et Iudaeorum; quos omnes apud se habet; nec prohibet vasallos suos ire in quamcumq<ue> sectam maluerint. multi populi chistianorum eorum, qui a tempore D. Thomae apostoli qui fuit doctor gentium orientalis Indiae, fidem acceperun<t> | et retinent, etsi mille superstitionibus ex malo gentium vicinio ferme obrutam, sed paucis abhinc annis purgatam diligentia Reverenstissimi archiepiscopi goensis dicti don frater Alexo de Menesses Ordinis Sancti Augustini viri probatissimi, sunt ditioni illius subiecti, sed patiuntur multa incommoda a rege et potissimo populo idolorum cultore. Omnes incedunt nudi, brevi panno ad ilia contexti. Arma defensiva, praeter clipeum, ignorant omnino, sed offensiva omnia ferme habent in <u>usu</u>, maxime nobiles, quorum plurimi ensem nudum et clipeum, quandam lanceam, quandam arcum sagittarium, quandam <u>bo<mb>ardulam</u> semper et ubique portant in | signum nobilitatis suae. | Nullo utuntur certo matrimonio, praeter regem et consequenter ignorant filios suos si quos habent, et ideo regulariter relinquunt bona sua filijs sororum, quos certo sciunt esse suos consobrinos.

King of Cochin

This king of Cochin professes idolatry, but he is a friend of the Christians and especially of the Muslims and of the Jews; all of whom he receives in his house. Neither does he forbid his vassals to join whichever religious creed they prefer. Many peoples of these Christians are subject to the king's power. The Christians were converted at the time of St. Thomas, the apostle, who was a learned man of the peoples of Eastern India and retained [their religion], although their faith was almost overwhelmed by a thousand superstitions coming from the bad neighboring tribes. The religion was, however, a few years ago, purified by the carefulness of the Venerable Sir Fray Aleixo de Meneses, archbishop of Goa, an excellent man. But these peoples [the Christians] suffer many inconveniences by the king and, particularly, by the peoples who worship idols. Everyone walks naked, covered by a light cloth on the groins. They completely ignore defensive weapons, except the shield, but the offensive weapons they have almost in daily employment, above all the noblemen, most of whom always and everywhere carry with themselves a bare sword and a shield, a kind of spear, a kind of bow, and a kind of small musket, as a sign of their nobility. They do not contract any clear marriage, except the king, and consequently they ignore their offspring, if they have one, and therefore, as a rule, they leave their patrimony to the offspring of their sisters, who they know for sure are their nephews. (EE/AH)

Echoing the detailed Latin inscription, the king is depicted as dark-skinned and dressed in a yellow-orange loincloth and red headgear, seated on a red blanket atop an elephant in the center. Two attendants at left and three at right, also dark-skinned and in similarly colored loincloths and hats, stand with swords, spears, and yellow shield with crescent moon motif.

De Bry's publication of Linschoten in *II Pars Indiae Orientalis* of 1599, plate XVIII is similar, although more elaborate, in its portrayal of the king upon an elephant, surrounded by his shield and spear-carrying attendants. This illustration does not appear in the original Dutch publication of 1596, indicating that it may have been taken from a different source. Diogo do Couto recounts Aleixo's dealings with the king of Cochin and the St. Thomas Christians in *Da Asia Decada XII*, which was written in the early years of the seventeenth century but not published until 1645.[155] The king of Cochin during the period described was Keshama Varma Rama, who ruled between 1565 and 1601.

[22] fol. 51: Reina de cochin. Pale yellow paper.

> Videas regina(m) tanto regi coniuncta(m) e(t) pedisse quas consimiles. | de qua non abs re erit dicere quod philosoph(us) alter de asino mandente | carduu(m). Talib(us) labriis tales lactucae.

Queen of Cochin

See the queen united to such a king and ask how they are similar. On this matter, it will not be amiss to say that which another philosopher said about a donkey chewing thistle: His lips have similar lettuce.[156] (BW)

The queen sits on a backless orange chair or table, flanked by two bare-breasted women in short, wrapped skirts, one red, the other pale yellow. The scene appears to be set in a landscape.

[23] fol. 53: Malabares. Red paper.

> Gens ista habitat littora maris India orientalis a civitate cochin usque ad Goensem, quae sunt Lusitano(rum) e(t) distant abimvicem centum Leucis. | Habent e(t) Lusitani aliqua praesidia intermedia. sed illis non obstantib(us) reliquus Litt(ora) maris habitant isti malavares, qui nudi e(t) inermes armis | defensivis, sunt armatis Lusitanis saepe fortiores. Habent enim aquilis velociora navigiola, quae ascendentes maria sulcant e(t) in navigantes grassantur nec sola | contenti praeda, cum eos capiunt, occident; etsi saepe etiam vice versa teneantur ipsi occidantur, vel ad triremes damnentur. Itaq(ue) officio sunt piratae, religione, mauri, morib(us) barbari. nec serunt faere nec metunt, sed toto hyeme; quo non licet mare petere; vivunt de praeda, quam in aestate habuerunt.

Malabars

This people inhabits the eastern shores of the Indian Ocean from the city of Cochin up to Goa, which are Portuguese and are a hundred leagues distant from one another. The Portuguese have another intermediary fort, but apart from those, the Malabars inhabit the rest of the shores of the ocean. They, naked and unarmed with defensive weapons, are often stronger than the armed Portuguese, for they have little boats faster than eagles, which rise up and plough through the water. And they prowl about in boats not content with booty alone: When they catch them, they kill them, although often it happens the other way around and they are caught and killed or condemned to the galleys. All in all, they are pirates in terms of work, Moors in religion, and barbarians in custom. They generally neither sow nor reap, but all winter, when they cannot take to the sea, they live off of booty, which they had from the summer. (BW)

Eight black men, one with long dress, while others wear only loincloths and carry shields and swords.

[24] fol. 55: Los comuries. Red paper.

Gens ista non longe sita est a promo<n>torio dicto de comorin. Illa autem est valde humilis et paucissimis contenta sed idolatriae dedita sicut et reliquae.

The Comuries

This people is located not far away from the promontory called the Comorin. It is, however, very poor and satisfied with very little but devoted to idolatry as like the others. (EE/AH)

Three men wear loincloths, one in the center with a bowl on his head.

[25] fol. 57: Gente del cavo de comurin. Pale yellow paper.

Istud promontorium est semper desertum, praeterquam tempore <le>gendi uniones ex ostreis, quibus mare illud abundat. Qua occassione singulis anni<s> mense februarij, paulo ante vel post, confluunt ad illud variae ac innumerae gentes ad emendum illos uniones, quos multi in natandi scientia valde periti legunt ex ost[re]is. Et ne maneant sub di<v>o interim dum id durat, domos/sibi palleas astruunt quibus cum recedunt ignem applicant ut comburantur.

People of Cape Comurin

This mountain ridge is almost always solitary, except in the season to collect large pearls from the oysters, which abound in that sea. In February of every year, or somewhat before or after that, many and diverse peoples converge to this place in order to buy those large pearls, which many very experienced in the art of swimming collect from the oysters. And so that they do not stay in the open sky while this period lasts, they build for themselves houses out of chaff to which they put fire when they leave in order to burn them up. (EE/AH)

Despite the caption, there are no people in this scene, which is a mountainous landscape in green (the only added wash), with two flimsy structures on land and a European transport ship, probably a *nao*, in black ink, floating offshore.

[26] fol. 59: Jabos qe pelean en campo. Red-gold paper.

Jaba est insula non longe a civitate Malaca sita Est aromatum ferax, sed maxime nucis indicae. Eius habi/tatores sunt religione Mauri, moribus inculti. Ob mutuas inimi/citias duella ruri agunt sicuti haec pictura ostendit.

Javanese who Fight in the Field

Java is an island situated not far from the city of Malacca. It is abounding in spices, but especially in Indian nut. Its inhabitants are Moors of uncultivated manners. Due to mutual enmity, they fight duels in the countryside, as shown in this picture. (EE/AH)

Two figures in loincloths and caps on horseback are jousting with shields and spears.

[27] fol. 61: Reina de garcopa. Pale yellow paper.

Videas reginam a portitoribus duci reti serica cubantem, sed nudam Qualis ipsa tales et vasalli, omnes quasi bruta animantia, et quod peius est daemonis mancipia.

Queen of Garcopa

Behold the queen laying down and being carried in a silken hammock, but naked. She is herself, as are her vassals, all almost animals, and what is worse, servants of the devil. (EE/AH)

The queen, bare-breasted and wearing a short skirt, is carried in a landscape on a palanquin with decorated red edge by two bare-chested men wearing ballooning short pants, one red and the other deep yellow. They are flanked by two other bare-chested males in short garments of the same color, brandishing swords and, in the second male, also a shield.

[28] fol. 63: Gente de Barcelos. Pale yellow paper.

Idolum est, quod fertur in curru processionaliter, mulieribus salt[r]at<r>icibus eius obsequio mancipatis, antecedentibus et subsequentibus ipsum.

People of Barcelor

It is an idol that is carried on a car in the form of a procession, while women are dancing who were bought for its sake [i.e., for the images' service], [and who are] walking before and after it. [Or: women who were bought to serve it [the idol]: to walk before and after it] (EE/AH)

A wheeled cart is pulled by two gray oxen, with a platform bearing a scaffold from which is suspended a figure grasping after two running figures with red and gray shields at the left. Two additional figures at the right in loincloths, one with a red shield, gesture toward the scene. The flesh of the figures is pink, the shields and wheels red, and the platform an orange achieved with the red pigment and yellow paper.

This scene appears to represent an antecedent of the annual Chariot festival held in spring on Chitra Pournima.

[29] fol. 65: Rei de Bisnaga. Gold paper with red back.

Bisnaga pars est orienta[lis] Indiae, quae tanto viget aest[u] quantum regis eius ornatus vi[dentur] arguere. Ipse autem cum omni g[ente] sua, quia idolorum cultor adhuc [callid] iori multo in inferno opprimet[ur].

King of Bisnaga

Bisnaga is part of eastern India, which is so lively in such hot weather as the ornaments of its king seem to demonstrate. But he himself with all his people, because he is still a worshipper of idols, will be castigated in hell, which is much hotter. (EE/AH)

The king in conical cap and loincloth is seated on a raised platform surrounded by attendants in short garments or loincloth and similar cap in front of curtains or a tent.

[30] fol. 67: Rei de dialcan. Gold paper with red back.

Rex de Dialcan est etiam vicinus Indiae orientali, quam et aliquando lacessivit bello, sed frustra Deo pro suis pugnante; est valde potens armis et equitatu et omni bellico apparatu. Est professione Maurus ac per consequens Christianis infestus.

King of Dialcan

The king of Dialcan is also a neighbor of Eastern India, against which he at a time waged war, but unsuccessfully since God fought for his people. He is very powerful in weapons and cavalry and all kinds of warfare. He is a declared Muslim and, consequently, hostile to Christians. (EE/AH)

As Engelsing points out, the "also" links this inscription to the previous one,[157] confirming that the original order of sheets is being followed here. The mustachioed king is seated within an ornate baldaquin with nine men in attendance, two seated on a decorated platform in the background and seven standing near the king.

[31] fol. 69: su mugger. Gold paper with red back.

Regina de Dialcan religione marito similis.

His Wife

The queen of Dialcan is similar to her husband in terms of religion. (BW)

The queen of Dialcan, in elaborate long dress, is flanked by a young woman in plainer long dress and a male child.

[32] **fol. 71**: Rei de seilan. Pale yellow paper and ghost image indicating reuse.

Insula de magna est longitudine et latitudine, fluviis multis irrigua; abundant gemmis et xilocasia, ita ut omnia fere montium eius arbusta sint xilocinnama | suavissimum de se spirantia odorem. Per quae passim vagantur elephantes, plures numero quam alibi reperiantur, et robore ac viribus potentiores. Sunt in ea aliqui populi fidelium | ex incolis eiusdem, quos patres D[ivi] Francisci XPO genuerunt. Sunt et aliquot Lusitanorum militum praesidia, quae a regulo isto et sibi adhaerentibus gentilibus,[158] quorum ingens numerus, passim oppug | nantur, et nunc cedit Victoria unis nunc aliis. Contigitque iam semel ex sexcentis milititbus Lusitanis, teneri ab inimicis 60 omnibus aliis desideratis. Sed et illi 60 abscissis naribus cum superioribus labiis libertate donati sunt | qui tamen postea non levem illis retribuerunt vindicta[m].

King of Ceylon

The Isle of Ceylon is large in length and breadth and is watered by many rivers. It is rich in precious stones and cinnamon so that almost all of the trees covering its mountains are cinnamon wood that exudes the sweetest fragrance. Elephants are everywhere to be found wandering through these trees, and they are more numerous than they can be found elsewhere, and more powerful in resistance and strength. Among the inhabitants of the island are some believers, whom the Franciscan fathers converted to Christ. There are also some garrisons of Portuguese soldiers, who are constantly attacked by this petty king and his Pagan followers, who are in a huge number. Sometimes victory is on one side, sometimes it is on the other, and it happened once that out of the six hundred Portuguese soldiers, sixty were retained by the enemies, whereas all the others were missed, but these sixty soldiers were set free after their nose and their upper lip had been cut out. Later, however, the same ones paid them back with no small revenge. (EE/AH)

Gray-skinned men in loincloths, one kneeling before the king, another holding a parasol over his head, stand with three bearing weapons. The scene is set in a landscape.

The first Franciscan mission to Ceylon was in 1543, its intention being the conversion of the king of Kotte, Bhuvenekabahu.[159] One massacre of 600 Portuguese and the mutilation of prisoners like that referred to in the text took place in 1544–1545, but Diogo da Couto also described the cutting off of noses and lips in his Decada XI, which covers the period 1588–1597.[160]

[33] fol. 73: Reina de seilan. Pale yellow paper.

> ecce regina(m) in ornatu regio, nullo faere alio praeter eu(m), que(m) a natura accepit. tales sunt insulae isti(us) incolae, quae | diutiis ac delitiis ita abundat, ut aliqui putarint in ea fuisse paradissu(m) Adami; quod tamen licet sit incertum vel poti(us) | videatur ridiculum, hoc tamen est mirum esse in ea monte(m) quemda(m) sua altitudine superante(m) nubes, qui vulgari Indor(um) ipsor(um) idiomate dicit(u)r pico de Adam.

Queen of Ceylon

Behold the queen in regal attire, with almost nothing other than that which she received from nature. Such are the inhabitants of this island, which abounds in blessings and delights to such an extent that some think that the paradise of Adam was on it. This, however; is doubtful or, rather, ridiculous, although one can see a certain mountain on it exceeding the clouds in height, which in the common tongue of those Indians is called the Peak of Adam. (BW)

The queen sits cross-legged on a table or backless chair, flanked by two female attendants, as in fol. 51, the queen of Cochin. In this scene set in a landscape, one attendant is bare-breasted and wears a knee-length skirt; the other is as in fol. 51, queen of Cochin, completely naked. Westermeier points out that word *pico* is Spanish, not Latin, and perhaps betrays the writer's native tongue.[161]

CHAPTER 3:
Inca Kings and Queen

The third series is comprised of nine watercolors depicting eight Inca kings, or Incas (*inkas*) and one queen, or *Coya* (*qoya*). Like the other two sets in ms. 1551, these drawings are mounted out of order despite the clear chronological identification of each in the inscriptions, suggesting that, like section 2, which is out of geographical order, the first to bind them did not read Spanish. Of the twelve historical Incas, all of whom had spouses recounted by early chroniclers, four are absent, and the only Coya represented is Chimbo Herma (more commonly Urma).[162] That Chimbo Herma is included suggests that her husband, Cinchi Roca, would have been part of the series, as would the remainder of the Coyas, making a total of twenty-four, of which thirteen must be lost. While the first two sets of ms. 1551 are executed on Asian papers mounted onto European paper, those in this section were drawn directly upon the same brand of European paper, which exhibits the same discoloration and wear as the other two, probably indicating the same date of manufacture and use, perhaps the same batch. This implies the prior existence of the first two sets, and at least a slightly later date for the Inca drawings, perhaps immediately prior to the first binding of the three together.

Ms. 1551, Section 3 and Other Contemporaneous Depictions of Incas

This series of Incas was first treated by Juan Carlos Estenssoro in 1994,[163] and has been investigated most recently by Sara González Castrejón.[164] Both discussions proceed from Estenssoro's hypothesis that, while serving as papal nuncio in Madrid between 1654 and 1658, Camillo Massimo II, the Roman antiquarian whose death inventory contained the first documentation of ms. 1551, copied these images himself or had copies made from original paintings sent to Philip II by Viceroy Francisco de Toledo in 1572, and hung in the Alcázar in Madrid until a fire destroyed them in 1734. Although a reasonable assumption, based on consideration of these drawings in isolation, evidence in the volume seen as a whole and within its Italian context points to a date probably a half-century earlier, as well as a different interpretation of their creation.

Three surviving sets of Inca portraits expanded the documentation of the mythical Incas from the exclusively textual to include the visual. Executed in Peru in the late 16th and early 17th centuries, all complement textual histories of the Inca that remained unpublished for centuries. Two are by Martín de Murúa (c. 1525–1618), a Basque Mercederian friar who arrived in Peru sometime in the 1570s, remaining there before his return to Spain with his manuscript around 1615. The earlier of the two is titled *Historia del origen, y genealogía real de los reyes ingas del*

Piru, and dated around 1590 (**fig. 3.1**). The second, *Historia general del Piru,* was completed around 1616 (**fig. 3.2**).[165] Both consist of text and some drawings by Murúa, and other drawings by Murúa's sometime associate, the native-born Felipe Guaman Poma de Ayala (c. 1535 until after 1615). The third series is in *El primer nuevo corónica y buen gobierno,* by Peruvian Guaman Poma, the completion of which dates to around 1615 (**Fig. 3.3**).[166] As Thomas B.F. Cummins has demonstrated, these sets all conformed to a single type of Inca representation in which:

> "Different artists who worked on these three manuscripts all employed the same set of iconographic and compositional conventions in their portrayals. The full-length figure is positioned in the foreground, at or only slightly back in the frame, and in most cases stands frontally, with his or her head turned slightly to the right or left. These are the conventions of royal Inca portraiture that proliferate in the late 16th and early 17th century, in both Peru and Spain."[167]

These conventions likewise apply to ms. 1551, section 3 (**fig. 3.4**). None of the extant portraits as copied from the set ordered in 1572 by Viceroy Francisco de Toledo and sent to Philip II in Madrid, which were half-length, not full-length, portraits. Nevertheless, Cummins asserts that,

> "The series of portraits in the manuscripts by Murúa and Guaman Poma are clearly a sequential development of the series commissioned by Toledo. Guaman Poma's uncolored drawings are accordingly accompanied by textual descriptions of the colors of various *uncu* and other Inca clothing. . . . these descriptions correlate to the colors used in the portraits of the Galvin manuscript."[168]

Ms. 1551 would also seem to be part of this sequential development from the Toledo paintings, even though it, like the other manuscripts, clearly did not copy them.

Each Inca and Coya in the earlier Murúa, Guaman Poma, and ms. 1551, stands upon a grass-covered knoll, with attributes in hand. The compositional format of single figure standing on a hillock may be seen in contemporaneous European costume books, for example, Cesare Vecellio's *Degli habiti, antichi et moderni di diversi parti del mondo,* first published in Venice in 1590, and reissued in 1598 with the addition of images of non-Europeans and their garments, including Mexican and Peruvian costumes.[169]

Texts and Images in Ms. 1551

The inscriptions below each figure in section 3 of ms. 1551 are written in a late 16th- or early 17th-century humanist cursive hand, identifying the figures by name and the venerable age they were said to have attained and describing their coronation attire, as well as a few salient features of their character and rule. Like the inscriptions in section 1, those in section 3 are neutral in their characterization of the Inca, omitting any reference to their ignorance of Christianity or other perceived barbarisms. The terminology for garments is Spanish, unlike the Quechua often employed by Guaman Poma. Ms. 1551 does not mention by name the native checkerboard patterned *tocapu,* although several of its Incas are shown wearing a more generalized form of it than the detailed motifs Guaman (and Murúa) favored.

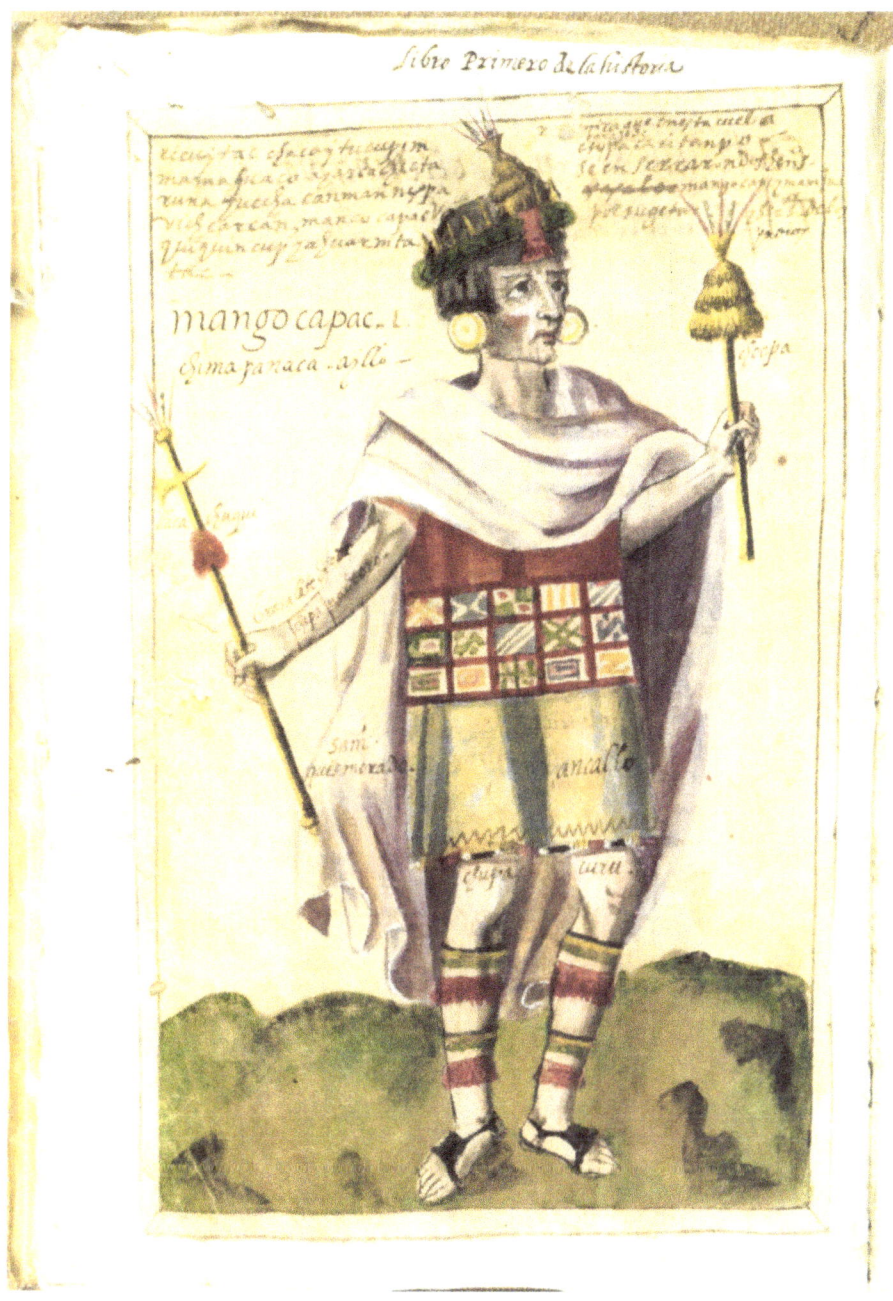

Figure 3.1 Martín de Murúa, *Manco Capac, Historia del origen, y gene-alogía real de los reyes ingas del Piru*, Peru, ca. 1590, Ireland, Seán Galvin collection, fol. 9v.

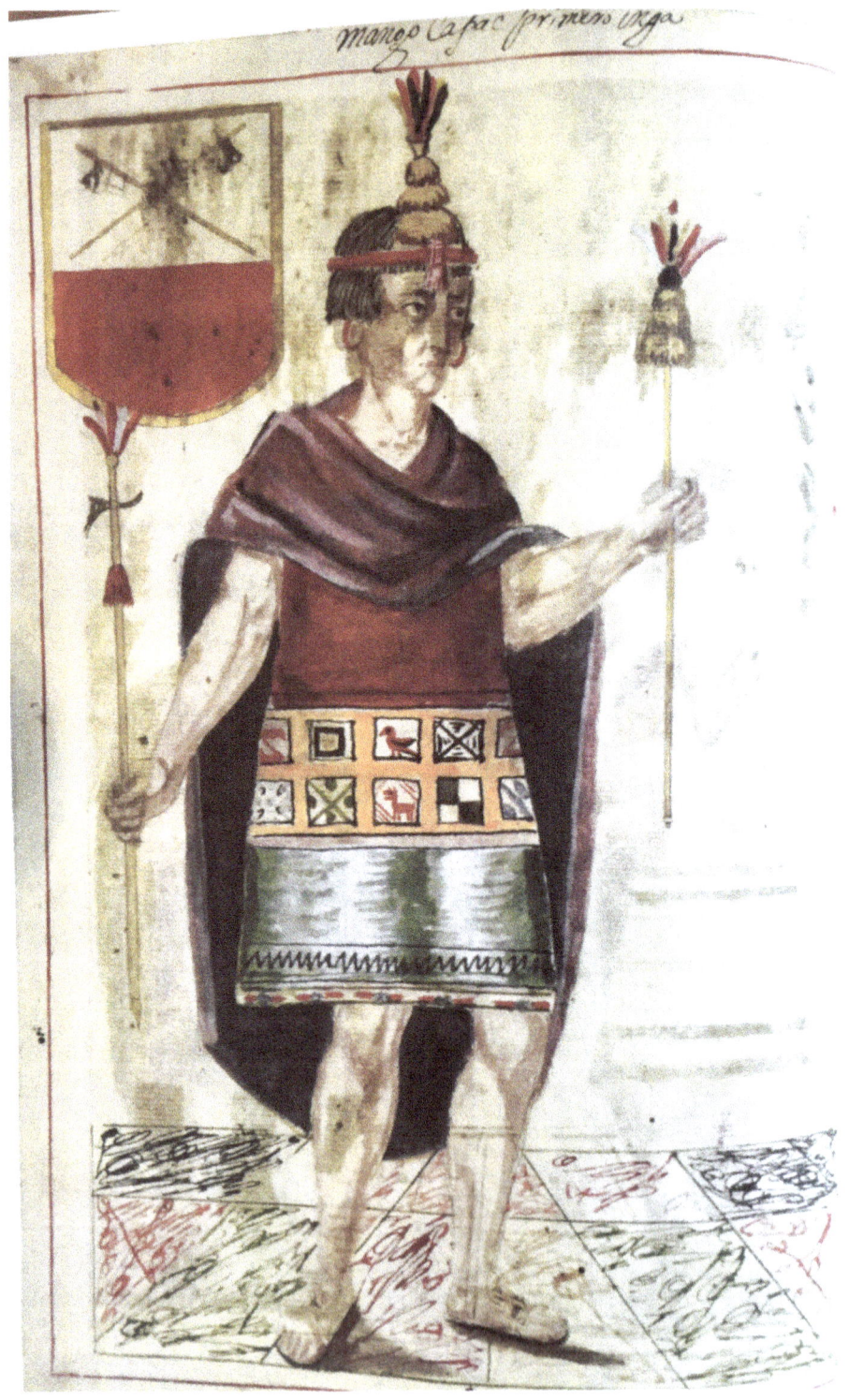

Figure 3.2 Martín de Murúa, *Manco Capac, Historia general del Piru*, Peru, 1616. Los Angeles, J. Paul Getty Museum, Ms. Ludwig XIII 16, fol. 21v.

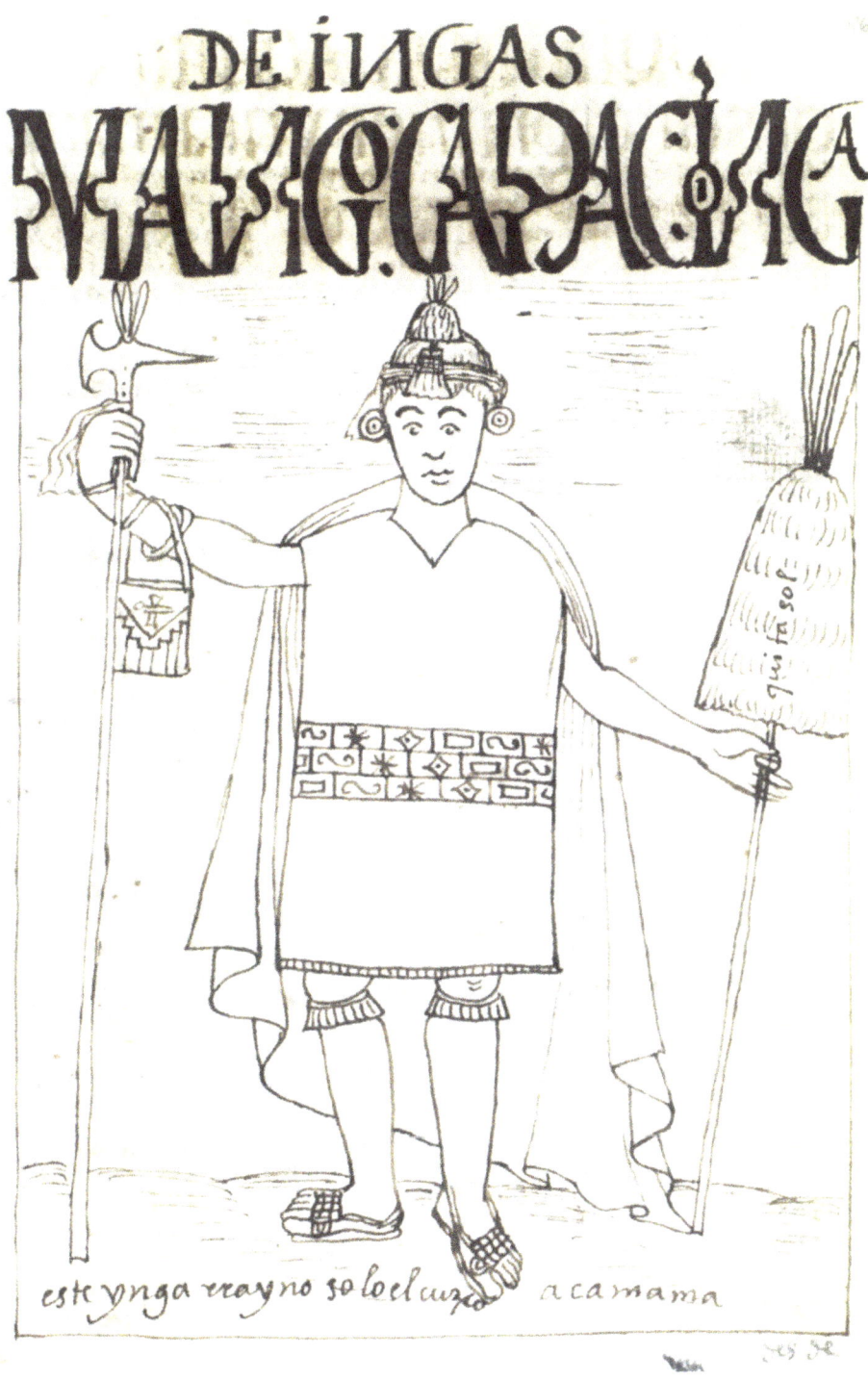

Figure 3.3 Felipe Guaman Poma de Ayala, *Manco Capac, Nuevo corónica y buen gobierno*, Peru, ca. 1615. Copenhagen, Kongelige Bibliotek, GKS 2232, fol. 86.

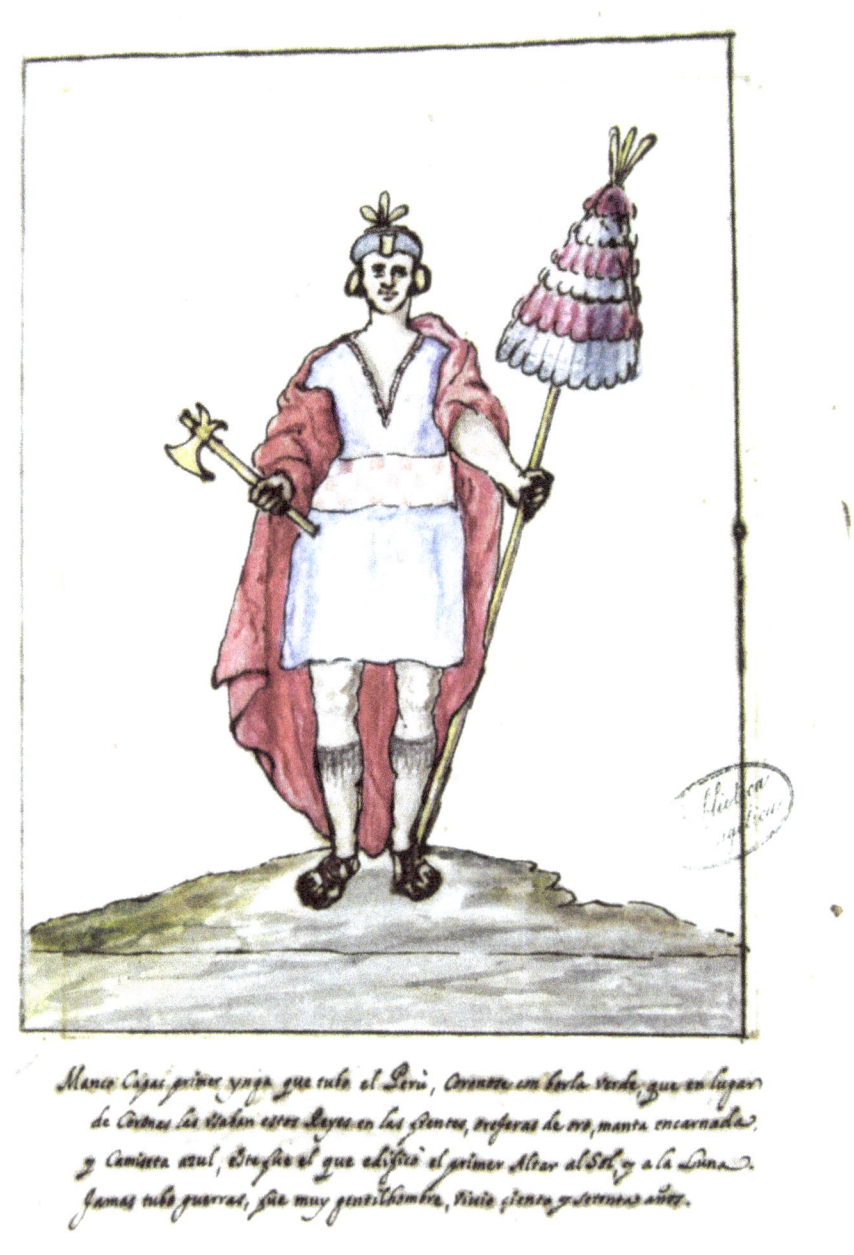

Manco Cápac primer ynga que tuto el Perú, coronese em borla verde, que en lugar de Coronas los usaban estos Reyes en las frentes, orejeras de oro, manta encarnada, y Camiseta azul, Bte fue el que edificó el primer Altar al Sol, y a la Luna. Jamas tuvo guerras, fue muy gentilhombre, vivió ciento y setenta años.

Figure 3.4   Artist unknown, *Manco Capac*. Rome, Biblioteca Angelica ms. 1551, section 3, fol. 77. On concession from the Ministry for Arts and Culture and Tourism. All rights reserved.

Although the elements of these written descriptions are similar to those in Guaman Poma and Murúa, the details sometimes differ. Manco Capac, for example, lived 160 years, according to Guaman Poma[170] and 170 according to the inscription for this ruler in ms. 1551 (**Fig. 3.4**). They also were slightly differently and uniquely spelled in some, as in "Chimba Herma" (fol. 76) and "lloque yuxaqui" in ms. 1551 (fol. 79), and the more widely accepted "Lloque Yupanqui" in Guaman,[171] and in ms. 1551 itself to identify the tenth Inca, Ingayupanqui, in folio 75. This would seem to indicate either a scribal error, perhaps by someone without knowledge of the language making a copy, or an author/scribe with a different, perhaps regionally based, knowledge of the language. This unusual orthographic variation is perhaps comparable to that of the use of Hieiteutl and Eccateutl in ms. 1551, section 1 (fols. 3 and 7).

On the other hand, some descriptions are remarkably close. One example is the rendering of Yaguar Guacac, who in both is characterized as wise and peaceable, with particular hatred of the rich and avarious, and the first to introduce fasts and penitences to the gods.[172] Similarly, Chimbo Herma in ms. 1551 (fol. 76), known as Chimba Urma in Guaman Poma,[173] is called, in the same words, beautiful, dark skinned, and thin. González, while noting these similarities of language between ms. 1551, section 3 and Guaman Poma, demonstrates that much of the descriptive text in the former, particularly that relating to color and garments, is almost identical to that in Buenaventura de Salinas y Córdova, *Memorial de las historias del nuevo mundo Pirú*,[174] published in 1631, and based, according to its author, on the lost notebooks of the Lima lawyer Francisco Fernández de Córdova (1580–1639), a younger contemporary of Guaman and Salinas. Pierre Duviols postulated that Guaman also took some of his texts from Fernández.[175]

Guaman said that he was working on his volume for thirty years when it was completed around 1615. If true, he was beginning his work around 1585, when Fernández was a small child and would not have written his lost text for another two decades. In addition, a number of minor discrepancies suggest the possibility of an earlier source for Guaman, Fernández, and ms. 1551. In the texts accompanying the illustration of Inca Yupanqui in ms. 1551 (fol. 75), for example, González observed that the tenth Inca is described as wearing a *camiseta tornazul* and a *manta verde* (**Fig. 3.5**). Salinas describes the reverse: a *manta de color tornasol* and a *camiseta verde*. Guaman Poma uses the term *torne azul* to describe the manta but omits the camiseta's color.[176]

Both Guaman and ms. 1551 employ a particular color term to describe the cape, as *tornazul* in ms. 1551, fol. 75 (**Fig. 3.5**), and *torne azul* in Guaman.[177] This is notable because not only is the image in ms. 1551 a representation of shot fabric, known in Spanish as *tornesol*, or "turn to the sun," but both are variants, or plays on words, that specify the shot fabric as blue, or "*torne azul*." As Elena Phipps has observed, tornesol fabric, which is made from contrasting colored yarns in warp and weft, changing color as it moves with light, was introduced into Peru in this period by the Spaniards, who had favored the fashion, especially in silk, in Europe. While the fabric often combined blue with another color to create the shimmering effect intended here in ms. 1551, folios 75 and 78, these appear to be the only instances, in Spain or the New World, of the word *azul* in place of *sol*.[178]

In addition to the depiction of tornesol, other folios also describe and illustrate colonial-era textiles worn by the pre-hispanic Incas. Mayta Capac (**Fig. 3.6**) wears a blouse with butterfly motifs, described in the text almost identically to that

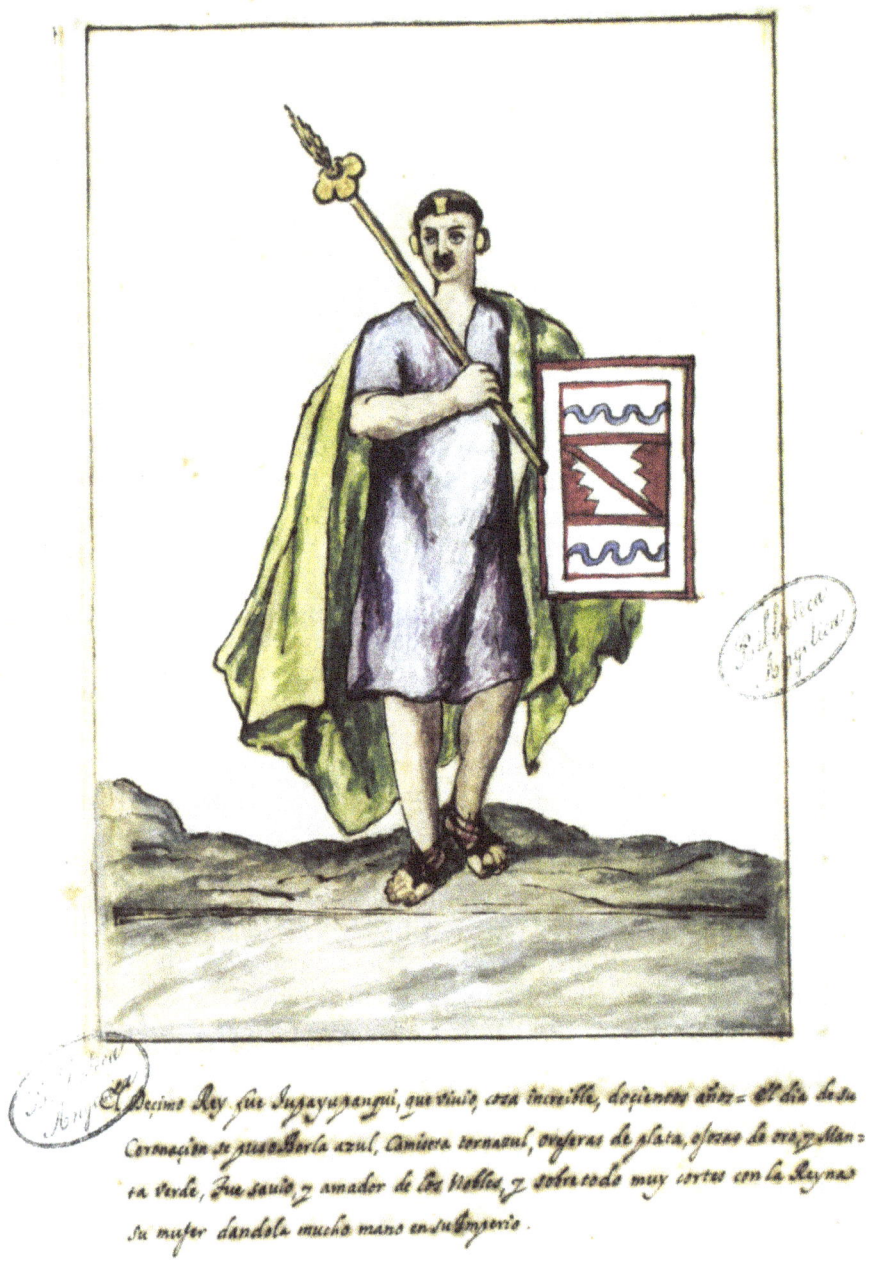

El Decimo Rey, fue Jugayupanqui, que viuio, cosa increible, docientos años = El dia de su Coronacion se pusa borla azul, Camiseta ternasul, orejeras de plata, ojotas de oro, y Manta verde, Fue sauio, y amador de los Nobles, y sobre todo muy cortes con la Reyna su muger dandola mucho mano en su Imperio.

Figure 3.5 Artist unknown, *Inca Yupanqui*. Rome, Biblioteca Angelica ms. 1551, section 3, fol. 75. On concession from the Ministry for Arts and Culture and Tourism. All rights reserved.

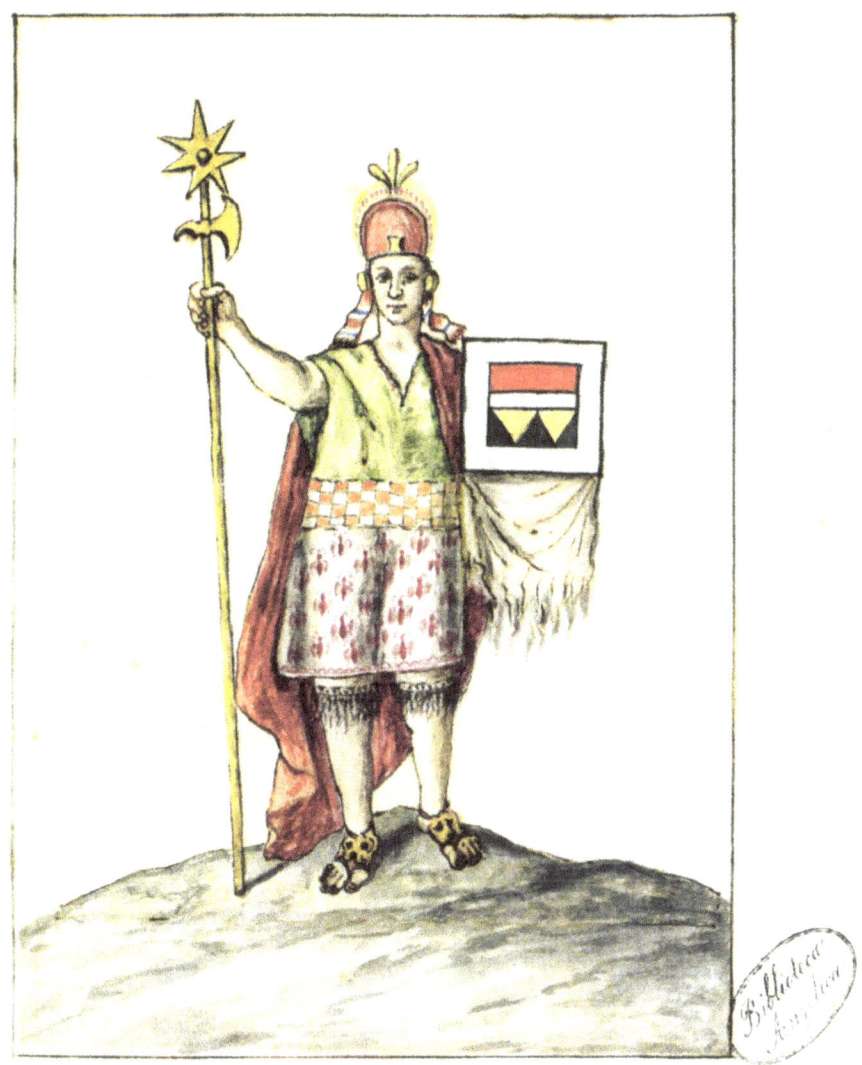

El quarto Rey fue Mayta Capac, que vivio çiento y beinte años, este se corono con borla azul Manta encarnada, y Camiseta blanca y verde, y salpicada con Maripozas carmesies. llamaronle el Maloncolico, aunque fue muy bravo para la Guerra, ques conquisto la Prouincia de los hearcos a llegar al zerro de Potosi = Deso grandes riquezas, tubo quarenta y dos niños con diferentes Mugeres.

Figure 3.6 Artist unknown, *Maytac Capac*. Rome, Biblioteca Angelica ms. 1551, section 3, fol. 74. On concession from the Ministry for Arts and Culture and Tourism. All rights reserved.

in Salinas.[179] Guaman Poma also illustrated butterfly motifs,[180] and the rare surviving textile examples with similar motifs date to the early colonial era, probably no later than the early 17th century, according to Phipps, thus further narrowing the most likely time period for the execution of the drawings.[181] Yaguar Guacac is described in the text as wearing a blouse with small lizards, but those motifs were not depicted in the image (fol. 82).

Like section 1 of ms. 1551, and in addition to the absence of lizards mentioned in folio 82, there are other discrepancies between text and image in which the text describes an element not pictured. Mayta Capac, for example, is shown wearing a red tassel, although his inscription says it is blue (**fig. 3.6**). Viracocha is not depicted with the bird feathers referred to in the inscription (fol. 78). Does this indicate the participation of an artist not following a scribe, comparable to section 1's text and image discrepancies?

The figure style, with black ink outlines (except for folios 81 and 82), lumpish knees, and classically inspired although awkwardly stiff poses, is reminiscent of late 16th- or early 17th-century Italian documentary drawings, particularly those of the Roman statues then being documented in the city by antiquarians such as Alfonso Chacón (**fig. 3.7**)[182] and others later collected by Cassiano dal Pozzo (1588–1657). A similar classicizing of American figures taken from an American source may be seen in the warrior figures, based on Bernardino de Sahagún's *Florentine Codex*, received by Francesco de' Medici by 1588, and appropriated by Lorenzo Buti in his ceiling fresco painted in 1588 in the Armeria of the Uffizi palace.[183]

Uniquely among the three sections of ms. 1551 and rarely among early visual and written portrayals, both the illustrations and inscriptions of the Incas in ms. 1551 emphasize the colors of garments. This contrasts with Guaman and Vecellio (c. 1530–1601), who described the colors in accompanying texts but did not color their images, and Murúa, whose images of Incas are varied and detailed in color but not explained in the accompanying texts, although the colors *morada, verde, azul,* and *carmesi* are specified in chapter 3 of his second book,[184] which describes but does not illustrate Inca costumes. The depiction of tornesol cloth is emphasized visually in folios 77 (**Fig. 3.4**) and 78 of ms. 1551, and the repeated use of the term *carmesi* to specify a carmine red, probably from cochineal, are additional indications of a late 16th- or early 17th-century date and European usage, before *cochinilla* became the preferred term for crimson, by this time generally made from the dye produced by the cochineal insect native to the New World.[185] In both Murúas and the Biblioteca Angelica manuscripts, the figures wear clearly defined Inca garments in a wide range of vivid hues: blue, violets, green, yellow, orange, and reds, the colors closely related to extant textiles from either the pre-Columbian or early colonial era, as Phipps has demonstrated.[186]

In the Angelica drawings, the colors are also described in detail in texts below the images as the only known Inca portraits to combine colored visual representations with corresponding written descriptions of colors,[187] which may imply instructions to an artist different from the scribe, not unlike Pignoria's inclusion of color descriptions provided by Aleandro of Asian figures in Cartari/Pignoria 1615. In a few instances, colors (but not generally motifs) chosen by Murúa or Guaman Poma and the artist of ms. 1551 coincide, as, for example, with the Getty Murúa (**fig. 3.1**), ms. 1551's (**fig. 3.6**) depictions of Mayta Capac, and some elements in the description of the same Inca given by Guaman Poma.[188] Like the differences in stance, garment motifs and attributes in the four series in most other portraits'

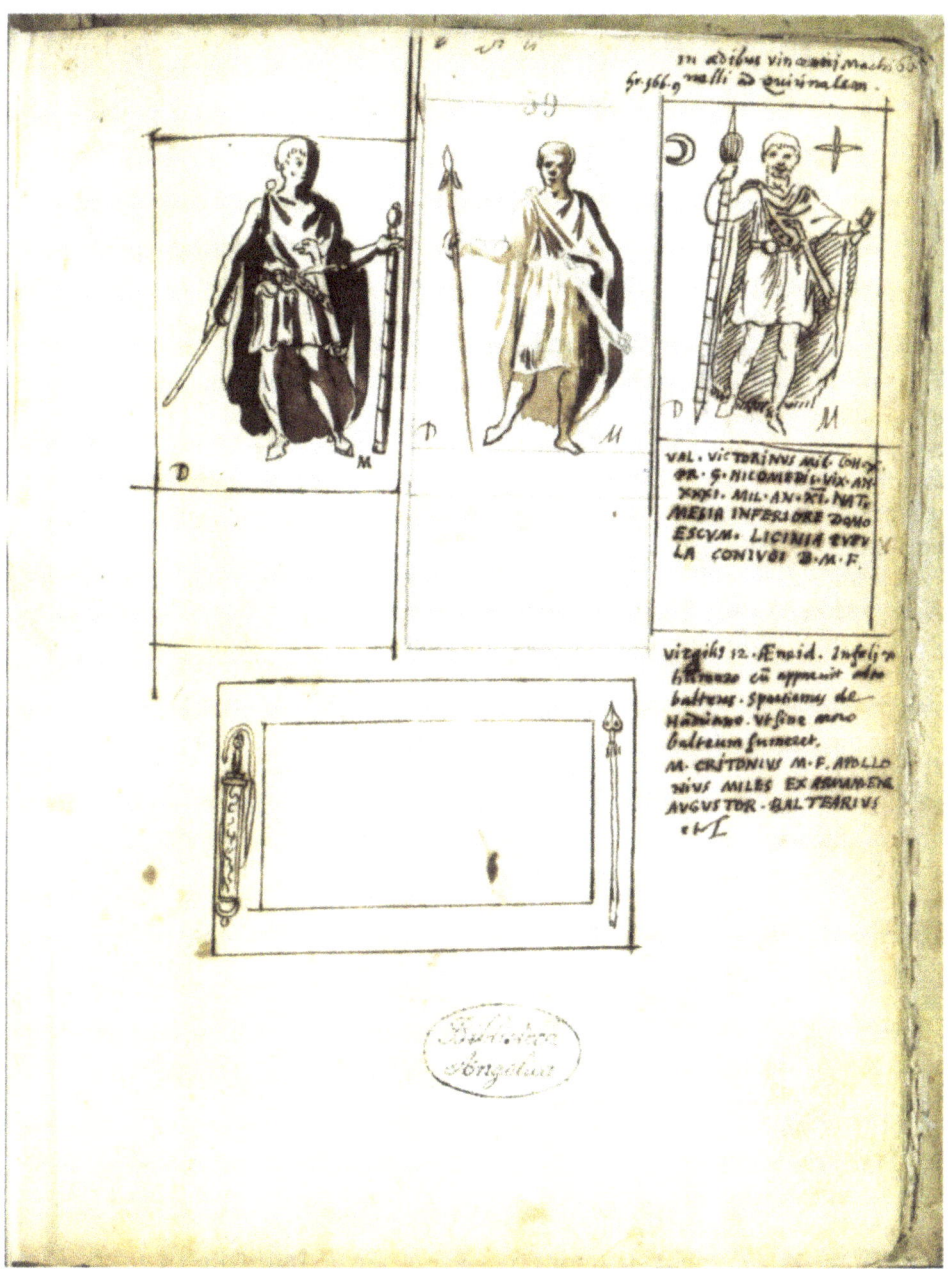

Figure 3.7 Artist unknown, sketches of Roman statues. Rome, Biblioteca Angelica, ms. 1564, fol. 59. On concession from the Ministry for Arts and Culture and Tourism. All rights reserved.

colors do not correlate, suggesting not only multiple pictorial sources but perhaps also a range of colors from which to select for garments or motifs worn by individual Incas for specific occasions.

The Origin of the Drawings

How would these drawings, or their sources if they are copies of originals, have made their way to Rome? Juan Carlos Estenssoro postulated that they were copies of the Inca portraits sent by Francisco de Toledo to Phillip II in Madrid, possibly made by the Italian artist Antonio Maria Antonozzi (or Antonazzi, active 1633–1682), who accompanied Camillo Massimo to Madrid while Massimo was papal nuncio to the court between 1654 and 1658. This is unlikely, based on several factors, including style, which Estenssoro does not address, but clearly places the drawings about 50 years earlier than the mid-17th century date of Massimo's stay in Madrid; the few surviving and very dissimilar works by Antonozzi;[189] and the fact that the Toledo portraits in Madrid were half-lengths, not full-length figures.[190]

Despite his devotion to the study of classical antiquity, there is no evidence that Camillo Massimo was interested in antiquities from the Americas (see Chapter 1). Throughout his adult life, Camillo made or commissioned drawings of Roman and Egyptian antiquities in his native Rome. While in Madrid, he made extensive descriptions of Philip IV's painting collections in all the royal palaces, never mentioning the Inca portraits in the Alcázar.[191] While surviving documentation in the Vatican places ms. 1551 in the Massimo family by the year of Camillo's death in 1677, it does not provide information on the date that ms. 1551 was acquired by the family, which possessed considerable wealth of centuries' longstanding.[192]

There are some clues to the drawings' possible origin. One possibility is that the drawings were a variant set, that is, one of full-length portraits in the same mode as Murúa's or Guaman Poma's sent directly from Peru to Cardinal Ferdinando de Medici by his cousin Francisco de Toledo. As Lia Markey has recently observed (and see Chapter 1), Ferdinando and his brother Francesco were both known to be interested in the New World, commissioning paintings that incorporated New World imagery for their palaces, Ferdinando's in Rome in 1576, around the time of Toledo's gift of Inca portraits to Phillip II in Spain.[193] Ferdinando, an avid collector of New World exotica, remained in Rome until his return to Florence as Grand Duke of Tuscany in 1587. The inventory made to document his move from Rome in that year includes several *quadri di pitture dell'Indie,* which Markey explained could refer to paintings or works on paper.[194]

The drawings' source material could also have reached Rome via José de Acosta, who spent from 1572 to 1585 in Peru, frequently in contact with Toledo. He wrote about the Incas in his *Historia moral y general* (1590) incorporating information derived from the historian Polo de Ondegardo, whose works, like those of Fernández de Córdoba, have not survived. Acosta, as mentioned, was in Rome in 1565 but more pertinently, again, after his time in Peru and Mexico in 1588 and from 1590 to 1592. If the drawings were not sent directly to the Medici in Rome in the 1570s, Acosta is the likely source because he alone was in Rome after a long period in Peru, rigorously accumulating knowledge of its history, as is the case with the Mexican deities of section 1. The works he is known to have studied, *Codex Ríos,* and especially the Tovar manuscript, are full of references and descriptions of garments and their colors, which Acosta would undoubtedly have understood as important signifiers, as is the case with ms. 1551.

It would seem that the drawings in this third section of ms. 1551 must be copies of earlier 16th-century originals, made after the Asian drawings in section 2 and therefore after the early years of the 17th century, when they were combined with the already existing drawings of sections 1 and 2 into a single volume. That might also account for the Italian feel of the awkward style. If the artist were Italian, or working in Italy, he might have copied or reworked an existing set of drawings, maintaining a Spanish text rather than translating it into Italian, like the first section of drawings in ms. 1551.

Antiquarians in this period freely traded among friends or copied their documentation of cultures. We have already seen in Chapter 1 that Girolamo Aleandro provided Pignoria with drawings of Asian objects in Rome and that Claude Nicolas Fabri de Peiresc asked for copies of drawings from Aleandro and borrowed drawings by Philips de Winghe from his brother Hieronymus de Winghe. As also discussed in Chapter 1, Lorenzo Pignoria recalled in a letter to Galileo of 1612 his visits to the princes of Rome and to the Pope, copying images of peoples of Asia and the New World, including Peru. Ms. 1551's Peruvian figures exhibit a thoroughly European, perhaps even more specifically late 16th- or early 17th-century Italian drawing style, one suggestive of a draughtsman whose main purpose was visual documentation of other works, demonstrating a passing familiarity with classicizing stylistic conventions, such as a contrappostal stance or heroic Roman pose commonly used in Chacón's workshop, and black pen lines to strengthen contours (**fig. 3.7**). Perhaps this series was produced by a member of Chacón's workshop between 1589 and Chacón's death in 1599, based on originals provided by Acosta in Rome.

Could the Peruvian images Pignoria copied in Rome be ms. 1551's third section or its source material, as an earlier set appears to have been his source for ms. 1551's section 1? Pignoria's interest in ancient cultures certainly extended to colors, as the inscriptions in the printed book provides them for many of the features of the Asian gods taken from ms. 1551, and his estate inventory listed a fragment of clothing dyed with the ancient murex purple.[195] This seems to be another example of the catalytic effect on antiquarians such as Massimo and Cassiano del Pozzo by earlier visual ethnographers in Rome and an intellectual connection between Acosta, Chacón, or his associates such as Winghe and Pignoria.

The Folios[196] (numbered in brackets in order as bound)

[1] fol. 74: Mayta Capac (**fig. 3.6**).

> El quarto Rey fue Mayta Capac, que vivio çiento y beinte años, se coronò con borla azul manta encarnada, y camiseta blanca y verde, y salpicada con mariposas carmesies. Llama = ron le el Malencolico, aunque fue muy bravo para la Guerra, pues conquistò la Provincia de los hearcos a llegar al zerro de Potosi = Dejo grandes riquesas, tubo quarenta y dos hijos con diferentes mujeres.

> The fourth king was Mayta Capac, who lived for 120 years, was crowned with a blue tassel [mascapaycha], red cape, and white and green blouse strewn with carmine butterflies. They called him the Melancholy, although

he was very brave in war, then conquered the province of Charcas to arrive at the Mountain of Potosi. He left great riches and had 42 children with different wives.

[2] fol. 75: Ingayupanqui (**fig. 3.5**).

El Deçimo Rey fue Ingayupanqui, que vivio, cosa increible, doçientos años = el dia de su coronaçion se puso Borla azul, camiseta tornazul, orejeras de plata, ojosas de oro, y Manta verde, Fue savio, y amador de los nobles, y sobre todo muy cortes con la Reyna su mujer dandola mucho mano en su Imperio.

The tenth king was Ingayupanqui, who lived, an incredible thing, 200 years. The day of his coronation he put on the blue tassel, shot blouse, silver earrings, gold sandals, and green cape. He was wise and a lover of the nobles and above all very courteous with the queen, his wife, giving her a large hand in his empire.

[3] fol. 76: Chimbo herma.

Chimbo herma mujer que fue de hinchirola [Cinchi Roca], fue muy hermosa, delgada, amiga de flores y maçetas.

Chimbo Herma, wife of Hinchirola [Cinchi Roca], was very beautiful, thin, friend of flowers and bouquets.

Like the depictions of wives in section 2, this one is the most cursory of those in its series. Guaman Poma writes that Chinbo Urma was the second Coya, wife of Cinchi Roca (fol. 123), while Chimpo Urma, according to Murúa (Getty fol. 30), was Coya to Mayta Capac, not Cinchi Roca, whose Coya was Chimpo Coya. Cinchi Roca is not among the drawings in this section of ms. 1551.

[4] fol. 77: Manco Capac (**Fig. 3.4**).

Manco Capac primer ynga que tubo el Perù, coronose con borla verde que en lugar de coronas las usaban estos Reyes en las frentes, orejeras de oro, manta encarnada, y camiseta azul, este fue el que edificò el primer Altar al sol y a la Luna. Jamas tubo guerras, fue muy gentilhombre, vivio çiento y setentas años.

Manco Capac, the first Inca that Peru had, crowned himself with a green tassel, which instead of crowns these kings used in the fronts, earrings of gold, red cape, and blue blouse. It was he who built the first altar to the sun and moon. He never had wars, was much the gentleman, and lived one hundred seventy years.

[5] fol. 78: Viracocha.

El octavo Rey fue Viracocha y ynga. Vivio çiento y viente y quatro años. Pusose el dia de su coronaçion borla azul y pluma de Papagaio pequeña, manta rosada y medio tornasolada con blanca, camiseta de lo mesmo y orejeras de oro. Fue blanco, y gentilhombre, de coraçon manso, y afable, des muy buen discurso, y tanto que estableció Ley general paraque se derivasen todos los ydolos y adoratorios, y se diesse La adoraçion a un solo dios verdadero, el qual deçia tras el sol dentro del çielo.

The eighth king was Viracocha, an Inca, who lived one hundred twenty-four years. He put on the day of his coronation a blue tassel of small bird feathers, a pink and semi-shot cape, a blouse of the same, and gold earrings. He was white and a gentleman of meek heart, affable, so well-spoken that he established the general law for which were derived all the idols and altars, and was given the adoration of a single true god, that which was given through the sun in the sky.

[6] fopl. 79: Lloqueyuxaqui.

El tercero rey del Peru fue Lloqueyuxaqui que bibio çiento y treinta años-tubo borla carmesi, manta amarilla, y camiseta morada, que mal axestado, y de civibil y perversa inclinaçion, no hiço açana ninguna, por lo que, y por floco, y viçioso fue aborreçido de todo su Reyno.

The third king of Peru was Lloqueyuxaqui (usually Lloque Yupanqui) who lived one hundred thirty years; had a carmine borla, yellow cape, and purple blouse; was maladjusted and of uncivil and perverse inclination; made no torment for which; and, weak and vicious, was not loathed by all his kingdom.

[7] fol. 80: Pachacuti.

El nono Rey fue Pachacuti que vivio ochenta y ocho años y los mas de ellos estuvo su Reyno afligidisimo con pestes y calamidades-coronose con borla rosada, pluma de oro, orejeras de plata, manta verde, camiseta naranjada. Fiscar con una onda por piedras pedaços, de oro masiço a sol este fue gran corredor.

The ninth king was Pachacuti who lived eighty-eight years, during which most of them his kingdom was highly afflicted with plagues and calamities. He was crowned with a pink tassel, gold feather, silver earrings, green cape, and orange blouse. To prod with a wave for bits of stone of solid gold of the sun, he was a great runner.

[8] fol. 81: Ingaroca.

El sexto Rey fue Ingaroca que vivio çiento y cinquenta y quarto años, el dia de su coronaçion se coronò con encarnada de plumas de pajaros, manta rosada, camiseta negra, llamavanle sus Vasallos el arrogante, y ablador por la aspereça y sonido de su voz con que hablava, la misma diçen tenia Alexandro Magno, fue baliente y animoso y inclinados a varios juegos y a mujeres y a desposeer a los vasallos de lo que tenian con color de leies y sostitutos.

The sixth king was Ingaroca who lived one hundred fifty-four years. The day of his coronation he crowned himself with red bird feathers, a pink cape, and a black blouse. His vassals called him "the Arrogant," for the harshness and sound of the voice with which he spoke, the same they say that Alexander the Great had. He was valiant and courageous and inclined to various games, to women, and to dispossess the vassals of what they had with the color of metals and substitutes.

[9] fol. 82: Jaquar guacac.

El septimo Rey del Peru fue Jaguar guacac con borla blanca, pluma de oro, camiseta negra y colorada, y manta açul salpicada de lagartijas, fue valiente Rey, savio, y rico, conpasivo, y Passiero, tubo particular aboreçiemento a los Ricos y avarientos, y fue el primero que introdujo los ayunos, y penitençias en honra de sus dioses a su modo haçia sus proçesiones.

The seventh king of Peru was Jaguar guacac with a white tassel, gold feather, black and red blouse, and blue mantle strewn with small lizards. He was a valiant king, wise and rich, compassionate, and a peacemaker. He had a particular loathing of the rich and avaricious, and he was the first to introduce the fasts and penitences in honor of his gods by way of processions.

Conclusion

Each of the three series of watercolors is visually and textually rich, with information supplied by eyewitnesses to the cultures they portray. In section 1, for example, ms. 1551 probably produced, through a collaboration among José de Acosta, Alfonso Chacón, and his artists, the most notable antiquarians and ethnographers in Rome and provides the only surviving colored representations of lost Asian objects then in Rome and a quarter century later published as black and white woodcuts in Cartari/Pignoria 1615. The drawings also add to both our reading of *Codex Ríos* and Cartari/Pignoria in their use of Nahuatl terms not in either. There is no previous study of the drawings in section 2, but just the awareness of their existence puts them in rarified company with the few other known illustrations of Asians produced in the late 16th century and adds to the visual documentation of places and peoples, such as Mongau and Sogau, not illustrated or described elsewhere. Similarly, the Inca rulers expand upon the small corpus of Inca portraits of this period, uniquely emphasizing color and garments, especially motifs, in text and image.

A superficial consultation of the drawings might suggest that the three sets have little to do with one another by virtue of their different subjects, scribes and authors, or artists. To the extent that these sets of drawings have been investigated previously, the scrutiny of the sets in isolation, and not from a visual or material perspective, resulted in a dating of the first to no earlier than 1615, and the last to the 1650s. Once all three sets and other related illustrated documents were examined together, earlier and similar dates became clear, at first simply based on a cursory examination of artistic and scribal styles. The growing suspicion followed, that these three sets of ethnographic drawings were actually linked, and set the direction for closer examination, as they were roughly contemporaneous and mounted on the same types of Asian and European papers. Despite being inscribed with Spanish texts, they were documented in Rome from the later 17th century and connected with other 16th- and early 17th-century ethnographic documents in Italy. Even the proximate catalogue numbers of this manuscript and another in Biblioteca Angelica with related images seemed to be more than coincidental. Most of these evidentiary elements are routine art historical concerns, so it is fair to say that the missing visual component of an interdisciplinary approach was critical to an understanding of the context of these watercolors.

There are also textual connections among the series, particularly pertaining to expression of cultural attitudes. Except for the Queen of Garcopa, a ruler in her own right, the queens in the Asian section and the one Coya in the Peruvian set are only briefly treated as indistinct adjuncts whose garments and personal qualities are not deemed worthy of detailed description. Unlike the derision of the peoples of section 2, the approaches to the Pagan figures of sections 1 and 3 are similarly descriptive, suggesting the eye of an eyewitness observer, such as Acosta, striving for some objectivity.

Jesuits in the later 16th century have not previously been credited with interest in visual documentation, except for Tovar in Mexico, although they did recruit European artists who trained Asians to establish a tradition of Christian imagery in both Asia and the Americas. Nevertheless, it was the Jesuits who were most likely responsible for the production, or at least the earliest assembly of all three sets of drawings in ms. 1551. They had direct access to and regularly used for their annual letters the Asian papers employed as supports for the drawings in sections 1 and 2. They were the only Europeans in all the Asian places depicted in section 2 and based in Rome, and José de Acosta, one of their most illustrious members, was probably involved in the creation of sections 1 and 3, the former an exploration of comparative religions in those regions using paper clearly identified with the Asians and a screenfold arrangement signaling the Americans.

The Jesuits at least played a role as interested consumers of visual materials depicting these new cultures. Casanatense ms. 1889, dated to the mid-16th century and exhibiting a similar focus on the appearance of Asian peoples, has not been attributed to the Jesuits, but it was sent in 1627 from the Jesuit College in Goa to Lisbon, another Jesuit capital, before winding up, like Angelica ms. 1551, in Rome, where both were first identified in non-Jesuit institutions in the later 17th century. Unless other Jesuit-illustrated mss. are discovered, we have evidence of Jesuit links only to Tovar in Mexico, ms. 1551 for Peru, and ms. 1551 and Casanatense for Asia. Tovar copied an Aztec historical and calendrical ms., but no Jesuit in the 16th century depicted contemporary Mexicans and their culture as systematically and exhaustively as Sahagún, and as they themselves apparently did in Asia. Nevertheless, the Jesuits, and perhaps most importantly José de Acosta, were certainly adding significantly to the early corpus of visual documentation of non-European cultures and contributing to Rome's central role in that endeavor.

Notes

1 Biblioteca Angelica ms. 1551: "Icones coloribus ornatae idolorum mexicanorum, Aeguptorum, Sinensim, Japanorum, Indorum addita declaration hispanica usque ad fmost fol 8: sequuntur usque ad fol. 74 effigies et usu barbarrum quarundam regionum a Asiae, Americae et Insularum cum declarationibus modo latinis, modo hispanicis A fo. 75 ad 82 meliori penicillo sunt iconas regum Peruvianorum subiectis notis biographicis hispanica lingua."

2 For a discussion of the Massimo book collections, see Juan Carlos Estenssoro, "Los Incas del Cardenal: las acuarelas de la colección," *Revista andina* 12, no. 2 (1994): 403–423.

3 It is difficult to determine the Asian country in which these papers might have been made. The papers are comparable to those apparently developed in China by the 1st century, but by the medieval era also made in other Asian regions. See Tsien Tsuen-Hsuin, "Chemistry and Chemical Technology, Part I: Paper and Printing," in *Science and Civilisation in China*, ed. Joseph Needham (London: Cambridge University Press, 1985), 5, 50, 76.

4 On the drawings in the first section, see, for example, Sonia Maffei, "Cartari e gli dèi del Nuovo Mondo: Il trattatello sulle *Imagini de gli dei indiani* di Lorenzo Pignoria," in *Arti Vincenzo Cartari e le direzioni del mito nel Cinquecento*, ed. Sonia Maffei (Rome: Genevra Bentivolio Editoria, 2013), 61–120; and Ewa Kubiak and Katarzyna Szoblik, "los Dioses mexicanos" en la seconda parte delle imagini de gli dei indiani (1615) de Lorenzo Pignoria como una imagen del mestizaje cultural, *VIII Encuentro internacional sobre barroco Mestizajes en diálogo* (La Paz: Unión Latina, 2017), 305–314. On the Peruvian drawings, see Estenssoro, "Incas del Cardenal."

5 Folio 11, depicting noble and common people of Japan, is reproduced with brief catalogue information in Nicoletta Muratore, ed., *da Palazzo Massimo all'Angelica: manocritti e libri a stampa di un'antica famiglia romana* (Rome: Fratelli Palombri, 1997), 57.

6 The vast and growing body of literature on contemporaneous European histories of the peoples of the Americas and Asia in this period includes, for the Americas, Stephen Greenblatt, *Marvelous Possessions: The Wonder of the New World* (Chicago: University of Chicago Press, 1991) and Karen Ordahl Kupperman, ed., *America in European Consciousness, 1493–1750* (Chapel Hill: University of North Carolina, 1995). For Asia, still the most comprehensive overview is Donald Lach, *Asia in the Making of Europe*, 3 vols. (Chicago: University of Chicago, 1965–1977).

7 Michele Mercati, *Degli Obelischi di Roma* (Rome: Domenico Basa, 1589).

8 José de Acosta, *Historia general y moral de las Indias* (Seville: Juan de León, 1590).

9 Duarte Lopes and Filippo Pigafetta. *Relatione del reame di Congo et delle circonvicine contrade: Tratta dalli scritti e ragionamenti di Odoardo Lopez Portoghese per Filippo Pigafetta* (Rome: Bartolomeo Grassi, 1591). See Cécile Fromont, *The Art of Conversion: Christian Visual Culture in the Kingdom of Kongo* (Chapel Hill: University of North Carolina, 2014), 133.

10 Vincenzo Cartari and Lorenzo Pignoria, *Le vere e nove imagini de gli dei delli antichi di Vicenzo Cartari* (Padua: Pietro Paolo Tozzi, 1615).

11 in Japan-Sinica 10, I–II, cited in Joseph Wicki and John Gomes, eds., *Documenta indica, Memorias de Africa e do Oriente. Monumenta Historica Societatis Iesu,* Volume XIV (1585–1588) (Rome: Institutum Historicum Societatus Iesu, 1979), 82.

12 according to Giacomo Filippi Tomasini, *de Vita, Bibliotheca et Museo Laurentii Pignorii canonici Tarvisini dissertatio* (Udine: Shiraci, 1639), 87. Red paper "the color of blood" is identified in the 17th century as Japanese by Pier Maria Terzago in his catalogue of the Settala collection in Milan. See Ronald Lightbown, "Oriental Art and the Orient in Late Renaissance and Baroque Italy," *Journal of the Warburg and Courtauld Institutes* 32 (1969), 257.

13 The Dutch East India Company began importing it to the Netherlands by the 1640s, at which point Rembrandt used lustrous yellowish Asian papers, consistent with a Japanese type called *torinoko* for some prints, and later, a series of drawn copies of Mughal miniatures. See Stephanie Schrader, "Rembrandt and the Mughal Line: Artistic Inspiration in the Global City of Amsterdam," in Stephanie Shrader, ed., *Rembrandt and the Inspiration of India* (Los Angeles: The J. Paul Getty Museum, 2018), 15–16, 25, n. 54.

14 Christian Feest, "Zemes Idolum Diabolicum. Surprise and Success in Ethnographic Kunstkammer Research," *Archiv für Völkerkunde* 40 (1986), 181–198, 191–193.

15 As identified by Lorenzo Pignoria in Vincenzo Cartari and Lorenzo Pignoria, *le vere e nove imagini*, Parte Seconda, VI.

16 Vicenzo Cartari and Lorenzo Pignoria, *Le imagini de gli dei de gli antichi: nelle quali sono descritte la religione de gli antichi li idoli, riti, & ceremonie loro, con l'aggiunta di molte principali imagini che nell'altre mancauano, et con l'espositione in epilogo di ciasceduna & suo significato* (Venice: Evangelista Deuchino, 1626).

17 Joanna Ostapkowicz and Lee Newsom, "Gods . . . Adorned with the Embroiderer's Needle: The Materials, Making and Meaning of a Taino Cotton Reliquary," *Latin American Antiquity* 23, no. 3 (2012): 300–326, 300–301.

18 Lauran Toorians, "The Earliest Inventory of Mexican Objects in Munich, 1572," *Journal of the History of Collecting* 6, no. 1 (1994): 59–67; 64.

19 Lia Markey, *Imagining the Americas in Medici Florence* (College Station: Pennsylvania State University Press, 2016). digital edition, loc. 1502.

20 "breve diceria in lingua spagnuola." Cartari/Pignoria 1615, XXVII.

21 Cartari and Pignoria *le vere e nove imagini*, Parte Seconda, XXIII.

22 "Un altra Imagine di Homopoca, o di simile deità mi è venuta per le mani. La quale però altri chiamano di Quetzalcoatl. & s'è havuta fuora di certi fogli, che furono Filippo Winghernio da Tornay, dottisissimo giovane. & esso asseriva d'haverla cavata da un Libro grande, ch'ènella Libreria Vaticana, compilato da F. Pietro de los Ríos." Cartari/Pignoria 1626, 550.

23 Mercati, *De gli obelischi di Roma*, 96: p. cxx digital: "à i tempi noſtri v ſi è veduto il medeſimo nel mondo nuouo tra gli habitatori del Mexico città principale della nuoua Spagna; - gna, a quali parendo troppa fatica il dipi'gnere tutî te le figure intiere: o-vero perche occupaffèro troppo. - fatica il dipignere tutte le figure intiere: ò vero occupassero troppo spatio; messero in uso dì figurare di molti animali' solamentei capi, & volendo dimoſtrare alcuna cosa, che per le sopradette figure non ſi poteſſe eſplicare, trouauano altro modo comedire, ſé voleuano esprimere le qualità dell 'animo, dipingevano un capo humano, il quale dimoſtrae nel viſo, per certi ſegni ſiſiognomici, ò bontà, ò contraria qualità dell'huomo. La morte dimostrauano con lac aluaria di un huomo: & per ogn'altra coſa ſimile, haueuano figure, proprie, riconoſciute tra' loro, come si può vedere 'in due libri della libraria Vaticana., ritratti da gli esſimplari istessi, venuti dal Mexico."

24 For an overview of and suggestions regarding the relationships between Ríos, ms. 1551, and Cartari/Pignoria 1615, see Ferdinand Anders, Maarten Jansen, and Luis Reyes García, *Religión, costumbres e historia de los angiquos mexicanos: libro explicativo del llamado Códice Vaticano A, Codex Vatic. Lat. 3738 de la Biblioteca Vaticana* (Graz: Akademishe Druck-und Verlagsanstalt, and Mexico, Fondo de Cultura Económica, 1996); and Eloise Quiñones Keber, "Collecting Cultures: A Mexican Manuscript in the Vatican Library," in *Reframing the Renaissance: Visual Culture in Europe and Latin America 1450–1650,* ed. Clare Farago (New Haven: Yale University, 1995), 229–242.

25 Ciacconius (Alfonso Chacón), "Raccolta di iscrizioni e imagini di pontefici e imperatori," Rome, Biblioteca Angelica, ms. 1564.

26 Ciacconius (Alfonso Chacón), *Historia utriusque belli datici a Trainano Caesare gesti quae in comumna eiusdem Romae visuntur, collecta* (Rome: Zanetrio and Tosi, 1576).

27 See, for example, Jean Seznec, "un Essai de mythologie comparé au début du XVIIe siècle," *Mélanges d'archéologie et d'histoire* 48, no. 1 (1931), 268–281.

28 Alejandro Recio, O.F.M., "'La Historia Descriptio Urbis Romae,' obra manuscrito de Fr. Alonso Chacón, O.P. (1530–1599)," *Anthologica annua,* Rome, Instituto español de historia eclesiastica (1968), 74.

29 Cartari/Pignoria 1615, XXXVII.

30 Ibid, XLII.

31 The two in ms. 1564, attributed to Winghe by Pignoria in Cartari/Pignoria 1626, on the other hand, are derived from the second and third sections, folios 35 and 58. This might suggest that those, dated 1592, were executed after ms. 1551, which comes entirely from the first section.

32 See, for example, Mary Miller and Karl Taube, *The Gods and Symbols of Ancient Mexico and the Maya* (London: Thames and Hudson, 2017), 142.

33 Antonio de Egaña, *Monumenta peruana,* vol. 2 (Rome, Archivum Romanum Societatis Iesu), 1958, Lima, 15 February, 157, doc. 26.

34 Eloise Quiñones Keber, *Codex Telleriano Remensis: Ritual, Divination, and History in a Pictorial Aztec Manuscript* (Austin: University of Texas Press, 1995), 240.

35 Cartari/Pignoria 1615, Part II, V.

36 Cartari/Pignoria 1626, 550.

37 The few colored drawings in ms. 1564, all found within the first 58 folios, include the two images from *Codex Ríos,* two manuscript illuminations in the Vatican Library, as well as several early Christian mosaic figures from the churches of Sant' Andrea, Santa Susanna, and St. John in the Lateran.

38 The scribal hands in 1551 and 1564 are different. The hand in 1564 is identical to one in a collection of documents called "Alfonso Chacón reports, 1578–1589," in the Getty Research Institute, Los Angeles (840005B). In this collection is a document in another hand, not the same as Biblioteca Angelica 1564 or 1551, but signed by Chacón. The only known autograph manuscript by Winghe is Brussels, Royal Library Albert I, inv. No. 17.872-3, written in a northern hand.

39 Mercati, *De gli Obelischi di Roma,* 96.

40 Acosta, *Historia general y moral de las Indias,* 1590, Book VII, chapter 19, 354.

41 Carpentras, Bibliothèque Inguimbertine 1875, f. 308. This was first noted by Cecilia Rizza in *Peiresc e l'Italia* (Torino: Giappichelli, 1965), 55. It was recently transcribed more fully in Sabine du Crest, "L' exotisme vu de provence au temps de Peiresc," *Sciences et Techniques en Perspective* II series 9, no. 1 (2005): 259–270, n. 17.

42 The history of this manuscript is confusing and has been the subject of much debate since its arrival in Rome. The most complete discussions of its historiography are in Anders, Jansen, and Reyes García, *Códice Vaticano A*; and Peter Mason, *The Lives of Images* (London: Reaktion Books, 2001), 133.

43 Eduardo Matos Moctezuma and Felipe Solis Olguin, *Aztecs* (London: Royal Academy of the Arts, 2002), cat. no. 346.

44 See especially Nancy Turner, "Accounting for Unfinished History: How Evidence of Book Structure Provides a New Context for the Making of the Galvin and Getty Murúas," in *Manuscript Cultures of Colonial Mexico and Peru*, eds. Thomas B.F. Cummins, Emily Engel, Barbara Anderson, and Juan Ossio (Los Angeles: Getty Research Institute, 2014), 86–87.

45 Anders, Jansen, and Reyes García, *Códice Vaticano A*, 30. The references to "our Spain" appear on folios 46r and 46v in one hand, 58r and 60v in the other.

46 "delle Capotecse, e delle Mextecse seguali io hò vedute." *Ríos*, 61r. Ibid.

47 "Asi esta todo hoy dia pintado en los Anales Mexicanos, cuyo libro tienen en Roma, y esta puesto en la Sacra Biblioteca o libreria Vaticana, donde un padre de nuestra Compania que habia venido de Mexico, vio esta y las demas historias, y las declaraba al bibliotecario de su Santidad, que en extremo gustaba de entender aquel libro que jamas habia podido entender." Acosta, *Historia natural y moral de las Indias*, libro VII, cap. XIX, 501. English translation in José de Acosta, *Natural and Moral History of the Indies,* ed. Jane E. Mangan (Raleigh and London: Duke University, 2002), 421.

48 Cartari/Pignoria 1615, XXIII.

49 Could the translation into Italian of Sahagún have been Chacón or Acosta shortly after its arrival in Rome? According to Markey, the *Florentine Codex* must have been in Rome by 1587, where it was translated, also imperfectly, as if by a nonnative speaker, into Italian for Ferdinando de' Medici. Lia Markey, "Istoria della terra chiamata la nuova spagna: The History and Reception of Sahagún's Codex at the Medici Court," in *Colours between Two Worlds: The Florentine Codex of Bernardino de Sahagún*, eds. Gerhard Wolf and Joseph Connors (Florence: Harvard University Press, 2011), 205–207.

50 Claudio M. Burgaleta, S.J., *José de Acosta, S.J. (1540–1600): His Life and Thought* (Chicago: Loyola Press, 1999), 53. Pedro Díaz was a founder of the same Jesuit College in Oaxaca, and he was, like Acosta, in Oaxaca and Rome (in 1578–1579). But there is as yet no evidence of his having investigated ancient cultures. See Anders, Jansen, and Reyes García, *Códice Vaticano A*, 14, note 2.

51 The third Jesuit in Rome after time spent in Mexico was Pedro de Hortigosa in 1584. Like Díaz, Hortigosa is not known to have been involved in the recording of native Mexican cultures.

52 The manuscript is believed to have been in Acosta's hands by 1587, when he left Mexico for Europe, and could have been in his possession in Rome while Acosta was studying *Ríos*. George Kubler and Charles Gibson, *The Tovar Calendar: An Illustrated Mexican Manuscript ca. 1585* (New Haven: The Connecticut Academy of Arts and Sciences, 1951), 9–11.

53 On Acosta's use of imagery, see Thomas Cummins, "From Lies to Truth: Colonial Ekphrasis and the Act of Cultural Translation," in *Reframing the Renaissance: Visual Culture in Europe and Latin America 1450–1650,* ed. Clare Farago (New Haven: Yale University Press, 1995), 152–174.

54 The entire Tovar Codex is available in digital format through the World Digital Library (wdl.org).

55 Jacques LaFaye, "Le manuscript Tovar dans la J. Carter Brown Library: attribution et filiation," *Mélanges de la Casa de Velázquez* 6 (1970): 363.

56 Acosta, *Natural and Moral History of the Indies*, 257, 259, 261, 284, 288, 307.

57 Antonio de Egaña, *Monumenta peruana* 2 (1910), doc. 26, no. 71, 278.

58 Claudio M. Burgaleta, *José de Acosta (1540–1600): His Life and Thought* (Chicago: Loyola Press, 1999), 62.

59 Los Angeles, Getty Research Institute Library, 840005b, folios 288–292.

60 Thomas James Dandalet, *Spanish Rome, 1500–1700* (New Haven: Yale University, 2001), 82–83.

61 A passage in *Ríos*, f. 55r, in the hand of the first translator, refers to the relation of ancient Mexicans to Jews, a connection to which Acosta did not subscribe, arguing instead, and for the first time, for the ancestry of Asians who walked to the Americas overland. This would suggest that the commentator here, whose knowledge of the culture of Mesoamerica was meager, as noted by Anders, Maarten, and Reyes (*Códice Vaticano A*, 31) was Chacón, a Dominican who may, like Diego Durán and other Dominicans, have ascribed a Jewish origin of the peoples of the New World.

It is difficult to attribute on the basis of handwriting, as so few manuscripts associated with Chacón, Acosta, and Winghe survive, and a number of scribes were likely to have been employed. Some of them, like those in the Getty Research Institute manuscript, display different hands but other evidence of Chacón's authorship.

62 Like the Italian in *Codex Ríos*, that of the Florentine Codex, now in the Hispanic Society in New York, as ms. B1479, is imperfect, suggesting that the translator's first language was not Italian. See Lia Markey, *Imagining the Americas in Medici Florence* (Chicago: The University of Chicago Press, 2016), loc. 2481.

63 Mercati, *De gli Obelischi di Roma*, 96.

64 Cartari/Pignoria 1615, Seconda Parte, XXXVII, XXXIX, and LXIII.

65 Galileo Galilei, *Le opera* (Florence: G. Barbera, 1966), Volume XI Carteggio 1611–1613: Letter 754, p. 319:

> "se costì nella galleria di S.A. Ser.ma overo appresso qualche gentil humo, si trovasse qualche idolo dell-Indie Orientali overo Occidentali, io receverei molta gratia ad haverne un poco di schizzo, di appresso del *quid rei e quid nominis*; Et rimborsarò la spesa del disegno di buona voglia," and

Letter 781, p. 339:

> "In galleria io stimavo che si fosse qualche idolo Indiano, perchè nella Vigna di S.A. in Roma io viddi pitture di que' paesi; et dale gallerie d'altri Principi io ho pure havuto qualche curiosità di questa sorte. Et noti V.S. ch'io no domando cose Egittie, ma Indiane, come della China, del Giapone, del Perù, Mexico, Nova Spagna, etc. Et questi idoli sono o di legno o di mistura, e molte volte miniati in carte con acquerelli [. . .] Se la Chimera di Galleria non portasse gran fattura per disegnarlo, io ne vederei volentieri un poco di copia."

66 The letter, said to be difficult to decipher, is reproduced in part in Maffei, "Pignoria," 74–75.

67 Fol. 10, ms. Vat. Lat. 10545.

68 That Peiresc consulted ms. 1564 is suggested by a collection of sketches in Bibliothèque Nationale de France nouv. acq. lat. ms. 2343, catalogued by Peiresc without evidence as if attributed by a former owner. In it are a number of drawings and inscriptions (fols. 45, 52, 65, 73, and 74) identical to figures in ms. 1564 folios 5, 34, 44, 45, 47, and 59). Although the artist and scribal hands are different, the scribal hand of the inscriptions on these drawings in BnF NAL 2343 is very close to Peiresc's hand in the album of drawings also in BnF, Rés. Est. Aa 54, for example, folio 52.

69 Bibliothèque National de France, gallica ms. 9450: "dello Schizzi del Sr. Winghemio, no sono fatto le stampe di già."

70 Fol. 258.

71 See Biblioteca Angelica ms. 1564 for examples of Roman, Mexican, and Egyptian deities known in Rome at the time. See also Chacón's transcription of the Chinese alphabet, "Alpha-betum Chinarum ut asservatur in Bibliotheca Vaticana," Getty Research Institute Library, "Alfonso Chacón reports, 1578–1589," leaf 283. This transcription is probably based on the very similar "Alphabeticum Idiomatis de Cina ex bibliotheca Vaticana Romae," London, British Library Lansdowne ms. 720, which Donald Lach asserts was in Rome by 1555 (Donald Lach, *Asia in the Making of Europe*, 3 vols. [Chicago: University of Chicago, 1965], II, book 3, 172).

72 For reproductions of all the images in ms. 1551, in order of their appearance in the vol-ume, see Maffei, "Cartari," 2013.

73 Mangau and Mignolo, Acosta, *Natural and Moral History,* 272, note 1.

74 Lach, *Asia in the Making of Europe*, II, 1, 88.

75 Cartari/Pignoria 1624, p. 570.

76 Ibid, 571.

77 Lightbown, "Oriental Art," 242–247.

78 See note 7.

79 In addition to the clear connection between mss. 1551 and 1564 in date and execution, there is other evidence against Maffei's argument that the drawings in ms. 1551 are traced from Cartari and Pignoria 1615. Her first point is that the drawing dimensions are identical to those of the printed version. But the printed version could just as easily have reproduced the drawings' dimensions through a tracing from them, as the other way around. It would be extremely difficult, if not impossible, to trace images from the printed book onto a folio that already had an image at least drawn, even if not yet painted, on its reverse side. Second, she asserts that the use of parallel lines to indicate shading (*tratteggio*) is a more common technique for woodcuts than for colored drawings that need only a darker wash to indicate volume. This is a tempting solution to the problem, especially because of the appearance of images from all regions, which Pignoria credits to different providers, Amulio via Malipiero in the case of the images from *Codex Ríos*, and Aleandro in the case of most of the Asian images. But the *tratteggio* in the drawings does not match that in the corresponding prints, and the employment of a *tratteggio* technique to depict shadows can be seen in many con-temporaneous Italian drawings. In fact, *tratteggio* is used in most of the figural drawings in Chacón's ms. 1564, clearly demonstrating that it was not reserved for printed images but was used in the very same workshop where ms. 1551, section 1, must have been produced. In addition, Peiresc suggests that Aleandro might have been the source for Pignoria's images from *Codex Ríos*, which would eliminate the problem of the two sources for Pignoria's illus-trations of both Mexican and Asian deities.

Other factors argue against the notion that ms. 1551 is a copy of Cartari and Pignoria 1615. The order of the numbered drawings neither corresponds to Pignoria's sequence nor follows that of *Codex Ríos*. Some of the details in the drawings, such as the red, ribbon-like ornaments on the Japanese headgear in no. 18, do not appear in Pignoria, and in a few instances, the identification of a figure in a drawing differs from Pignoria. For example, as mentioned, the figure in no. 5, ms. 1551, is identified as Hometeo[tl] or hieitleutli, whereas in Pignoria he is Homoyoca or Hometeutle. Why would a copyist change the names, and how would he know how to create a new word out of Nahuatl components?

The highly saturated palette of some of the Mexican images in 1551 and all of the colored illustrations in 1564 are continued throughout the Asian images in 1551 and correspond, with a few omissions, in Pignoria's description, quoting from Aleandro, his source for the Asian images. The palette, like that of 1564, is attributed to Chacón and Winghe. It is therefore difficult to imagine how a copyist of black and white woodcuts working after 1615 would have used the same palette as an artist working at least 16 to 23 years before, or no later than Chacón's or Winghe's death. Also, the pinks, greens, and ochres in ms. 1551 are too similar, albeit not always in the same locations, to those of the source figures in *Codex Ríos*. In addition, details in the drawings taken directly from *Codex Ríos* do not appear in the prints, for example in no. 5. How would a tracer know these details in the Vatican manuscript, and why copy the secondhand source if he did? How would he remember the colors in *Codex Ríos* while tracing from Pignoria?

A tracer from Pignoria after 1615 would also not likely have known of, much less copied, the screenfold format of a pre-Columbian manuscript, which was not a format in European manuscripts and would not likely have introduced the discrepancies in identification, or made the novel implied cultural comparisons discussed above between the inscription and image in numbers 2, 8, and 14. If errors, these would point to a revision after the inscriptions were written and not ignorance, which, if made by a tracer, would have been easily avoided by looking at the identifications in the printed book at hand.

80 David Jaffé, "Two Bronzes from Poussin's *Studies of Antiquities*," *J. Paul Getty Museum Journal* 17 (1989): 39.

81 Caterina Volpi, "Lorenzo Pignoria e il suoi correspondenti," *Nouvelles de la république des lettres* 12 (1992): 118.

82 Bibliothèque National de France, gallica ms. 9540.

83 For an extensive discussion of Camillo's antiquarian and collecting interests, see Lisa Beaven, *An Ardent Patron: Cardinal Camillo Massimo and his antiquarian and artistic circle* (London: Paul Holberton, 2010).

84 Ibid, fig. 29a, 244.

85 Barbara Mundy, personal communication, May 7, 2018.

86 Acosta, *Natural and Moral History*, 315.

87 Cartari/Pignoria 1615, VI. Sergio Botta also points out Pignoria's observation of a perversion of Christianization in the Mexican god in this passage, and in Pignoria's vision in general. See Sergio Botta, "Il corpo universale degli dèi americani: per una teoria visuale del politeismo nell'opera di Lorenzo Pignoria," *Civiltà e Religioni* 3 (2017): 54.

88 Peter Mason, "The Purloined Codex," *Journal of the History of Collections* 9, no. 1 (1997): note 133.

89 Lightbown, "Oriental Art," 245, fig. 28b.

90 Ibid, 244, fig. 30d.

91 Ibid, 246, fig. 29e.

92 Ibid, 246, fig. 30e.

93 Ibid, 244, fig. 27b.

94 Ibid, 245, fig. 4.

95 Ibid, 246, fig. 28d.

96 Ibid, fig. 29b.

97 Ibid, fig. 30a.

98 See, for example, all folios in which a king is depicted, identified as "rei," rather than "rey;" fol. 17, where Virrei, not virrey, is the spelling for viceroy. My thanks to Eduardo Engelsing for confirming that this is likely Portuguese, rather than a simple spelling variant in Spanish.

99 Latin inscriptions in the 25 folios identified after each translation with initials "EE/AH" were transcribed and translated with elegance and important insights by Engelsing of the University of Western Washington and Antoine Haacker of the University of Wroclaw. The translations and transcriptions of the 8 folios identified with the initials "BW" were beautifully executed, with enlightening interpretations of Latin usage, by Burton Westermeier of Yale University.

100 I am indebted to Engelsing for his discovery that a virrey was a flat-bottomed boat common to the Philippines by the early 17th century, cited as such in the English translation of Antonio de Morga, *History of the Philippine Islands* (Mexico: 1609), vol. 1, by Emma Helen Blair, *The Philippine Islands, 1493–1898.* 4 vols. (Cleveland: Arthur Clark, 1915), vol. 2, 26.

101 "paucis abhinc annis."

102 In addition is a series of panoramic views of coastlines from Africa to China produced by the Portuguese cartographer Francisco Rodrigues in the first half of the 16th century. The drawings are bound with an early manuscript copy of Tomé Pires, *Suma Oriental*, in the Chambre des Députés, Paris, ms. 1248. See Armando Cortasão, *The Suma Oriental of Tomé Pires and the Book of Francicso Rodrigues.* 2 vols. (London: Hakluyt Society, 1944), vol. 2, 290–306.

103 "Boxer Codex," Indiana University, Lilly Library, Ms. II, LMC 2444.

104 Jan Huygen van Linschoten, *Itinerario: Voyage oft schipvaert van Jan Huygen van Linschoten* (Amsterdam: Corneliuz Claesz, 1596).

105 Johann Theodor and Johann Israel de Bry. *II Pars Indiae Orientalis, in qua Johan Hugonis Linscotani navagatio in Orientem* (Frankfurt, 1599); *III Pars Indiae Orientalis* and *IV Pars Indiae Orientalis* (Frankfort, 1601).

106 Lach, *Asia in the Making of Europe*, II, 94.

107 See Ernst van den Boogaart, *Civil and Corrupt Asia: Image and Text in the Itinerario and the Icones of Jan Huygen van Linschoten* (Chicago: University of Chicago, 2003), 3–5.

108 Ibid, 40, note 54.

109 Ibid, 9.

110 Johannes Theodor and Johannes Israel De Bry, *VII Pars. Nauigationes duas, Primam, trium Annorum, a Georgio Spilbergio, trium nauium praefecto, Ann. 1601. ex Selandia in Indiam Orientalem susceptam: Alteram, nouem Annorum, a Casparo Balby, Gemmario Veneto, Anno 1579. ex Alepo Babyloniam versus . . . continens . . . Auctore M. Gotardo Arthvs Dantiscano. Omnia elegantiβimis in aes incisis iconibus illustrata & in lucem emiss* (Frankfort, 1606), plate XXII.

111 Jeremiah P. Losty, "Identifying the Artist of the Codex Casanatense 1889," *Anais de Historia de Alem-Mar*, XIII (2012), 13–40.

112 See entry for ms. 1551, section 2, folio 25.

113 "Boxer Codex," *Filipino Heritage: the Making of a Nation* IV, ed. Alfredo R. Roces (Philippines: Lahing Pilipino Publishing, 1977).

114 John N. Crossley, "The Early History of the Boxer Codex," *Journal of the Royal Asiatic Society* (Third Series) (2014), 24, 115–124. doi:10.1017/S1356186313000552.

115 Charles R. Boxer, "A Late Sixteenth-Century Manila Manuscript," *Journal of the Royal Asiatic Society of Great Britain & Ireland* (New Series) 82, nos. 1–2 (April 1950), 37–49. http://dx.doi.org/10.1017/S0035869X00103302

116 George Bryan Souza and Jeffrey Scott Turley, *The Boxer Codex: Transcription and Translation of an Illustrated Late Spanish Manuscript Concerning the Geography, Ethnography and History of The Pacific, Southeast Asia and East Asia* (Leiden: Brill, 2015), 31.

117 These include: the Jesuit correspondence between 1580 and 1597 (see Joseph Wicki, *Documenta indica: Memorias de Africa e do Oriente. Monumenta Historica Societatis Iesu*, 12–18 (Rome: Archivum Romanum Societatis Iesu, 1972–1988), with 14 places, in Barcelor, Mogor, Cambaya, Japan, various temples, St. Thomas, Fishery Coast, Bisnaga, Malaca, Cochin, Ceylon, Pegu, Goa, and Ormuz; Mendoza (1585), with 11 places: Philippines, Tartars, Japan, Malaca, St. Thomas, Bisnaga, Nicubar, Cochin, Goa, Cambaya, and Ormuz; Alessandro Valignano, writing in 1577, in Ibid,13 (1975), 1–134, with 9 places: Goa, Cape Comurin, Bisnaga, Cochin, Cambaya, Malaca, Ceilan, Hormuz, and Japan; Luís de Guzmán, *Historia de las missiones que han hecho los religiosos de la Compañia de Iesus, para predicar el Sancto Euangelio en la India oriental, y en los reynos de la China y Iapon.* (Alcalá: Biuda de Juan Gracian, 1601), with 13 places: Cambaya, Ceylon, Bisnaga, Mogor, Malaca, Maluccas, Goa, Fishery Coast, St. Thomas, Pegu, Hormuz, Cochin, and Japan; Giovanni Pietro Maffei, *Historiarum Indicarum libri xvi* (Venice, 1588), with 9: Cambaya, Goa, Malaca, Brahmans and sacerdotes, St. Thomas, Cochin, Comurin, Idalcan, and Pegu. For an overview of the early secular and religious accounts by Europeans of Asian cultures, the best source is still Lach, *Asia in the Making of Europe*, I, 1.

118 Letter to Rome from Amboyna, May 1546, in Henry James Coleridge, *The Life and Letters of St Francis Xavier*. 2 vols. (London: Burns and Oates, 1881), 1, 381.

119 Wicki, *Documenta indica*, XVII, p. 35 digital.

120 Ibid.

121 Ibid, XVIII, 34 digital.

122 Ibid, XVII, 65 digital.

123 Ibid.

124 Ibid, 457–459 digital.

125 Ibid, 505 digital.

126 Personal communication, April 17, 2018.

127 Johannes Theodor de Bry, *Indiae Orientalis Pars Undecima: qua continetur I. Duarum navigationum, quas [. . .] in Indiam Orientalem Ann. 1501. Dn. Americus Vesputius instituit, historia. II. Vera atque hactenus inaudita Angli cujusdam relatio [. . .]. III. Descriptio regionis Spitzbergae [. . .]. Nunc primum latio donata, atq [. . .] in aes incisis imaginibus illustrata / Sumptibus atq* (Oppenheim, 1619).

128 His "Sumario de las cosas que pertenecen a la Provincia de la India Oriental y al govierno della, compuesto por el Padre Alexandro Valignano Visitador della y dirigido a Nuestro Padre General Everardo Mercuriano en el año de 1579," was originally written in Italian in 1577 (Goa 31), revised and translated into Spanish in 1580 and 1583 (Goa 6 and 7). All are in the Archivium Romanum Societatis Iesu. John J. Coyne, S. J. (trans), Josef Franz Schütte, *Valignano's Mission Principles for Japan.* 2 vols. (Gujarat: Sahitya Prakash, India, 1980), vol. I, 122–123.

129 On the scope of Valignano's duties as Jesuit visitor, see M. Antoni J. Üçerler, S. J., "Alessandro Valignano: man, missionary, and writer," *Renaissance Studies* 17, No. 3 (2003): 340–341.

130 Wicki and Gomes, *Documenta Indica* XIII, "Sumario 1577" (Spanish trans 1579), 198.

131 See Gauvin Alexander Bailey, "The Jesuits and the Grand Mogul: Renaissance Art at the Imperial Court of India, 1580–1630," *Freer Gallery of Art Occasional Papers* 2 (1998): 29–30.

132 Sanjay Subrahmanyam, *Europe's India: Words, People, Empires 1500–1800* (Cambridge: Harvard University, 2017), 15.

133 Blair, *Philippines,* 4, 61.

134 Antonio de Morga, *History of the Philippine Islands from their discovery by Magellan in 1521 to the beginning of the VII Century; with descriptions of Japan, China and adjacent countries* (1609), trans. and ed. El H. Blair and J. A. Robertson (Cleveland: Arthur Clark, 1915), 2, 301–302.

135 According to Westermeier, this is a nonstandard spelling of the word for "water;" standard would be "aquam." Personal communication, July 30, 2018.

136 Westermeier notes that this is another nonstandard spelling of the word for "water." Personal communication, July 30, 2018.

137 "The verbs 'pr[a]esentari' (to be in sight) and 'confortari' (to strengthen much; and usually in its active form, 'confortare') are attested in later Latin. Similarly, the postposition of the modifier 'valde' (very) is a sign of ecclesiastical Latin." Engelsing, personal communication, April 17, 2018.

138 The translators are not sure of the meaning of the words in italics.

139 John Huyghen van Linschoten, *The Voyage of John Huyghen Van Linschoten to the East Indies, From the Old English Translation of 1598,* 2 vols. (New York: Burt Franklin, 1884), 1, 294–295.

140 *Informatione del regno et stato del Gran Re di Mogor, della sua persona, qualita & costume . . .* (Rome, 1597). See Lach, *Asia in the Making of Europe,* I, 455.

141 Antonio de Monserrate, *The Commentary of Father Monserrate, S. J. on his Journey to the Court of Akbar,* trans. J.S. Hoyland ed. and S. N. Banerjee (New Delhi: Asian Educational Services, 2003).

142 Ibid, 190.

143 See Fergus Nicoll, *Shah Jahan* (New Delhi: Penguin Books, 2009), 44.

144 Monserrate, *Commentary,* 196.

145 See, for example, Ibid, 76 and 199.

146 Engelsing (personal communication, May 30, 2018) comments that, "As with previous documents (see, e.g., f23), the page seems to have been cut after the text was written

on it, and part of it is missing. Therefore, for the supplanted readings in brackets, cau-
tion is recommended. For example, the suggestion "ab <aliis>" (by others) could also be
"<haereticis>" (by the heretics), and the passage would read: "On which account they are
considered by the heretics to be saints . . ."

147 Johannes Theodor and Johanes Israel De Bry. *Pars VII. Nauigationes duas, Primam,
trium Annorum, a Georgio Spilbergio, trium nauium praefecto, Ann. 1601. ex Selandia in
Indiam Orientalem susceptam: Alteram, nouem Annorum, a Casparo Balby, Gemmario
Veneto, Anno 1579. ex Alepo Babyloniam versus . . . continens . . . Auctore M. Gotardo
Arthvs Dantiscano. Omnia elegantiβimis in aes incisis iconibus illustrata & in lucem emiss*
(Frankfort, 1606), plate XXII.

148 Engelsing points out that: "A brief explanation is in place about the pronouns in the
Latin text that indicate the three figures: the elephant, the priest, and the man on the
ground. The use of the pronoun 'altera,' which is usually used in a group of two, 'altera . . .
altera . . . , to describe the priest after noting the figure of the elephant indicates that the
elephant and the priest stand as a connected pair. It could be translated as 'the first' and
'the second' [figure]. In this sense, the pronoun 'alia,' which means 'the other,' presents the
iron figure as something apart from the first two." Personal communication, June 15, 2017.

149 Goa, St. Paul's College, 1563.

150 Cartari and Pignoria 1615, p. XXVII. Diogo do Couto provides a lengthy description of
Elephanta in his contribution to *Da Asia*, which he began to write in 1580 but was not published until 1645. See João de Barros e Diogo do Couto, *Decada quarta da Asia: dos feitos
que os portugueses fizeram na conquista e descobrimento das terras, & mares do Oriente.*
12 vols. (Lisbon: Regia Officina Typografica, 1788). Decada VII, 250–261. For a discussion
of the early European accounts of Elephanta and other Indian temple complexes, see Partha
Mitter, *Much Maligned Monsters: A History of European Reactions to Indian Art*. Revised
edition (Chicago: University of Chicago, 1992), 31–38.

151 Monumentae Historica Societatis Iesu, *Memorias do Africa e do Oriente*, 15, 1981, Doc.
40A, 166 (digital).

152 Linschoten, *Itinerario*, and De Bry, *Indiae Orientalis*, 2 and 4.

153 Mitter, *Monsters*, 34.

154 Letter to Rome from Amboyna, May 1546, in: Henry James Coleridge, *The Life and
Letters Of St Francis Xavier*, 10 vols. (London: Burns And Oates, 1881), I, 381.

155 Barros and Couto, *Da Asia, Dos Feitos, Decada XII,* Book II, Chapter III, 171–172 and
Chapter IV, 185; and Book III, Chapter IV, 270.

156 Westermeier (personal communication, August 1, 2018) explained that this charm-
ing reference is to a Latin proverb meaning that every group has its own tastes. Laura
Gibbs observed that a fable of Aesop, "*similes habent labra latucas*, 'the lips have lettuce
to match,' . . . seems to have been associated with the motif of donkeys eating thistles."
Laura Gibbs, *Aesopica: Aesop's Fables in English, Latin and Greek* (Oxford: Gibbs
Index, 2002 and mythfolklore.net), Fable 533. This Latin proverb was popular throughout the 16th century, perhaps first in Andrea Alciato (Alciati), *Emblematum libellus*
(1531), emblem 86.

157 Engelsing, personal communication, July 31, 2018.

158 Engelsing, personal communication, February 21, 2018, advised that "'Gentiles,' in "ad-
haerentibus gentilibus,' by itself may mean "of the same clan, race. In ecclesiastical Latin,
however, it is frequently used to mean "heathen" or "Pagan." This may bolster the argument
that the inscriptions were added by a religious person, probably Jesuit.

159 C. Gaston Perera, "The First Evangelical Mission of the Franciscans to Ceylon," *Journal of the Royal Asiatic Society of Sri Lanka*, New Series, vol. 53 (2007): 153.

160 Diogo do Couto refers to those who cut off noses and lips in *da Asia*, Decade V, Book V, Chapter 8. See Donald Ferguson, "The History of Ceylon from the Earliest Times to 1600 AD, as related by João de Barros and Diogo do Couto," *Journal of the Royal Asiatic Society, Ceylon Branch,* vol. XX, no. 60 (1908), no. 60, 1–445, 106; and Diogo do Couto, *Da Asia Decada XI,* 175.

161 Personal communication, August 1, 2018.

162 Missing are second Inca Cinchi Roca, Capac Yupanqui (fifth), Huayna Capac (eleventh), and Huascar (twelfth).

163 Juan Carlos Estenssoro, "Incas del Cardenal," 403–442, 413–414.

164 Sara González Castrejón, "Las efigies de los Incas en el Ms. 1551 de la Biblioteca Angelica (Roma) y los 'cuadernos de mano' de Francisco Fernández de Córdova," in A. Vázquez Varela, A. Ballone, H. Cowie, F. Eissa-Barroso, and S. Gonzalez, *Élites, representación y redes atlánticas en la Hispanoamérica moderna* (Michoacan: El Colegio de Michoacan, A.C., 2018), 57–109.

165 Accession, no. 83. MP.159.

166 Kongelike Bibliotek, Copenhagen, ms. GK2232.

167 Thomas B. F. Cummins, "The Images in Murúa's *Historia general del Piru*: an Art Historical Study" in *The Getty Murúa: Essays on the Making of Martín de Murúa's "Historia general del Piru,"* J. Paul Getty Museum Ms. Ludwig XIII, 16, eds. Thomas B.F. Cummins and Barbara Anderson (Los Angeles: Getty Research Institute, 2008), 147–174, 165.

168 On Inca portraits and their circulation, particularly those commissioned by Viceroy Francisco de Toledo, see Ibid, 164–170.

169 For a fuller discussion of these drawings in relation to European costume books, Guaman Poma and Murúa, see Barbara Anderson, "Colors of the New World for Consumption of the Old," in Gabriela Siracusana and Agustina Rodríguez Romero eds., *Materia Americana. The "body" of Spanish American images (16th to mid-19th centuries)* (Buenos Aires: EDUNTREF, 2020 [forthcoming]).

170 Fol. 87.

171 Ibid, fol. 96.

172 Ibid, fol. 105.

173 Ibid, fol. 123.

174 Buenaventura de Salinas and Córdova, *Memorial de las historias del nuevo mundo Pirú; Méritos, y Excelencias de la ciudad de Lima, Cabeça de sus ricos, y estendidos Reynos, y el Estado presente en que se halla. Para inclinar a la magestad de su Católico Monarca don Felipe IV, Rey poderoso de España, y de las Indias, a que pida a Su Santidad la Canonización de su Patrón Solano* (Lima, Gerónimo de Contreras, 1631).

175 Pierre Duviols, "En Busca de los fuentes de Guaman Poma de Ayala: realidad e invención." *Historica*, XXI, no. 1 (1997): 27–52, 30–31.

176 González, "Efigies," 72.

177 Ibid, 111.

178 On *tornesol* fabric in Peru, see Elena Phipps, "Tornesol: A Colonial Synthesis of European and Andean Textile Traditions," in *Approaching Textiles, Varying Viewpoints: Proceedings from the Seventh Biennial Symposium of the Textile Society of America, Santa Fe, New Mexico, 2000* (Earleville, Md: Textile Society of America, 2000), 221-30.

179 González, "Efigies," 32.

180 See, for example, the butterflies on the mantle and skirt hem of the ninth queen, Mama Ana Uarque, (f. 136). The motifs are not described in his text. See also f. 242, for the month of April: ABRIL, *CAMAI, INCA RAIMI Quilla,* where the hem of the dress of a woman behind the Inca is similarly strewn with butterflies. On f. 254, for the month of September, SETIENBRE, *COIA RAIMI Quilla,* the lower area of the tunic of a male figure is likewise dotted with the insects.

181 See the tunic for a statue of the Christ Child, Alto Peru, late 16th- 17th century. La Paz, Bolivia, Patrimonio Cultural de Bolivia in custody of Museo Nacional de Etnografía y Folklore (316). Elena Phipps, Johanna Hecht, and Cristina Esteras Martín, *The Colonial Andes: Tapestries and Silverwork and Andean Textile Traditions, 1580*-1830 (New Haven: Yale University Press, 2004), 143-146-147, and 273-276.

182 See Chapter 1, on ms. 1551, section 1.

183 Lia Markey, *Imagining the Americas in Medici Florence,* University Park: University of Pennsylvania Press, 2016, Kindle edition: loc. 2603 and figures 68 and 69.

184 fol. 226v.

185 I have discussed the use and description of colors in these manuscripts in Anderson, "Colors of the New World," [2020]. See also, Elena Phipps, Nancy Turner, and Karen Trentelman, "Colors, Textiles, and Artistic Production in Murúa's *Historia general del Piru*," in Cummins and Anderson, *The Getty Murúa*, 125-146, 129.

186 Ibid, 125–133.

187 The colors of the Coya Chimba Herma's garments (fol. 76) are not mentioned in the accompanying inscription, which appears to be unfinished.

188 fol. 99.

189 The few known works by him, which do not exhibit similarities with the Angelica watercolors (quite possibly because of the difference in subject), are illuminations in papal liturgical books, long thought to be lost from the Vatican, but recently discovered in Toledo. See Elena de Laurentiis, "The Liturgical Codices of the Seventeenth-Century Papal Court and the Illuminated Manuscripts of Pope Urban VIII in Toledo (Spain)," in *The Lost Manuscripts from the Sistine Chapel: An Epic Journey from Rome to Toledo,* eds. Elena de Laurentiis and Emilia Anna Talamo (Dallas: Southern Methodist University, 2011), 29–56.

190 Estenssoro, "Incas del Cardenal," 407–413. See Anderson, "Colors of the New World," [2020].

191 For a thorough discussion of Camillo Massimo's collecting and scholarship, see Lisa Beaven, *An Ardent Patron: Cardinal Camillo Massimo and His Antiquarian Artistic Circle* (London: Paul Holberton, 2010), particularly 137–177.

192 Nicoletta Muratore, *da Palasso Massimo all'Angelica: manoscritti e libri a stampa di un'antica famiglia romana* (Rome: Fratelli Palombi Editore, 1997), 29–38.

193 Markey, *Imagining,* loc. 1865 and 2044.

194 Ibid, loc. 2176.

195 "Segmenta veftium cum oris purpureis antiquis." Filippo Tomasini, *Bibliothecae Patavinae,* 87; F. Zen Benetti, "Per la biografia di Lorenzo Pignoria, erudite padovano," in *Viridarium floridum: Studi di stori Veneta offerti dagli allieva a Paolo Sambin,* eds. Maria Chiara Billanovich, Giorgio Cracco, and Antonio Rigon (Padua: Antenore, 1984), 317–336, 87.

196 Illustrations and transcriptions were first published by Juan Carlos Estenssoro, in "Los Incas del Cardenal," 413–414. I have transcribed them here, with minor corrections in diacritics and orthography, for easier access.

Bibliography

Manuscripts:

Artist and Scribe unknown. "Boxer Codex," Indiana University, Lilly Library, Ms. II, LMC 2444.

Chacón, Alfonso. "Alfonso Chacón reports, 1578–1589." Los Angeles, Getty Research Institute, 840005B.

_____. (Ciacconius). "Raccolta di iscrizioni e imagini di pontefici e imperatori." Rome, Biblioteca Angelica, ms. 1564.

_____. and workshop (?). "Icones coloribus ornatae idolorum mexicanorum, Aeguptorum, Sinensim, Japanorum, Indorum addita declaration hispanica usque ad fmost fol 8: sequuntur usque ad fol. 74 effigies et usu barbarrum quarundam regionum a Asiae, Americae et Insularum cum declarationibus modo latinis, modo hispanicis A fo. 75 ad 82 meliori penicillo sunt iconas regum Peruvianorum subiectis notis biographicis hispanica lingua." Rome, Biblioteca Angelica, ms. 1551.

Peiresc, Claude Nicolas Fabri de. Carpentras, Bibliothèque Inguimbertine 1875, letter 1809.

Ríos, Pedro de los. Codex Vaticanus A. Rome, Biblioteca Apostolica Vaticanus, Codex Vaticanus (3738).

Published works:

Acosta, José de. *Historia general y moral de las Indias*. Seville: Juan de León, 1590.

Alciato, Andrea (Alciati). *Emblematum libellus*. Augsburg: Heinrich Steyner, 1531.

Anders, Ferdinand, Maarten Jansen, and Luis Reyes García. *Religión, costumbres e historia de los antiguos mexicanos: libro explicativo del llamado Códice Vaticano A, Codex Vatic. Lat. 3738 de la Biblioteca Vaticana*. Graz: Akademishe Druck-und Verlagsanstalt, and Mexico, Fondo de Cultura Económica, 1996.

Anderson, Barbara. "Colors of the New World for Consumption of the Old." In *Materia Americana. The "body" of Spanish American images (16th to mid-19th centuries)*, edited by Gabriela Siracusano and Agustina Rodríguez Romero. Buenos Aires: EDUNTREF, [2020].

Bailey, Gauvin Alexander. "The Jesuits and the Grand Mogul: Renaissance Art at the Imperial Court of India, 1580–1630." *Freer Gallery of Art Occasional Papers* 2, (1998).

Barros, João de, and Diogo do Couto. *Da Asia, Dos Feitos, Que Os Portuguezes Fizeram Na Conquista, E Descubrimento Das Terras, E Mares Do Oriente*. 12 vols. Lisbon: Regia Officina Typografica, 1788. *Decada VII*.

Beaven, Lisa. *An Ardent Patron: Cardinal Camillo Massimo and His Antiquarian and Artistic Circle*. London: Paul Holberton, 2010.

Benetti, F. Zen. "Per la biografia di Lorenzo Pignoria, erudite padovano." in *Viridarium floridum: Studi di stori Veneta offerti dagli allieva a Paolo Sambin*, edited by Maria Chiara Billanovich, Giorgio Cracco, and Antonio Rigon, 317–336. Padua: Antenore, 1984.

Boogaart, Ernst van den. *Civil and Corrupt Asia: Image and Text in the Itinerario and the Icones of Jan Huygen van Linschoten*. Chicago: University of Chicago, 2003.

Botta, Sergio. "Il corpo universale degli dèi americani: per una teoria visuale del politeismo nell'opera di Lorenzo Pignoria." *Civiltà e Religioni* 3 (2017), 39–69.

Boxer, Charles R. "A Late Sixteenth-Century Manila Manuscript." *Journal of the Royal Asiatic Society of Great Britain & Ireland* (New Series) 82, nos. 1–2 (April 1950), 37–49. http://dx.doi.org/10.1017/S0035869X00103302.

Bry, Johann Theodor and Johann Israel de. *II Pars Indiae Orientalis, in qua Johan Hugonis Linscotani navagatio in Orientem*. Frankfort, 1599.

_____. *III Pars Indiae Orientalis*, and *IV Pars Indiae Orientalis*. Frankfort, 1601.

_____. *Pars VII. Nauigationes duas, Primam, trium Annorum, a Georgio Spilbergio, trium nauium praefecto, Ann. 1601. ex Selandia in Indiam Orientalem susceptam: Alteram, nouem Annorum, a Casparo Balby, Gemmario Veneto, Anno 1579. ex Alepo Babyloniam versus . . . continens . . . Auctore M. Gotardo Arthvs Dantiscano. Omnia elegantißimis in aes incisis iconibus illustrata & in lucem emissa*. Frankfort, 1606.

_____. *Pars XI: qua continetur I. Duarum navigationum, quas [. . .] in Indiam Orientalem Ann. 1501. Dn. Americus Vesputius instituit, historia. II. Vera atque hactenus inaudita Angli cujusdam relatio [. . .]. III. Descriptio regionis Spitzbergae [. . .]. Nunc primum latio donata, atq; [. . .] in aes incisis imaginibus illustrata / Sumptibus atq.* Oppenheim, 1619.

Cartari, Vincenzo, and Pignoria, Lorenzo. *Le vere e nove imagini de gli dei delli antichi di Vicenzo Cartari*. Padua: Pietro Paolo Tozzi, 1615.

_____. *Le imagini de gli dei de gli antichi: nelle quali sono descritte la religione de gli antichi li idoli, riti, & ceremonie loro, con l'aggiunta di molte principali imagini che nell'altre mancauano, et con l'espositione in epilogo di ciasceduna & suo significato*. Venice: Evangelista Deuchino, 1626.

Coleridge, Henry James. *The Life and Letters of St. Francis Xavier*. 2 vols. London: Burns and Oates, 1881.

Cortasão, Armando. *The Suma Oriental of Tomé Pires and the Book of Francisco Rodrigues*. 2 vols. London: Hakluyt Society, 1944.

Crest, Sabine du. "L' exoticisme vu de provence au temps de Peiresc," *Sciences et Techniques en Perspective* II series 9, no. 1 (2005): 259–270.

Crossley, John N. "The Early History of the Boxer Codex." *Journal of the Royal Asiatic Society*, Third Series, 24 (2014): 115–124. doi:10.1017/S1356186313000552.

Cummins, Thomas B.F. "From Lies to Truth: Colonial Ekphrasis and the Act of Cultural Translation." in *Reframing the Renaissance: Visual Culture in Europe and Latin America 1450–1650*, edited by Clare Farago. New Haven: Yale University Press, 1995, 152–174.

_____. "The Images in Murúa's *Historia General del Piru*: An Art Historical Study." in *The Getty Murúa*, edited by Thomas B.F. Cummins and Barbara Anderson. Los Angeles: Getty Publications, 2008, 147–174.

Dandalet, Thomas. *Spanish Rome, 1500–1700*. New Haven: Yale University, 2001.

Documenta indica: Memorias de Africa e do Oriente, edited by Joseph Wicki and John Gomes. *Monumenta Historica Societatis Iesu,*12–18. Rome: Archivum Romanum Societatis Iesu, 1972–1988.

Duviols, Pierre. "En busca de los fuentes de Guaman Poma de Ayala: realidad e invención." *Historica* XXI, no. 1 (1997): 27–52.

Egaña, Antonio de. *Monumenta peruana.* 3 vols. (Rome: Archivium Romanum Societatis Iesu, 1958), vol. 2.

Estenssoro, Juan Carlos. "Los Incas del Cardenal: las acuarelas de la colección Massimo." *Revista andina* 12, no. 2 (1994), 403–423.

Feest, Christian. "Zemes Idolum Diabolicum. Surprise and Success in Ethnographic Kunstkammer Research." *Archiv für Völkerkunde* 40 (1986), 181–198.

Ferguson, Donald. "The History of Ceylon from the Earliest Times to 1600 AD, as related by João de Barros and Diogo do Couto." *Journal of the Royal Asiatic Society, Ceylon Branch* XX, no. 60 (1908): 1–445.

Fromont, Cécile. *The Art of Conversion: Christian Visual Culture in the Kingdom of Kongo.* Chapel Hill: University of North Carolina, 2014.

Galilei, Galileo. *Le opera.* Florence: G. Barbera, 1966, Volume XI Carteggio 1611–1613.

Gaston Perera, C. "The First Evangelical Mission of the Franciscans to Ceylon." *Journal of the Royal Asiatic Society of Sri Lanka*, New Series 53 (2007): 153–202.

The Getty Murúa: Essays on the Making of J. Paul Museum Ludwig XIII, 6, edited by Thomas B. F. Cummins and Barbara Anderson. Los Angeles: The Getty Research Institute, 2008.

Gibbs, Laura. *Aesopica: Aesop's Fables in English, Latin and Greek.* Oxford: Gibbs Index, 2002 and mythfolklore.net.

González Castrejón, Sara. "Las efigies de los Incas en el Ms. 1551 de la Biblioteca Angelica (Roma) y los 'cuadernos de mano' de Francisco Fernández de Córdova." In *Élites, representación y redes atlánticas en la Hispanoamérica moderna,* edited by A. Vázquez Varela, A. Ballone, H. Cowie, F. Eissa-Barroso, and S. Gonzalez Castrejón. Michoacan: El Colegio de Michoacan, 2018, 57–109.

Guzmán, Luís de. *Historia de las missiones que han hecho los religiosos de la Compañia de Iesus, para predicar el Sancto Euangelio en la India oriental, y en los reynos de la China y Iapon.* Alcalá: Biuda de Juan Gracian, 1601.

Jaffé, David. "Two Bronzes from Poussin's *Studies of Antiquities.*" *J. Paul Getty Museum Journal* 17 (1989), 39–46.

Kubler, George and Charles Gibson. *The Tovar Calendar: An Illustrated Mexican Manuscript, ca. 1585.* New Haven: The Connecticut Academy of Arts and Sciences, 1951.

Lach, Donald. *Asia in the Making of Europe.* 3 vols. Chicago: University of Chicago, 1965–1977.

LaFaye, Jacques. "Le manuscrit Tovar en la J. Carter Brown Library: attribution et filiation." *Mélanges de la Casa de Velázquez,* 6. Chicago: University of Chicago, 1970, 359–370.

Laurentiis, Elena De. "The Liturgical Codices of the Seventeenth-Century Papal Court and the Illuminated Manuscripts of Pope Urban VIII in Toledo (Spain)." In *The Lost Manuscripts from the Sistine Chapel: An Epic Journey from Rome to Toledo,* edited by Elena de Laurentiis and Emilia Anna Talamo. Dallas: Southern Methodist University, 2011.

Lightbown, Ronald. "Oriental Art and the Orient in Late Renaissance and Baroque Italy." *Journal of the Warburg and Courtauld Institutes* 32 (1969), 228–279.

Linschoten, Jan Huyghen van. *Itinerario: Voyage oft schipvaert van Jan Huygen van Linschoten.* Amsterdam: Corneliuz Claesz, 1596.

_____. *The Voyage of John Huyghen Van Linschoten to the East Indies, From the Old English Translation of 1598.* 2 vols., New York: Burt Franklin, 1884.

Lopes, Duarte and Filippo Pigafetta. *Relatione del reame di Congo et delle circonvicine contrade: Tratta dalli scritti e ragionamenti di Odoardo Lopez Portoghese per Filippo Pigafetta.* Rome: Bartolomeo Grassi, 1591.

Losty, Jeremiah P. "Identifying the Artist of the Codex Casanatense 1889." *Anais de Historia de Alem-Mar,* XIII (2012), 13-40.

Maffei, Giovanni Pietro. *Historiarum Indicarum libri xvi.* Venice, 1588.

Maffei, Sonia. "Cartari e gli dèi del Nuovo Mondo: Il trattatello sulle *Imagini de gli dei indiani* di Lorenzo Pignoria." in Sonia Maffei. *Arti Vincenzo Cartari e le direzioni del mito nel Cinquecento.* Rome: Genevra Bentivolio Editoria, 2013, 61-120.

Markey, Lia. *Imagining the Americas in Medici Florence.* College Station: Pennsylvania State University Press, 2016.

_____. "Istoria della terra chiamata la nuova spagna: the History and Reception of Sahagún's Codex at the Medici Court." in *Colours between Two Worlds: The Florentine Codex of Bernardino de Sahagún.* Edited by Gerhard Wolf and Joseph Connors. Florence: Harvard University Press, 2011, 199-220.

Mason, Peter. "The Purloined Codex." *Journal of the History of Collections,* 9, 1 (1997), 1-30.

_____. *The Lives of Images.* London: Reaktion Books, 2001.

Matos Moctezuma, Eduardo, and Felipe Solis Olguin. *Aztecs.* London: Royal Academy of the Arts, 2002.

Mercati, Michele. *Degli Obelischi di Roma.* Rome: Domenico Basa, 1589.

Miller, Mary and Karl Taube. *The Gods and Symbols of Ancient Mexico and the Maya.* London: Thames and Hudson, 2017.

Mitter, Partha. *Much Maligned Monsters: A History of European Reactions to Indian Art,* revised edition. Chicago: University of Chicago, 1992.

Monserrate, Antonio de. *The Commentary of Father Monserrate, S.J. on his Journey to the Court of Akbar.* Translated by J.S. Hoyland and edited by S. N. Banerjee. New Delhi: Asian Educational Services, 2003.

Morga, Antonio de. *History of the Philippine Islands from their discovery by Magellan in 1521 to the beginning of the XVII Century; with descriptions of Japan, China and adjacent countries* (1609), edited and translated by El H. Blair and J. A. Robertson. Cleveland: Arthur Clark, 1915.

Nicoll, Fergus. *Shah Jahan.* New Delhi: Penguin Books, 2009.

da Palazzo Massimo all'Angelica: manocritti e libri a stampa di un'antica famiglia romana, edited by Nicoletta Muratore. Rome: Fratelli Palombri, 1997.

Ostapkowicz, Joanna, and Lee Newsom. "Gods . . . Adorned with the Embroiderer's Needle": The Materials, Making and Meaning of a Taino Cotton Reliquary, *Latin American Antiquity* 23, no. 3 (2012), 300–326.

Phipps, Elena. "Tornesol: A Colonial Synthesis of European and Andean Textile Tradi-
tions." In *Approaching Textiles, Varying Viewpoints: Proceedings from the Seventh
Biennial Symposium of the Textile Society of America, Santa Fe, New Mexico, 2000.*
(Earleville, MD: Textile Society of America, 2000, 221–230.

——, Johanna Hecht, and Cristina Esteras Martín. *The Colonial Andes: Tapestries and
Silverwork and Andean Textile Traditions,* 1580–1830. New Haven: Yale University
Press, 2004.

——, Nancy Turner, and Karen Trentelman. "Colors, Textiles, and Artistic Production
in Murúa's *Historia general del Piru.*" In *Making the Getty Murúa,* edited by Thomas
B. F. Cummins and Barbara Anderson, 125–146. Los Angeles: Getty Publications,
2008.

Quiñones Keber, Eloise. "Collecting Cultures: A Mexican Manuscript in the Vatican
Library." In *Reframing the Renaissance: Visual Culture in Europe and Latin America 1450–1650,* edited by Clare Farago, 229–242. New Haven: Yale University Press,
1995.

——, *Codex Telleriano Remensis: Ritual, Divination, and History in a Pictorial Aztec
Manuscript.* Austin: University of Texas Press, 1995.

Recio, Alejandro, O.F.M. "'La Historia Descriptio Urbis Romae,' obra manuscrito de Fr.
Alonso Chacón, O.P. (1530–1599)." *Anthologica annua* (1968), 43–102.

Roces, Alfredo R., ed. "Boxer Codex," *Filipino Heritage: The Making of a Nation,* vol. IV.
Philippines: Lahing Pilipino Publishing, 1977.

Rizza, Cecilia. *Peiresc e l'Italia.* Torino: Giappichelli, 1965.

Salinas and Córdova, Buenaventura de. *Memorial de las historias del nuevo mundo Pirú;
Méritos, y Excelencias de la ciudad de Lima, Cabeça de sus ricos, y estendidos Reynos,
y el Estado presente en que se halla. Para inclinar a la magestad de su Católico
Monarca don Felipe IV, Rey poderoso de España, y de las Indias, a que pida a Su
Santidad la Canonización de su Patrón Solano.* Lima, Gerónimo de Contreras, 1631.

Schütte, Josef Franz. *Valignano's Mission Principles for Japan.* Translated by John J.
Coyne, S. J., 2 volumes (Gujarat: Sahitya Prakash, India, 1980) 1, 122–123.

Seznec, Jean. "Un essai de mythologie comparé au début du XVIIe siècle." *Mélanges
d'archéologie et d'histoire* 48, no. 1 (1931), 268–281.

Schrader, Stephanie. "Rembrandt and the Mughal Line: Artistic Inspiration in the Global
City of Amsterdam." In *Rembrandt and the Inspiration of India,* edited by Stephanie
Schrader, 5 28. Los Angeles: The J. Paul Getty Museum, 2018.

Souza, George Bryan, and Jeffrey Scott Turley. *The Boxer Codex: Transcription and Translation of an Illustrated Late Spanish Manuscript Concerning the Geography, Ethnography and History of the Pacific, Southeast Asia and East Asia.* Leiden: Brill,
2015.

Tomasini, Giacomo Filippi. *de Vita, Bibliotheca et Museo Laurentii Pignorii canonici Tarvisini dissertatio.* Udine: Shiraci, 1639.

Toorians, Lauran. "The Earliest Inventory of Mexican Objects in Munich, 1572." *Journal of
the History of Collecting* 6, no. 1 (1994), 59–67.

Tsuen-Hsuin, Tsien. "Chemistry and Chemical Technology, Part I: Paper and Printing." In
Science and Civilisation in China, edited by Joseph Needham, 5. London: Cambridge
University Press, 1985.

Nancy Turner. "Accounting for Unfinished History: How Evidence of Book Structure Provides a New Context for the Making of the Galvin and Getty Murúas." In *Manuscript Cultures of Colonial Mexico and Peru*, edited by Thomas B.F. Cummins, Emily Engel, Barbara Anderson, and Juan Ossio, 85–115. Los Angeles: Getty Research Institute, 2014.

Üçerler, M. Antoni J. "Alessandro Valignano: man, missionary, and writer." *Renaissance Studies* 17, no. 3 (2003), 340–341.

Volpi, Caterina. "Lorenzo Pignoria e il suoi correspondenti." *Nouvelles de la république des lettres* 12 (2002), 71–127.

Index

NOTE: Page numbers followed by "f" indicate figures.